Longman Handbooks for Language Teachers

A Framework for Task-Based Learning

Jane Willis

Pearson Education Limited
Edinburgh Gate, Harlow, Essex CM20 2JE, England
and Associated Companies throughout the world.

www.longman.com

First published 1996
Ninth impression 2005

Set in Palatino
Printed in Malaysia, PJB
Produced for the publishers by de Henseler Books
Designed and illustrated by Oxprint Design, Oxford

ISBN 0582 25973 8

Acknowledgements

We are grateful to the following for permission to reproduce
copyright material:

Cobuild Ltd for extracts from *COBUILD ENGLISH COURSE,
Student book level 1 & Teacher book levels 1, 2 & 3* by J & D Willis;
Guardian Media Group plc for text article 'Cold Store'; extracts &
headline from 'The boy who came out from the cold' in *THE
GUARDIAN*; Thomas Nelson & Sons Ltd for extracts from
TALKING TO LEARN: The Shropshire Talk Project (1987) by Bain,
Francis & Matthews. We have been unable to trace the copyright
holder of the article 'Spiders' in *The Daily Telegraph* 24.1.94. and
would appreciate any information which would enable us to do so.
We are also grateful to The BNC. The British National Corpus is a
collaborative initiative carried out by Oxford University Press,
Longman, Chambers Harrap, Oxford University Computing
Services, Lancaster University's Unit for Computer Research in the
English Language, and the British Library. The BNC project
received funding from the UK Department of Trade and Industry
and the Science and Engineering Research Council and was
supported by additional research grants from the British Academy
and the British Library.

Contents

Acknowledgements

Initial inspiration and support for task-based language learning came from Prabhu in Bangalore, John Sinclair in Birmingham and staff and students of many nationalities at the British Council Teaching Centre in Singapore under Dave Willis. There have been many people both inside and outside the Cobuild Project in Birmingham who have recorded, piloted and reported on tasks and task-based learning and to all these people I am truly grateful.

It was Arlene Gilpin who finally gave me the impetus to start writing this book, and Dave Willis, my husband, who, with patience and understanding, kept me going right to the end, reading and commenting on drafts of every chapter and suggesting revisions.

Initial versions of seven chapters were piloted with future Spanish teachers of English at León University in northern Spain – my thanks to them, and to Professor Chamosa and the Departamento de Filología Moderna. The book has greatly benefited from detailed feedback and enthusiastic encouragement from those who read the complete manuscript: Melanie Butler, Jeremy Harmer and Seth Lindstromberg, and from those who have read and commented on individual chapters and helped with revisions and appendices: Margaret Allan, Paul Barnes, Brahim Bouattia, Charlie Brown, John Coston, Corony Edwards, Pauline Foster, Ronnie Holdsworth, Katie Jennings, Juares Lopes, Steve Mann, Nicki Marshall, Jaimis Silveira, Richard West and Sue Wharton, together with their colleagues, trainee teachers and students. Many of these people have had considerable experience of implementing and using TBL in the UK, USA, Australia, Ireland, Spain and Brazil, and I have both enjoyed their professional companionship and benefited greatly from their advice and feedback.

Staff and students from Aston University Language Studies Unit have also contributed in many ways. Distance Learning Masters students, especially those in Turkey, together with teachers and trainers from the British Council Teaching Centres in Istanbul and Izmir have undertaken task-based learning projects, short and long term, and have kept me in touch with their findings and their progress.

My greatest appreciation goes, as always, to my family, who have put up with my absences, my long week-ends of writing, and with whom I have resolved to spend far more time enjoying myself in the coming years.

Jane Willis

Introduction

The aim of communication tasks is to stimulate real communication in the target language. Many textbooks include tasks of this kind. There are also resource books full of imaginative tasks. But typically, such tasks are used at the end of a methodological cycle, rather than being central to that cycle, or are used as the basis for separate speaking skills lessons.

This book on task-based learning (TBL) shows how tasks can be used as the central focus in a supportive methodological framework. The aim of the task is to create a real purpose for language use and provide a natural context for language study. Students prepare for the task, report back after the task and then study the language that arises naturally out of the task cycle and its accompanying materials.

The framework offers a rich but comprehensible exposure to language in use, through listening and reading, and provides opportunities for both spontaneous and planned speaking and writing. It provides learners with the motivation to improve and build on whatever language they already have.

This task-based framework takes into account what we know about how people learn languages. We know, for example, that practice of language forms does not necessarily make perfect. We know that people cannot learn a language without plenty of opportunities for real language use. It is also important that the language that they are exposed to and that they use reflects the kind of language they want to learn. For example, if this includes spontaneous spoken language (which is very different from planned written language), then that is what they need to hear and study. We also know that too much emphasis on small-group communication without any call for accuracy may result in learners' grammar fossilising; some learners develop fluency at the expense of accuracy. The TBL framework is designed to resolve all these issues.

Task-based learning combines the best insights from communicative language teaching with an organised focus on language form. Although the examples in this book are based on English, TBL is valid for the teaching of any target language, second or foreign.

How to use this book

Each chapter begins with a focus page which introduces two or three of the main themes and concepts. Its aim is to help readers reflect on relevant language-learning or teaching experience which they can draw on while reading the chapter. It can also be photocopied and used on teacher-training courses to stimulate discussion of these concepts. The questions on the focus page are exploratory – there are often no set answers – but the issues they raise are important ones and will be further developed in the chapter.

Many chapters refer to the resources materials which have been gathered together in the Appendices for ease of use. These are also photocopiable.

At the end of most chapters there are suggestions for activities to help develop specific teaching skills. There are also recommendations for further reading.

I hope you and your learners enjoy working with task-based learning. I hope, too, that you gain professional satisfaction from overcoming initial difficulties (there are always some!) and seeing the difference that TBL can make in the language classroom.

Jane Willis, Birmingham, March 1996

What are your views on language learning?

*Rate these statements **A**, **B**, **C** or **D** according to how far you agree with each of them. Note your reasons, and any evidence to support your decisions. Then share your views with a colleague and try to reach agreement.*

A Agree strongly   **B** Agree   **C** Don't really agree   **D** Disagree

1 You can learn to speak a foreign language quite well without lessons. ☐

2 Many secondary students who have studied a foreign language leave school unable to communicate in it. ☐

3 Learners often go on making the same error even after being corrected many times. ☐

4 If students learn the rules of grammar they are quickly able to use them. ☐

5 You must use the language freely to learn to speak it, even if you make a lot of errors. ☐

6 Teachers should always correct student errors. ☐

7 Reading widely is one of the best ways to learn another language. ☐

8 People of all intellectual abilities can successfully learn another language. ☐

9 The younger you are the better you will learn another language. ☐

10 Extroverts make better language learners. ☐

Did You Know?

Most of the world's people speak two languages in their everyday lives.

Multilingualism is the natural way of life for hundreds of millions.

Mother-tongue speakers of English number over 300 millions.

English, Chinese and Spanish are the three most widespread languages.

Over half the world's business is conducted in English between non-native speakers.

80 per cent of the world's scientists write in English.

75 per cent of the world's mail is written in English.

Over 400 million speak English fluently as a second or foreign language.

Language learning: creating the best environment

This chapter provides the rationale for task-based learning. It explores how natural language learning processes can enhance learning in the classroom.

We begin with a questionnaire which focuses on concepts and issues in foreign language learning. After discussing these, and the principles behind them, we consider different individual learning styles.

We then identify three basic conditions for natural language learning which, combined ideally with a fourth, instruction, provide an optimum learning environment.

Finally we show how the teacher-centred classroom tends to have fixed interaction patterns which inhibit natural learning. This underlines the need for alternative patterns of interaction which centre on the learner rather than the teacher. We suggest that task-based learning can fulfil this need.

1.1 Beliefs about language learning

We all have strongly held beliefs about the ways that foreign or second languages are learnt – beliefs which are based on our own experience as language learners and as language teachers. It is well worth examining those beliefs, together with the experience that lies behind them. This is what the questionnaire in Focus 1 is designed to help you do.

Most teachers who do this questionnaire find they agree with six or seven statements and disagree with three or four. But your answers may well be different because they are based on different experiences.

How does this examination of our beliefs help us to understand how people learn another language? Or, more importantly perhaps, to understand why people don't learn one? We will now discuss each statement in turn.

1 You can learn to speak a foreign language quite well without lessons.

Most of us know or know of people who have learnt to speak a foreign language quite fluently without any teaching at all: people who travel and work abroad a lot; people who stay in their own country but who mix with speakers of another language. Even quite young children, who drop out of school, often classed as 'unteachable,' become unofficial tourist guides and end up managing to communicate in several foreign languages. They are not always totally accurate, but they achieve a level of language ability that is entirely adequate for their needs.

What is it that helps people like this to learn? For one thing, they are usually very motivated – they have a pressing desire to communicate and to get their meaning across. They receive a lot of exposure – they hear the language in use and pick up expressions they need. And they have many opportunities to speak and experiment with the language. Their interlocutors do not expect them to be perfect, and will often support their attempts to communicate by suggesting words and phrases.

It is, then, quite possible for people to learn a lot without having lessons. Classroom instruction is not a necessary condition for learning.

2 Many secondary students who have studied a foreign language leave school unable to communicate in it.

Unfortunately this is often the case. In language schools all over the world the largest group of students consists of people who have studied English at school but who feel they know nothing and want to start again. Many British school leavers have failed to learn French or German in much the same way. They have a small battery of formulaic phrases, but are unable or too shy to put them to use. Although many of them pass their examinations successfully, they find they cannot cope in conversation with a fluent speaker.

One reason why this happens is because much of their exposure consists of written language at sentence level: they are used to reading textbook exercises and hearing carefully-scripted dialogues. Many have been exposed to little real spoken interaction other than instruction-focused teacher talk.

We can say therefore that some people learn a language naturally without classroom instruction. On the other hand, many people do not learn one in spite of being taught.

This is not to say that classroom instruction is useless; indeed there is evidence to suggest that instruction does help. For example, learners who have had formal instruction and who then spend time in the country concerned are likely to achieve a higher degree of accuracy than those who have not had formal instruction.[1] But language lessons on their own bring no guarantee of success. Formal instruction is rarely a sufficient condition for learning a language.

What is it that prevents students learning? Most teachers would say that lack of motivation is the main problem. Learners are often keen at the beginning of their course, but in the second and third years motivation drops. Students complain they find lessons boring, and get depressed when they lose marks because they make mistakes. In large classes it is difficult to give individuals enough chance to use the language naturally. Adults feel shy about talking in front of the class. Speaking is rarely tested, and exams based on grammar often result in a lot of direct grammar teaching with focus on form rather than meaning.

There are many more reasons, too, which will come to light gradually throughout this book.

3 Learners often go on making the same error even after being corrected many times.

You don't have to sit long in any staffroom before you hear the cry: 'But I've taught them that so many times and they are still getting it wrong!' Sometimes students seem to master a grammar point successfully in a lesson, and get it right when doing an exercise on it; they even reproduce it in a test or exam. But they often fail to use it correctly when expressing themselves freely. In other words, this temporary mastery seems to happen when they are paying conscious attention to form (i.e. the surface pattern), but not when they are trying to communicate and paying attention to meaning. There is, then, a lot of evidence that practice activities, such as drilling a particular language pattern, do not necessarily 'make perfect', especially when it comes to communication.

The distinction that Stephen Krashen, an influential American linguist, made between acquisition and learning is a useful one here. Acquisition is the subconscious process that happens naturally and leads to fluency; learning being the conscious process. In a situation like the one above, you could say that students have learnt the target form, in that they can reproduce it in a controlled situation when consciously applying the rule, but that they have not yet acquired it, in that it has not become part of their internalised language system. Few people now accept Krashen's claim that formally learnt knowledge will never become part of a learner's deployable language. But until a new item has been properly acquired, it will not be freely available for use. So until then, learners are likely to continue expressing their meanings in ways which are not in accordance with the grammar of the target language.[2]

The proverb 'Practice makes perfect', then, does not always apply to learning grammar. And this raises another question. Should we really be aiming at perfection in our learners? If their only aim is to pass a grammar test, then some exam practice, where conscious knowledge is applied, will probably pay off. But it is most unlikely to result in fluency. In other cases, instead of aiming at the unachievable goal of perfection and falling short, might it not be more realistic and useful to spend less time on practising isolated patterns and more on helping learners to increase their vocabulary (words and phrases being generally far easier to learn) and deploy the language they have?[3]

4 If students learn the rules of grammar they are quickly able to use them.

This depends partly on what we mean by the word 'grammar'. There are many ways in which this word is used. We can say that children have normally acquired the basic grammar of their mother tongue by the age of four. This is grammar as an internalised system, which is acquired subconsciously, and is difficult to describe in words even for adults. In fact, it is often impossible to explain precisely what the rules are. As N S Prabhu writes: 'Developments in grammatical theory and description had shown clearly that the internal grammatical system operated subconsciously by fluent speakers was vastly more complex than was reflected by, or could be incorporated into, any grammatical syllabus…'.[4]

People who write letters to newspapers complaining about split infinitives (e.g. *I want to totally ban them* rather than *want to ban them totally*) are basing their complaints on the prescriptive grammar rules they were taught at school. Grammarians, who set out to describe how a language system works by looking at how people actually use it, write descriptive grammars which are often used for reference purposes. Pedagogic grammars aim to classify language for teaching purposes, so the rules they give are attempts to simplify and generalise. These are the kinds of rules to which the statement above refers. There are often exceptions to the rules that are given in coursebooks and pedagogic grammars, as we shall see in Chapter 7.

It also depends on what is meant by the word 'learn' (see Statement 3 above). Sometimes even rules that are easy to explain and practise take a long time to acquire and thus to become incorporated into language use. The rule that there must be an *–s* ending on the verb in the third person singular of the present simple tense in English is simple, but even advanced learners sometimes say *She work*, or overcompensate and put *–s* endings where they are not needed. In English, the form of the possessive adjectives *his* and *her* relate to the gender of the possessor. In languages where nouns have genders they usually agree with the noun. Students quickly learn this rule but continue to say things like *His husband* for some time. Other rules are conceptually more difficult, like the uses of the present perfect tense in English, and learners require a lot of exposure before they begin to use such features correctly.

Explanation of rules only helps if the learner has sufficient experience of the target language to make sense of it, in which case there may be no need for the explanation at all. Sometimes learners begin to use new language to which they have been exposed without having had any rule explained or even any practice of the pattern. They just acquire it naturally.

What is interesting is that there are many common errors that all learners tend to make, no matter what their mother tongue is. Even more interesting is the evidence that shows that all learners seem to acquire grammatical features in a similar order regardless of the sequence in which they have been taught. For example, *–ing* forms come early on, but the third person *–s* very late.

So, one thing seems quite clear – a rule will not become internalised until the learner's developing language system can accommodate it. And, for individual learners, we have no way of knowing when that might be. So once learners have learnt to recognise and pronounce the new pattern, there is little point in trying to speed up the learning process by extra practice, which is what most coursebooks seek to provide. Classroom time may be better spent in other ways: increasing exposure, (which will provide more examples of patterns that learners may recognise), expanding their repertoire of useful words and phrases and getting them to use language themselves. This is what task-based learning is all about.

5 You must use the language freely to learn to speak it, even if you make a lot of errors.

Certainly this is how you learn to speak when acquiring another language naturally. Because you are in situations where meaning is paramount, you have to try to get it across, making use of whatever words and phrases you have at your disposal. In classrooms, many speaking activities involve students in producing a given form or pattern, or expressing a given function, rather than saying what they feel or want to say.

Free use involves a far broader range of language and gives learners richer opportunities for acquiring. They need chances to say what they think or feel, and to experiment in a supportive atmosphere with using language they have heard or seen without feeling threatened. They need chances to test the hypotheses they have formed about the way language works, to try things out, to see if they are understood. They are bound to get some things wrong at first. But they will gradually get more accurate as their repertoire of language increases. A task-based learning framework aims to provide opportunities for learners to experiment, both with spoken and written language.

6 Teachers should always correct student errors.

Most teachers disagree with this. If you actually tried to correct every error, including those of stress and pronunciation, the lesson would come to a standstill and learners would become demotivated. Many students say they won't risk speaking in or out of class because they are afraid of making mistakes or being corrected in public. So when will they ever get the chance to learn by speaking freely?

When children are learning to speak their first language, parents are usually encouraging, or even ecstatic, if their child comes out with a new expression, no matter how imperfect. Parents sometimes rephrase what children say but in a very positive way. They rarely respond by saying 'That was a good try but you made two mistakes, so say it again.'

Few teachers correct students when they are doing an activity in pairs or small groups aimed at confidence building and fluency. In those situations students rarely take in a correction anyway. In the privacy of a small group, with the teacher monitoring from a distance, learners are more likely to experiment and take risks with new language if the atmosphere is supportive.

There are, however, times when students need to be accurate. Apart from the obvious requirements of examinations, learners feel the need for accuracy when they perform in public, that is, if what they say is going to be recorded, or if they are preparing an oral presentation, or a piece of writing for public display. Preparing drafts gives them a chance to check things they are not sure about, and time to work out new and better ways of expressing what they mean. So it is important that learners are challenged to be accurate at times, because this helps them to consolidate and improve their language.[5]

Ideally, the classroom should be managed so that opportunities for both kinds of language use – private and public – are available and distinct from each other. Students should know when they can use language freely without worrying about getting things wrong, and when they need to be accurate.

7 Reading widely is one of the best ways to learn another language.

Teachers often feel strongly that extensive reading does help, although students often say they don't have time! Many successful learners find that reading is an excellent way of extending vocabulary, learning new phrases and consolidating grammar.

Like extensive listening, reading provides rich exposure to language in use. Both are valuable, but reading is more controllable than listening, and allows time for reflection. You can read fast or slowly; you can go back and read things again. Good students often treat texts as learning opportunities and go back over the same pages several times, working out meanings and noting down new words and useful phrases.

Some people manage to gain an excellent reading knowledge of a language but never learn to speak it. This is usually because they either have no need or opportunity to speak, or do not hear the language used. Conversely, other people never learn to read at all, but speak quite fluently. This is often the case when languages have different alphabets and learners rely on spoken input. The most successful learners make use of all the opportunities for exposure they are offered, and reading is usually one of them.

8 People of all intellectual abilities can successfully learn another language.

Everyone is born with an innate ability to learn a language. As we saw in Focus 1, the majority of the world's people have to learn two languages just to go about their daily life. Few fail in these circumstances. It is mainly in formal instruction (where the focus is on learning about the language rather than interacting in the language) that intellectual ability (aptitude) seems to matter.

It is worth remembering that some students are less sensitive to grammatical niceties but better at memorising, while others use more cognitive strategies. Either way of learning can be successful and some learners practise both. Research shows that high-quality teaching can nullify aptitude differences.[6] So we can hope that if we re-create natural learning conditions in the classroom, all learners will learn. This is precisely what task-based learning aims to do.

9 The younger you are the better you will learn another language.

Some experts believe that there is a 'critical period': that children who begin to learn a new language before puberty will learn better; that after puberty, it is more difficult to attain native-like fluency and pronunciation. In fact, it depends a lot on the circumstances.[7]

Adults usually learn faster to begin with because they use more cognitive and metacognitive strategies. Children have better memories and rely less on cognitive strategies. They are even less likely than adults to benefit from formal grammar teaching, though simple consciousness-raising activities designed as games or puzzles to suit their stage of cognitive development seem to help. With children, teachers often use more active methods, reflecting their ability to imitate and rote-learn and to speak without being self-conscious. Both adults and children benefit from involvement in games and problem-solving activities, but obviously of different types. Exposure and involvement are critical for all age groups.

10 Extroverts make better language learners.

Many people who write about second language learning make the point that language is intimately bound up with human behaviour and personality.[8] Language learning, therefore, requires investment of the whole person and positive attitudes to it are important. For the teacher, this means encouraging self-esteem, which in turn gives learners the confidence to adopt beneficial risk-taking learning strategies.

Extroverts often appear to be more active learners, and more willing to take risks with language; however, introverts who are silent in class are often listening well, thinking hard and learning as much – if not more. Other personality factors also come into play: people who are tolerant of ambiguities tend to do well, while shy or anxiety-prone students may do less well and will benefit from small group or pairwork, which is less threatening.

In this section we have examined some commonly held beliefs about learning and explored evidence for those beliefs. Some is evidence we have noticed ourselves as learners or teachers, some has been noted by researchers into language acquisition. Both kinds of evidence contribute to the theories we hold about language-learning processes.

1.2 How learners differ

We now turn from examining learning processes to examining individual learners and in particular how their ways of learning can be different.

Factors such as previous learning experience, cognitive style and motivation, as well as aptitude, age and personality, which were discussed above, may all affect an individual's learning style and strategies. Motivation will be dealt with separately in 1.3.3.

Research into these factors has produced conflicting findings and generated much controversy. It has not produced much in the way of clear guidelines for teachers.[9] Most of these factors cannot be changed by the teacher, anyway, but it is important to recognise them, and we can often rough-tune classroom activities to suit as many people as possible.

1.2.1 Learning strategies	Different types of learners adopt different strategies for learning successfully. Good learners tend to have more strategies than weak ones, and they use them more regularly.

It is generally agreed that good language learners have a strong reason for learning the language, and will:

- seek out opportunities to use the target language and make maximum use of them, focusing on communication of meaning rather than on form;
- supplement natural learning with conscious study, e.g. by keeping a notebook for new words;
- respond positively to learning situations, avoiding anxiety and inhibitions;
- be able to analyse, categorise and remember language forms and monitor errors;
- be prepared to experiment with language and be willing to take risks;
- be flexible and capable of adapting to different learning conditions.[10]

O'Malley and Chamot (1990) identified three main types of strategy: 'metacognitive' (e.g. organising one's learning, monitoring and evaluating one's speech, etc.); 'cognitive' (e.g. advance preparation for a class, using a dictionary, listing/categorising new words, making comparisons with other known languages, etc.) and 'social' (e.g. asking for help, interacting with native speakers, etc.).

Teachers can help by making students aware of such strategies, and encouraging their use. Previous educational experience may have resulted in learners having a very limited range of strategies. In cases such as these, students may benefit from actual training in particular strategies. Certainly encouraging students to become self-reliant will raise the quality of their classroom learning and make it easier for them to carry on learning after their course has finished. [11]

1.2.2 Analytic and holistic learners

Learners' cognitive styles may vary, too. A distinction is often made between analytic learners who prefer a deductive approach (give them a rule and let them deduce other examples from it) and holistic learners, who prefer an inductive approach (give them examples, and let them induce the rule). However, much research on cognitive styles and second language success is, in the end, inconclusive. Indeed, it has been suggested that learners should be exposed to a variety of approaches in order to broaden their learning styles.

Task-based learning, with its holistic approach, would seem, in its purest form, to favour the styles of holistic learners. The broader framework suggested in this book tries to take all types of learners into account. Chapter 9 will give advice on helping learners who have difficulties in adapting.

No matter what strategies or styles your learners use, it is generally agreed that there are certain essential conditions to be met that are vital for all language learners. These are outlined in the next section.

1.3 Four conditions for language learning

From now on I shall use the word 'learn' in its general sense, and not distinguish between acquiring and learning, unless otherwise stated.

The many research studies into foreign language learning have, to some extent, produced conflicting results. It is often argued that we don't yet know enough to be sure that one method is better than another. However, there are certain basic principles that can help us select and devise useful classroom activities that are most likely to stimulate learning. So under what conditions does effective language learning take place?

Most researchers would agree that in order for anyone to learn a language with reasonable efficiency, three essential conditions must be met. These are basic enough to apply to all learners, regardless of their individual cognitive styles. There is also one additional condition that is desirable, though not essential. These conditions are summarised in the following diagram:

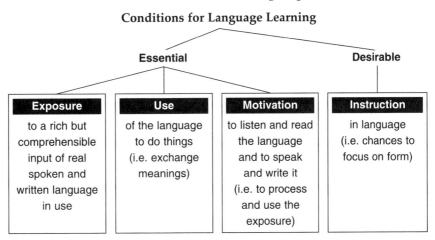

Conditions for Language Learning

	Essential		**Desirable**
Exposure	**Use**	**Motivation**	**Instruction**
to a rich but comprehensible input of real spoken and written language in use	of the language to do things (i.e. exchange meanings)	to listen and read the language and to speak and write it (i.e. to process and use the exposure)	in language (i.e. chances to focus on form)

1.3.1 Exposure

All good language learners take full advantage of their exposure to the target language in use. This might involve listening, or reading, or both. It may be a conscious process, or largely subconscious. It involves grappling with meaning (trying to make sense of whatever they hear and read) and observing how others express the meanings that they want to be able to express. This leads on to noticing small chunks of language typically used in particular contexts, for example *It doesn't matter*; *I don't know*; *What I think is…* It involves isolating particular words and phrases, discovering what they mean and noting how they are used. It is only when such features are noticed, processed in the learner's mind and understood that they are likely to become part of their internalised language system.[12]

One important question is what sort of real language benefits learners most? For beginners, rich input such as randomly chosen radio programmes will just be noise. No matter how motivated, beginners are unlikely to be able to notice and pick out anything comprehensible, and therefore will not learn from them.

However, if learners initiate a conversation, they are likely to use strategies to adjust the input to suit their level of comprehension. For example, simply looking blank will often cause the speaker to rephrase and try again. Knowing what the topic and the purpose of the conversation are, the learner can make sensible predictions about meaning, and check anything they are not sure of having understood correctly. This modified exposure thus becomes comprehensible input and should help acquisition.[13]

If learners select a radio programme of a familiar type on a familiar topic and can guess at the kinds of meanings that are likely to be expressed, and how the discourse will proceed, they will have a better chance of catching something they can understand and subsequently learn from. They are modifying their input by careful selection.

A similar kind of modifying can apply to reading too. By selecting a familiar genre and style of text on a familiar topic, and by reading and re-reading as we discussed in Statement 7 above, parts of the input become comprehensible. Deciphering instructions given in a foreign language is a good example of this, especially if they are relevant to some task in hand.

Teachers commonly modify their speech to suit their learners and help them understand. Repeating, rephrasing, stopping to explain a vital new word are all part of the natural co-operative communication process. Non-native teachers are generally much better at this than native speakers, because they have a greater appreciation of their learners' difficulties. Often this modification is done quite unconsciously, and it is beneficial so long as it is not carried too far.

There will, for example, be problems if everything is always said very slowly and clearly, for there are likely to be distortions of common intonation patterns, and learners will never get used to coping with natural speech. Some teachers, in their attempts to simplify, tend to address adult learners as if they were children. Other native-speaker teachers have been known to converge their speech so far towards their learners' systems that they produce ungrammatical and quite strange discourse – a kind of classroom pidgin. Obviously learners fed on a diet of impoverished input are not going to acquire anything resembling a nationally or internationally acceptable version of the target language. Neither will they be able to understand the language when they hear it used outside the classroom. So as teachers we must be aware of how we modify our classroom language.

An internationally acceptable version of the target language does not have to be a native-speaker variety. Well over half the people in the world who speak English are non-native speakers. Over half the world's business is conducted in English between people whose first language is not English.

What about the linguistic simplification of reading texts? This has been a controversial issue, and it depends very much on how the simplification is done.

There may be no overall advantage in simplifying texts. Systematic simplification removes certain features of a text, for example by rewriting complex noun groups or breaking up grammatically complex sentences into a series of two or more simple ones. Such simplification, by definition, deprives learners of the opportunity to become familiar with the original forms, which may occur frequently in the target language. Nor does simplification necessarily make the task of comprehension easier. Rewriting a complex sentence as a series of simple ones entails the omission of explicit markers like *because*, *so* and *although*. The price of grammatical simplicity, therefore, may be the obscuring of meaning. Finally there is the risk of the text becoming a distorted sample of the target language – one which learners subsequently have to unlearn.

It is essential that learners are ultimately exposed to the variety of language they will need to understand and use outside the classroom. This might be language they will need in order to study other subjects, to use at work, or for pleasure. If they need to write reports, they will need to read and study reports to find out how these are typically written. If they wish to become fluent in informal, spontaneous conversation, they will need to experience samples of spontaneous conversation.

Some language students, especially younger learners, might not know what language they will need later. In this case it is best to select a range of materials that will give them a varied language experience, and to choose things they enjoy in order to sustain their motivation.

A final point is that in research on second language acquisition, the quality of the exposure has been found to be more important than the quantity. Quality does not just mean good pronunciation but a variety of types of language use, e.g. informal chat as well as formal monologue, and a range of different kinds of writing. In other words, exposure to a restricted diet of simplified or specially written texts, sentence-level examples and scripted dialogues is not enough. This is why the words 'rich' and 'real' appear in the diagram on page 11.

In 1.4 and 2.3 we will explore further the issue of 'quality' exposure and look more closely at the differences between classroom and non-classroom interaction and between spontaneous and planned language. In Chapters 5 and 7 we shall look at ways to select and exploit reading and listening texts.

1.3.2 Use of language

As well as input, output is now generally considered essential for language development, especially if learners wish to speak and/or write in the target language. If learners know that in class they will be expected to make real use of the target language themselves, this leads them to pay more attention to what they hear and read, and to process the input more analytically, noticing useful features of language. Thus output can encourage intake.[14]

Some teachers believe that real beginners need an initial silent period where they are not called upon to speak the language until they have had a certain amount of exposure to it. This gives them time to get the feel of it, and to acquire naturally, in an unpressured atmosphere, a stock of words and phrases they can then use when they do begin to speak. Some learners, however, feel frustrated by an imposed silent period and want to start speaking as soon as possible. Teachers should be sensitive, and accept but not force early contributions from their beginners (see Chapter 8).

As we discussed in Statements 5 and 6 above, learners need opportunities to communicate what they want to say and express what they feel or think. Using language for real purposes (for example to get things done, share experiences and socialise) gives learners chances to recall and use the language they know already. It is important, especially with less confident learners, to create a positive, supportive, low stress atmosphere that encourages creativity and risk-taking.

Through interaction, learners have the chance to acquire the range of discourse skills they need in order to manage their own conversations, and to control the level and kind of input they receive. These discourse skills include:

- opening and closing a conversation, i.e. introducing a topic and saying how it is relevant and 'winding down' a topic to prepare for saying good-bye and leaving;
- interacting and turn-taking, i.e. recognising possible pause points and ensuring that people will listen; even interrupting politely, to clarify or challenge what someone has said;

- organising the discourse in advance in order to sustain a longer speaking turn, e.g. *Well, I think there are two things you ought to think about. One is…*;
- reaching agreement co-operatively and shifting the topic.

Learners also need the experience of communicating in a variety of situations, for example in different size groups and for different audiences, since different linguistic strategies are appropriate in different circumstances.

There is evidence, then, that learners who are encouraged to communicate are likely to acquire a language faster and more efficiently. Teachers have also noted ample evidence that learners who are pushed or challenged to 'go public' will strive harder to improve and reach a higher level of accuracy.[15]

However, practice activities that are not meaning-focused, such as acting out dialogues, where the main aim is to practise specific forms and functions, have been found inadequate ways of promoting learning by themselves. All too often students do them on automatic pilot without really having to think about what they mean.

1.3.3 Motivation

The third essential condition students need is motivation to learn: motivation to process the exposure they receive, and motivation to use the target language as often as possible, in order to benefit from exposure and use.

Learners' motivation may be integrative (they may admire and identify with the target language and culture) or purely instrumental (they see the target language as a means to an end, such as further study or a good job) or it may be both. Other motivating factors include travel, seeking new friendships and simply acquiring knowledge.[16]

Even if language students have no personal long-term motivation, as is often the case in school, teachers can select topics and activities that serve to motivate them in the short term. If an activity can stimulate interest and involvement for, say, the next ten minutes of a lesson, students may learn something during that time.

Success and satisfaction are key factors in sustaining motivation. If students feel they have achieved something worthwhile, through their own individual effort, they are more likely to participate the next time. Hence the need for teachers to set achievable goals, and to highlight students' successes.

Early on, or when confidence is low, teachers may select simple communicative activities that students can achieve with success, for example, exchanging phone numbers in order to make a class telephone directory. Praise and encouragement will help to raise motivation. As we discussed earlier, there is no point in expecting accuracy early on, and to correct more than is absolutely necessary only undermines confidence and reduces motivation, especially when the focus is on trying to communicate.

Sometimes, though, students gain both confidence and satisfaction from activities like repeating after the tape or the teacher. In this case, spend a little time each lesson doing such activities. Children especially enjoy learning songs, poems and even dialogues by heart. Adults sometimes feel this helps them to improve their pronunciation. It may help them to notice new sounds and intonation patterns, which could raise their awareness of phonological features. Later, learners will benefit from activities presenting a higher degree of challenge, both cognitive and linguistic.

Obviously, if students can be motivated sufficiently to seek out opportunities for exposure to and use of the target language outside the classroom, so much the better. Writing to pen-friends, reading, and even playing computer games in the target language will give learners valuable language experience.

Exposure, use and motivation, then, are three essential conditions for language learning. One without the others, or even two without the third, will not be sufficient. All three can be met outside the classroom, as we saw above. Learners can learn a language quite successfully by living, working or socialising in an environment where the target language is used, simply because these three conditions naturally coincide.

However, the level of accuracy thus attained depends greatly on the uses to which such learners need to put their language. Some become almost indistinguishable from native speakers; others, however, manage to communicate but with poor syntax, simply because in their social or professional circles this level of language attainment is acceptable. Such learners are likely to fossilise and cease to improve unless they have a reason to become aware of language form.

So, we have a fourth condition: instruction, which, although not totally essential, is highly desirable.

1.3.4 Instruction

It is generally accepted that instruction which focuses on language form can both speed up the rate of language development and raise the ultimate level of the learners' attainment.

What instruction does not seem to do is change the learners' developmental sequence (see Statement 4 above). In other words, students will not necessarily learn what we teach them when we teach them. Neither does it change the order in which linguistic features begin to occur accurately in spontaneous talk, which is why students often do not appear to learn from error correction. However, given adequate exposure and the right conditions, their language systems will develop along similar lines to those of people who acquire the language naturally.

So, would one solution be to construct a syllabus that reflects the natural order of acquisition? This unfortunately presents many problems. Firstly, we do not yet know enough about it; studies are restricted to certain morphemes, like *–ing*, *–ed* and *–s* endings, and some developmental sequences involving negatives, interrogatives and relative clauses.[17] But language involves far more than this and we have little idea of the order in which other features may be acquired. To restrict learners to those features we know are learnable at each stage would seriously distort the sample of language to which they were exposed. And besides, how do we know which learners are at which stage? Learners in the same class may well be at different stages in the developmental sequence, and so would not benefit from such restricted input or focus.

This last problem occurs with any lockstep approach to teaching grammar where students are expected to produce the target structure themselves. Spending twenty minutes on presenting and practising one single structure to perfection is likely to benefit only the very few learners who happen to be ready to use it. Some may know it already and it might be beyond the grasp of the rest. For these students, such practice is largely a waste of time.

The same is probably true of narrowly focused pronunciation drills. For most students, improving pronunciation is a slow organic process. They need to be aware that particular sounds exist, but not made to feel stupid if they cannot yet distinguish or produce them.

In what ways, then, can instruction help? It can certainly help students notice specific features of the target language. It can give students the opportunity to process grammatical and lexical patterns, and to form hypotheses about their use and meaning. Learners are then more likely to recognise these features occurring in the input they are exposed to. For example, once they have had their attention drawn to the use of the words *thing* and *things* in spoken phrases such as *The thing is…* they may start to notice other common phrases such as *The important thing is…* or *and things like that*. Subsequently, each time they notice a phrase with the word *thing*, they stand to gain a new insight into its use. These all become learning opportunities.

Sometimes they notice a new piece of evidence which disconfirms a hypothesis, and changes the whole picture they have of a particular form. For example, if they have learnt about the past simple, and have begun to recognise past tense verbs, they will use the past simple for everything that has happened in the past (a process that researchers refer to as overgeneralisation). Then one day, they notice verb phrases that seem also to refer to the past, but with *have / has* – the present perfect. So their former hypothesis about the past simple is disconfirmed. They now need to look out for examples of both tense forms, and examine evidence of when they are used. This leads to a restructuring of their current system to accommodate the new evidence, and drives their language development forward.

Activities aimed at promoting awareness of language form, making students conscious of particular language features and encouraging them to think about them are likely to be more beneficial in the long run than form-focused activities aimed at automating production of a single item.

If we offer learners as rich a language menu as they can cope with, we can give them plenty of opportunities to notice useful features.[18] We can help them by setting consciousness-raising activities (see Chapter 7) to highlight specific aspects of language that occur naturally both in their reading and listening texts. We can give them a chance to ask about other features they notice for themselves.

During such activities, individual learners' differences can more easily be catered for, and different levels of learners can be accommodated. Setting learners to investigate specific linguistic features allows them to process them in their own time, at their own level. Phrases and words that individuals want to remember can be written down, new words can be looked up; phrases and patterns that students think might come in useful can be practised quietly. Learners will probably all be learning something different.

We find, therefore, that activities that raise learners' awareness of and make them think about language form, together with activities like planning and drafting a public presentation, are likely to be more beneficial in the long run than activities automating the production of specific patterns. Michael Long summed this up nicely by recommending a focus on form (in general) rather than a focus on forms.[19] We must remember, however, that focus on form, or instruction is not an essential condition for learning.

In the next section we take a closer look at a typical teacher-centred classroom environment, to see to what extent the three conditions that are essential for language learning are generally met.

1.4 Classrooms as learning environments

This last section will reveal how the very nature of classroom interaction can easily restrict the learning opportunities open to the language learner – even though our whole teaching aim is to reproduce the essential conditions for learning, and thus to enlarge and open up those opportunities.

It describes typical features of classroom interaction showing how this differs from real-world interaction. It shows how and why teachers may need to change typical teaching routines to give learners a fairer share of the interaction with more opportunities to acquire discourse skills and to experiment with the target language themselves.

1.4.1 The power of the teacher

Which of these two exchanges is more typical of a language classroom?

Excuse me. What's the time?
Erm... Five past five.
Thanks.

Okay. Who can tell me the time? Yes? Ana.
Erm... Five past five.
Good. Five past five. Yes.

Most people immediately recognise the second as being a classroom exchange. In fact, classroom interaction is typically made up of three-part exchanges in which the teacher initiates, a student responds, and the teacher gives some feedback. And if the teacher gives no feedback, the learners take this as a negative sign and go on trying to answer until some feedback occurs.

There are many ways in which classroom interaction differs from everyday, real-life conversation. Let's start by looking at the normal roles of the teacher as exemplified by the second exchange above.

- The teacher alone has the power to nominate a topic: *Okay. Who can tell me the time?* (Imagine if a student started by saying *Okay* to the teacher!).
- The teacher controls the turn-taking, by nominating a student (*Ana*), or selecting by gesture or eye contact and saying *Yes?*
- The teacher initiates most exchanges, which may involve:
  - informing the class about something
  - directing students to do or say something
  - eliciting a response (asking a question that she normally knows the answer to – these are often called display questions)
  - checking that something has been done.
- The teacher finally evaluates the response, in this case: *Good.*

In other words, it is the teacher who controls the openings and closings of every classroom topic or activity, who controls the turn-taking, and who initiates almost every exchange.[20]

For teachers this power is reassuring. It allows them to exert a large measure of control over the language produced by students. However, for the student trying to learn a language for the purposes of communication, it is another matter. It is true that they will get a fair amount of exposure if the teacher uses the target language for most of the lesson, but this exposure will be of a limited nature. And what opportunities will students have to use English for themselves and to acquire discourse skills such as those described in 1.3.2?

1.4.2 The constraints on the student

It is true that students occasionally ask questions to check meanings and spellings, but research based on hours of classroom recordings, even recordings of so-called conversation classes, reveals that the role of the student in teacher-led classroom interaction is generally that of responding.

Since responding is one third of the typical three-part exchange, and since all students share this one third between them, an average student in a class of 30 will get half a minute's speaking time in a 45-minute lesson. With 4 x 45 minute lessons a week for 36 weeks a year, each student will get one and a quarter hour's talking time a year. This is in fact a generous estimate; it does not allow for times in class where the teacher is in 'lecture' mode, or when students are reading, writing or listening.

If 10 minutes of every lesson is used for pair interaction (all pairs working simultaneously), this allows each learner an extra 20 minutes' speaking a week or 12 hours per year, making a total of around 13 hours. This at least is some improvement.

We also need to consider the quality of student talking time. In how many of those responding moves will students be actually communicating, i.e. saying what they think or feel? Often responding involves learners in repeating a pattern, or saying a word or phrase to show they know it. Even in pairwork, much of the talking is based on form-focused exercises or dialogues from textbooks, where students practise the target forms or display linguistic knowledge.

We see, then, that most of the opportunities for language use are taken by the teacher. Generally, learners in a teacher-led classroom get hardly any chances to manage their own conversations, exercise discourse skills, or experiment with, and put to meaningful use whatever target language they can recall.

1.4.3 Changing the balance

In task-based learning, communication tasks (where language forms are not controlled) involve learners in an entirely different mental process as they compose what they want to say, expressing what they think or feel.

Tasks remove the teacher domination, and learners get chances to open and close conversations, to interact naturally, to interrupt and challenge, to ask people to do things and to check that they have been done. Much of this will involve composing in real time. The resulting interaction is far more likely to lead to increased fluency and natural acquisition than form-focused exercises that encourage learners to get it right from the beginning.[21]

If students are to learn how to communicate efficiently, it is vital for them to have more equal opportunities for interaction in the classroom. Teachers need to find ways to relinquish much of the linguistic control and to motivate students to interact more freely and more often in the target language. Learners need more chances to use the target language with each other, not just to practise forms, but also to achieve results. These chances constitute learning opportunities. The teacher dominated initiation – response – feedback pattern needs to be used less often.

In order to meet fully the three essential conditions for learning, then, we need to create more opportunities for students to use the target language freely in the classroom, and thus to provide a more even balance of exposure and use. Carefully selected tasks will provide the stimuli for learners to take part in complete interactions and help to meet the third condition, motivation.

1.5 Summary

This chapter began by examining various beliefs about foreign and second language learning and appraising those beliefs in the light of recent research. We found out why learners often fail to learn what we teach them. We found that learning is a gradual, organic process and, given the right conditions, will happen even without a teacher.

We looked at strategies successful learners use, examined some ways in which learners differ, and suggested that they may benefit by becoming aware of a wider range of learning styles and strategies.

We said that to create an effective learning environment in the classroom, we need to meet three essential conditions: the provision of exposure to the target language; the provision of opportunities for learners to use the target language for real communication; and the provision of motivation for learners to engage in the learning process. In addition, focused instruction – drawing attention to language form – will help learners to improve more rapidly and to continue improving.

We finally reflected on the quality and type of language that learners typically meet and use inside a teacher-centred classroom. We found that the typical routine of teacher-initiated three-part exchanges offered learners an impoverished language input, and very little chance to use the target language individually other than in single responses.

This chapter illustrates some of the principles underpinning a task-based approach to language learning. It focuses on conditions in which people do and do not learn, and argues the need to depart from traditional classroom routines.

The task-based learning framework that is described in the following chapters aims to help you to manage classroom interaction so as to maximise opportunities for learners to put their limited language to genuine use, and to create a more effective learning environment.

Reflection

1 Look back at the questionnaire in Focus 1. In the light of what you have read and thought about in this chapter, do you now feel you would like to change any of your answers? Which and why?

2 What are the implications of what you have read here for your teaching situation? List three things you will try to do next time you teach a class or start with a new group. If possible, compare your list with someone else's.

3 If you have learnt a foreign or second language, think back to that experience. What learning strategies did you use? Which might you use now? How would you rate yourself in terms of cognitive style, motivation and aptitude?

4 In his book *Principles of Language Learning and Teaching*, H. Douglas Brown summarises the six broad learning strategies employed by the good language learners that were studied by Naiman *et al.* (1978):

1 Find a learning style that suits you.
2 Involve yourself in the language-learning process.
3 Develop an awareness of language both as a system and as communication.

4 Pay constant attention to expanding your language knowledge. Make guesses about things you do not know, check your beliefs against the language you hear and read.

5 Develop the L2 as a separate system. Do not relate everything to the L1.

6 Recognise that learning is very demanding both in effort and psychologically.

Compare the above list with the list in 1.2.1. What similarities are there? Are there any differences?

5 Naiman *et al.*'s 'good language learner' research is based in North America. How far do you believe it is representative of students you have taught?

Observation

1 Observe a lesson from the learners' point of view to calculate the balance achieved between exposure, free use of language, and instruction focused on language form. Use a three-column layout as in the example below. Write down in the appropriate column what the students are doing. Tick the activities that seem to motivate most students. Sometimes, for example in pairwork, where they are talking and listening, you will use more than one column. Make a note of the times at which students change what they are doing.

Lesson Observation

Exposure	Use of Language	Instruction
(Ss listening/reading)	(Ss speaking/writing freely)	
10.03 T. explains what lesson is about, and what ss will be doing. Ss listen.		
10.06 T. introduces topic and class brainstorm on ideas in picture.	10.09 Six ss, J F D R P, D, A, offer comments about picture.	a few new words (class pronunciation practice)
10.14 T. writes words and phrases on board and chats about some.		Pronunciation of some of words and phrases. Ss write some down. S queries, e.g. 'Can we say...?'
10.22 T. gives final task instructions.	10.23 Ss start task in twos.	

---

2 Draw a large plan of the class, making a square for each student. Each time a student speaks, put a dot for a single word or short phrase, a short line for a longer utterance or a longer line for a sustained turn, i.e. several sentences.

3 Observe a lesson where the main focus is on speaking. Pick one average student and try to write down everything he/she says (without making it obvious who you are focusing on). If you observe in a group with other teachers, make sure you each choose different students. Discuss what you find out from doing this.

Further reading

For a short and well exemplified introduction to first and second language acquisition written for language teachers, containing some interesting samples of classroom data and another questionnaire to try out, read *How Languages are Learned* by P Lightbown, and N Spada, 1993, OUP.

For a fuller but extremely readable analysis of findings relevant to language teachers, with end-of-chapter vignettes on methodology and classroom applications, read *Principles of Language Learning and Teaching* by H Douglas Brown, 1994, Prentice Hall Regents.

Notes

1 C Doughty, 1991.
2 Krashen's theories are clearly summarised in P Lightbown, and N Spada, 1993, pp. 26–29 and H Douglas Brown, 1994, pp. 279–82.
3 P M Lightbown, 1985, pp. 173–89.
4 N S Prabhu, 1987, p. 17.
5 P Skehan, 1996.
6 J Carroll, 1965 as reported in D Larsen-Freeman, and M H Long, 1991, p. 207.
7 See P Lightbown and N Spada, 1993, pp. 11–12 and pp. 41–52 for more on the effects of age.
8 See H Douglas Brown, 1994.
9 For more discussion see P Lightbown and N Spada, 1993, Chapter 3, or H Douglas Brown, 1994, Chapter 6.
10 Adapted from R Ellis, 1986, pp. 122–123.
11 See G Ellis and B Sinclair, 1989, for more on learner training.
12 R W Schmidt, 1990.
13 D Larsen-Freeman and M H Long, 1991, pp. 134–44.
14 P Skehan, 1994, pp. 177–78, where he summarises work by M Swain, 1985.
15 P Skehan and P Foster, (in preparation).
16 V Cook, 1991, p. 73.
17 For interesting examples see P Lightbown and N Spada, 1993, pp. 57–68.
18 Identifying what these are would largely be the job of the syllabus designer, who would need to ensure that by the end of a course students had been alerted to a thorough and balanced coverage of useful items. But students will doubtless add items they like or need.
19 M Long and G Crookes, 1992.
20 J Sinclair and M Coulthard in M Coulthard (ed), 1992.
21 P Lightbown and N Spada, 1993, pp. 104–105.

FOCUS 2

From topic to task

FAMILIES

1. **Family surveys**   Find out whether your partner's family has more girls and women than boys and men. *Time: 3 min.*
2. **Family tree**   Tell each other the names of your close family, and then draw a family tree for your partner's family. Finally, show it to your partner to check. *Time: 4–5 min.*
3. **Family photos**   Take turns to tell the others about each person in your photo. Put all the photos away. See how much the others can remember about the people in your family. Which person in each family was remembered the best? *Time: 8–10 min.*

   Next lesson – Write as much as you can remember about one of the people in someone else's photo. Do not say who they are. Ask the others to read it and identify the person.
4. **Family members**   How many ways of classifying these family members can you find? e.g. adults/children. Work in twos. *Time: 2–3 min.*

   > ■ father ■ baby ■ grandparents ■ aunt ■ daughter ■ mother ■ brother
   > ■ cousin ■ uncle ■ grandmother ■ parents ■ children ■ son ■ sister

5. **Family birthdays**   Write the dates of four birthdays of people in your family, including yours. Now try to find someone who has the same birthday as someone in your family. Whose are the closest? *Time: 3–5 min.*

Discussion Points

(a) For each topic, say which task might be the easiest and which the most difficult. Why?

(b) Choose any three tasks. Work out what opportunities for speaking, listening, reading and writing each could offer.

(c) Look at the tasks on this page. How would you define the term "task"?

SCHOOL

6. **Teachers** Think of a teacher you remember well. Tell your partner about him or her. Do your two teachers have anything in common? Why do you remember them? Finally, write up what you can remember about your partner's teacher for the class to read.
7. **Subjects** What used to be your favourite and least favourite subjects at school and why? Compare your reasons for liking/not liking them.

WORK

8. **Manager qualities**   Which are the most important qualities in a small company manager? Add four more to the list below, then rank them, starting with the most important. Justify your choice.

   > ■ normally patient   ■ strict on deadlines   ■ sense of humour
   > ■ listens to everyone   ■ knows the competition
   > ■ helps with personal problems

9. **Company in distress**   This task requires company data such as graphs and charts showing downturn in sales, increasing head count, escalating costs, reduced marketing budgets. Can you decide on two alternative courses of action the Managing Director might consider taking? Draft a list of recommendations for both.

N.B. See Appendix A for a useful classification of task types with further examples.

2 Aspects of tasks

> This chapter explores what we mean by tasks in task-based learning (TBL) and looks at different aspects of their use. We include an overview of task types and illustrate a range of materials tasks can be based on.
>
> We then turn to language use in the task cycle. We identify differences between spontaneous spoken language and planned written or spoken language, arguing that learners need to recognise and practise both types. We ask how far the language of a particular task can be predicted.
>
> Finally, we summarise the learning opportunities that TBL offers students.

2.1 Defining tasks

In some books, the word 'task' has been used as a label for various activities including grammar exercises, practice activities and role plays. As I shall show in this section, these are not tasks in the sense the word is used here.

In this book tasks are always activities where the target language is used by the learner for a communicative purpose (goal) in order to achieve an outcome.

2.1.1 Goals and outcomes

The sample tasks in Focus 2 arise out of three different topics. Any topic can give rise to a wide variety of tasks. One job of the course designer and teacher is to select topics and tasks that will motivate learners, engage their attention, present a suitable degree of intellectual and linguistic challenge and promote their language development as efficiently as possible.

You will notice that all the tasks illustrated have a specified objective that must be achieved, often in a given time. They are 'goal-oriented'. In other words, the emphasis is on understanding and conveying meanings in order to complete the task successfully. While learners are doing tasks, they are using language in a meaningful way.

All tasks should have an outcome. For example, outcomes of some of the sample tasks in Focus 2 would be the completed family survey, the final version of the family tree and the identification of the best-remembered person in the photograph.

The outcome can be further built on at a later stage in the task cycle, for example, by extending the pairs family survey to the whole class to discover how many families are predominantly male or female.

It is the challenge of achieving the outcome that makes TBL a motivating procedure in the classroom.

An example of an activity that lacks an outcome would be to show students a picture and say *Write four sentences describing the picture. Say them to your partner.* Here, there is no communicative purpose, only the practice of language form.

It is often possible, though, to redesign an activity without an outcome so that it has one. In the above example, if the picture is shown briefly to the students then concealed, the task could be: *From memory, write four true things and two false things about the picture. Read them out to see if other pairs remember which are true.* The students would be thinking of things they could remember, (especially things that other pairs might have forgotten!) and working out how best to express them to challenge the memories of the other pairs. To achieve this outcome they would be focusing first on meaning, and then on the best ways to express that meaning linguistically.

2.1.2 Meaning before form

An important feature of TBL is that learners are free to choose whatever language forms they wish to convey what they mean, in order to fulfil, as well as they can, the task goals.

It would defeat the purpose to dictate or control the language forms that they must use. As the need arises, words and phrases acquired previously but as yet unused will often spring to mind. If the need to communicate is strongly felt, learners will find a way of getting round words or forms they do not yet know or cannot remember. If, for example, learners at a very elementary level want to express something that happened in the past, they can use the base form of the verb, and an adverb denoting past time, like *I go yesterday, Last week you say…*

The teacher can monitor from a distance, and, especially in a monolingual class, should encourage all attempts to communicate in the target language. But this is not the time for advice or correction. Learners need to feel free to experiment with language on their own, and to take risks. Fluency in communication is what counts. In later stages of the task framework accuracy does matter, but it is not so important at the task stage.

Learners need to regard their errors in a positive way, to treat them as a normal part of learning. Explain to them that it is better for them to risk getting something wrong, than not to say anything. If their message is understood, then they have been reasonably successful. If they remain silent, they are less likely to learn. All learners need to experiment and make errors.

Language then, is the vehicle for attaining task goals, but the emphasis is on meaning and communication, not on producing language forms correctly.

We will now look at two activities and evaluate them as tasks in the TBL sense.

Controlled language practice

A controlled practice activity involving repetition of target patterns is not a task, even if this is done in pairs. For example, in activities like: *Change the verb forms from present simple to past simple* or *In pairs, ask and answer questions using 'Do you like …?' 'Yes, I do/No, I don't'*, the emphasis is closely focused on getting students to produce the right forms. Meaning is of secondary importance.

Role plays

The term 'role play' includes a wide range of activities, some of which do have outcomes to achieve, some of which do not.

Some role plays are actually problem-solving tasks. In a business simulation based on a case study, where a team of people each take the point of view of a company employee and argue their case to solve a problem, they would genuinely be trying to convince one another. The outcome would be the solution of the problem. This counts as a task.

Similarly a shopping game, where students play the roles of shopkeepers and customers, can have an outcome. Customers must buy the things on their 'shopping lists', keeping within a set budget. Shopkeepers must try to be the first to sell out of goods, but also to make a profit. This is likely to involve bargaining sequences where students really do mean what they say, as they try to succeed in the task. Here again there is an outcome for each side to achieve.

However, there are other role plays where students are simply acting out pre-defined roles with no purpose other than to practise specified language forms. These are not tasks. While acting, students are unlikely to be meaning what they say. And if there is no outcome to achieve, they have no real reason to set themselves goals of trying to convince someone or explaining something fully. There is no challenge – they can simply avoid confronting linguistic problems and concede the argument without suffering penalties.

Recordings of classes where students are preparing and performing this kind of role play show that there is often far more real communication at the planning and rehearsal stages, especially where students with the same role are put together in groups to plan their strategies, than during the role play itself.[1]

2.1.3 Tasks and skills practice

Some approaches to language teaching talk in terms of four separate skills: listening, speaking, reading and writing. Skills lessons are principally designed to improve one single skill and often supplement grammar teaching. Other approaches talk in terms of integrated skills. With the exception of reading or listening for pleasure, it is rare for anyone to use one skill in isolation for any length of time. If you are talking to someone you will be both observing their reactions and listening for their responses; as you listen to them, you'll be composing what you want to say next. Writing usually involves reading, checking and often revising what you have written.

Teachers following a task-based cycle naturally foster combinations of skills depending upon the task. The skills form an integral part of the process of achieving the task goals; they are not being practised singly, in a vacuum.

The task objectives ensure there is always a purpose for any reading and note-taking, just as there is always an audience for the speaking and writing. Carrying out a task demands meaningful interaction of some kind.

If you are aware of your learners' current or future language needs, you can select or adapt tasks that help them to practise relevant skills. Some learners may need English for academic purposes, so tasks involving reading and listening, note-taking and summarising are bound to be helpful. Some students may need translating or oral interpreting skills and tasks can be devised to practise these, for example, hearing a news item in one language and comparing it with a news summary in the other. For those who need only to pass a written examination, but also want to socialise in the target language, you could use text-based tasks with written outcomes, and discussion at various points in the task cycle.

2.2 Varieties of task

Whereas Focus 2 illustrates how individual topics can be exploited to give rise to many different tasks, Appendix A sets out six main types of task that could be adapted for use with almost any topic. For each type, examples of topics or themes are given. You could, for example, keep to the topic in the coursebook, and go through the list of task types to see if any are appropriate. For beginners, select a simple task type that involves only one or two processes (see Chapter 8 for examples).

All types of task can involve reading as well as speaking, and many lead naturally into a writing phase. There are more examples of text-based tasks in Chapter 5.

2.2.1 Six types of task

We shall briefly now introduce each type. For more details and examples, please read the following section in conjunction with Appendix A. Numbered tasks are those shown in Focus 2.

1 Listing

Listing may seem unimaginative, but in practice, listing tasks tend to generate a lot of talk as learners explain their ideas. In Focus 2, tasks 1, 2, 3, 5 and 8 involve listing at some stage.

The processes involved are:
- brainstorming, in which learners draw on their own knowledge and experience either as a class or in pairs/groups
- fact-finding, in which learners find things out by asking each other or other people and referring to books, etc.

The outcome would be the completed list, or possibly a draft mind map.

2 Ordering and sorting

These tasks involve four main processes:
- sequencing items, actions or events in a logical or chronological order
- ranking items according to personal values or specified criteria (Tasks 8 and 9)
- categorising items in given groups or grouping them under given headings (Task 2)
- classifying items in different ways, where the categories themselves are not given (Task 4).

3 Comparing

Broadly, these tasks involve comparing information of a similar nature but from different sources or versions in order to identify common points and/or differences (Task 7). The processes involved are:

- matching to identify specific points and relate them to each other (end of Task 3)
- finding similarities and things in common (Tasks 5 and 6)
- finding differences

4 Problem solving

Problem-solving tasks make demands upon people's intellectual and reasoning powers, and, though challenging, they are engaging and often satisfying to solve. The processes and time scale will vary enormously depending on the type and complexity of the problem.

The classification in Appendix A starts with short puzzles such as logic problems. Real-life problems may involve expressing hypotheses, describing experiences, comparing alternatives and evaluating and agreeing a solution. Completion tasks are often based on short extracts from texts, where the learners predict the ending or piece together clues to guess it. The classification ends with case studies, which are more complex, entail an in-depth consideration of many criteria, and often involve additional fact-finding and investigating, as in Task 9.

5 Sharing personal experiences

These tasks encourage learners to talk more freely about themselves and share their experiences with others. The resulting interaction is closer to casual social conversation in that it is not so directly goal-oriented as in other tasks. For that very reason, however, these open tasks may be more difficult to get going in the classroom. Section 2.2.2 below discusses their value more fully. In Focus 2, Tasks 6, 7 and possibly 8 may well include some social personal talk.

6 Creative tasks

These are often called projects and involve pairs or groups of learners in some kind of freer creative work. They also tend to have more stages than other tasks, and can involve combinations of task types: listing, ordering and sorting, comparing and problem solving. Out-of-class research is sometimes needed. Organisational skills and team-work are important in getting the task done. The outcome can often be appreciated by a wider audience than the students who produced it.

The classification in Appendix A starts with children's activities such as model making, and goes on to ideas for creative writing. Social and historical research and media projects may be longer-term tasks spread over a whole day or done in short spells over some weeks.[2]

In real-life rehearsals pairs or groups of students predict, plan and rehearse what they could say in typical real-life situations (e.g. buying stamps). They then perform their dialogue in front of the class, and/or record it. Next, they either hear a recording of a real-life parallel dialogue, or, if they are in an English-speaking area, they go to the place (e.g. the post office) and take notes of what people actually say. If possible, they also take part in a similar situation themselves (e.g. buy the stamps) with another student taking notes. Finally, students compare the real-life versions with their own prepared scripts.

2.2.2 Closed and open tasks	Closed tasks are ones that are highly structured and have very specific goals, for example, *Work in pairs to find seven differences between these two pictures and write them down in note form. Time limit: two minutes.* These instructions are very precise and the information is restricted. There is only one possible outcome, and one way of achieving it. Most comparing tasks are like this.

Open tasks are ones that are more loosely structured, with a less specific goal, for example, comparing memories of childhood journeys, or exchanging anecdotes on a theme.

Other types of task come midway between closed and open. Logic problems usually have a specific goal and one answer or outcome, but learners have different ways of getting there. Ranking tasks and real-life problem-solving tasks have specific goals, too (e.g. to agree on a prioritised list or on a solution), but each pair's outcome might be different, and there will be alternative ways of reaching it.

Open, creative tasks can still have an outcome for students to achieve. This could be to listen to each other's anecdotes and then decide which one was the most frightening or dramatic. Because the range of learners' experience is so wide, and the choice of anecdote is entirely up to them, the precise outcomes will be less predictable.

Generally speaking, the more specific the goals, the easier it is for students to evaluate their success and the more likely they are to get involved with the task and work independently. It is often the goal and outcome that provide the motivation for students to engage in the task, which then becomes for them a learning opportunity.

However, we must not forget that much interaction outside the classroom is not so directly goal oriented. In real life, people often talk just to get to know someone better, or to pass the time of day – there is a far greater proportion of experiential, interpersonal and open ended talk. Our ultimate aim is to prepare students for this.

Tasks with specific goals are good ways of encouraging students to interact in the target language in the language classroom. If, however, some groups of learners begin to talk naturally amongst themselves in the target language even if they are digressing from the task goals, we should do everything we can to encourage it. If students are still working on a task, using the target language, long after the time limit you set, let them be. Their language development is more important than your lesson plan.

2.2.3 Starting points for tasks	This section gives a general overview of five possible starting points. Combinations of these can also be used.

Personal knowledge and experience

Many tasks are based primarily on the learner's personal and professional experience and knowledge of the world. Most of the tasks illustrated in Focus 2 come into this category. The exceptions are Task 9 where starting-point data is given, and 4 and 8 which start from lists. With a group learning for a specific purpose, (e.g. hotel reception skills), tasks can be based on their professional knowledge and experience.

Problems

Here the starting point is normally the statement of the problem. Students are likely to engage better in the task and interact more confidently if they have had a few minutes' individual thinking time before they come together to discuss possible solutions.

Many tasks can be made more challenging by introducing constraints. These can be given at the beginning or, occasionally, to raise the degree of challenge and spontaneity, announced half-way through.

Visual stimuli

Tasks can be based on pictures, photographs, tables or graphs, e.g. Tasks 3 and 9 in Focus 2. Pictures can be used as a basis for 'Spot the difference' games. Initially pairs can work together to spot and describe the differences. Later, each person only sees one picture and they have to describe their picture to each other to find the differences.

Find seven differences. (*Collins Cobuild English Course* Level 1)

For elementary students, games like 'Describe and arrange' and 'Describe and draw' can be done with the teacher describing while students arrange or draw pictures. A more challenging task is to give students three or four pictures from a magazine: one of a person, one of a place and one of an object, and challenge them to develop a story-line that links them all. The outcome arises out of the comparisons of the various story-lines. Individual planning time is recommended for all tasks such as this one that require imagination.[3]

Real objects can be useful too, for example, twelve objects on a tray which learners have 15 or 20 seconds to try to memorise, makes the popular memory challenge, 'Kim's Game'.

Short video sequences, shown without the sound track with pauses every few seconds, can stimulate a lot of speculation and prediction. A ten-second video extract, preferably with some action (shown with or without the sound track), can be used as a memory challenge. Ask students, after they have seen it just once, to recall and list the actions they saw, in the right order. They then tell each other what they remembered. (They might even argue about whose order is correct, but the teacher must not be tempted to say who is right!). Their answers are checked by watching the extract again.

Spoken and written texts

Recordings of spoken English, extracts from video recordings and reading texts can also make good task material. Some EFL books make a clear distinction between 'listening comprehension' and 'reading comprehension' activities but most types of task can be done with either spoken or written text, or a mix of both (see Chapter 5). Selected examples follow:

- Learners read or listen to the first part of a story; are given a few additional clues and are asked to discuss and write an ending.
- Learners spot differences between an original news item (written or on an audio or video recording) and a written summary of it containing one or two factual inaccuracies.
- Learners spot differences between a written story and a version read aloud by the teacher with some of the events in a slightly different order.

In order to complete the goals in all these tasks, students are reacting to the content and processing the text for meaning.

Children's activities

Action games, miming and guessing, and even livelier playground games like hopscotch and ball games are all popular and effective with younger learners (see Chapter 8). Children enjoy making things, drawing and colouring, practising magic tricks, preparing snacks, and doing simple science experiments. If the instructions are available only in the target language, and the necessary materials can only be obtained if they ask in the target language, such activities stimulate a natural need to understand and use it. Many can be broken down into smaller stages, forming a series of tasks, each enriched with teacher talk in the target language. A review or report afterwards (e.g. on a wall poster) will stimulate a different variety of target language use.

Combinations of starting points

Combinations of two or more starting points: text and personal experience, for example, are especially useful in some cases. A questionnaire could deal with a controversial topic. Students would read the statements, then discuss each one, saying whether they agree or disagree and giving evidence from their own experience. The questionnaire format gives a clear step-by-step agenda to the task, thus making it easier to complete satisfactorily.

Other tasks (e.g. 3 and 9 in Focus 2) can be based on a combination of visual data (photographs, graphs and diagrams) and personal or professional experience, while problem-solving tasks are often based on a written text, in combination with a map, chart or table of some kind.

2.3 Language use in tasks

Tasks provide opportunities for free and meaningful use of the target language, and thus fulfil one of the key conditions of learning. But what kind of language can we expect of learners doing tasks? Unfortunately, we are so used to working with written language, that we often do not realise what spoken language is actually like. This is because it happens fast, and we don't normally see it written down. All too often learners think they need to speak in full sentences. But do we, in fact, compose spontaneous speech in sentences? And what are the differences between spontaneous spoken language and written language? The next section attempts to answer some of these questions.

2.3.1 Spontaneous language

Let us look now at two tasks, one open and one closed, that were done, spontaneously, by native-speakers, recorded and then transcribed.[4]

A is an extract from an open task where Rachel and Chris are comparing experiences of sea journeys. B is from a closed task; David and Bridget are playing a 'Spot the difference' game co-operatively, i.e. both can see both pictures, and David is writing down the differences they find to make a key for another pair. The pictures for this task were in Section 2.2.3 above.

A

Chris: *Are you a good sailor? Have you ever been seasick?*

Rachel: *Yeah I have been seasick, once. But I haven't sailed very much. Except in a –*

Chris: *Was that on a long journey?*

Rachel: *Yeah. In fact I'm quite a good traveller normally. But this was erm – er – not on a long journey, no. It was about twenty miles. And erm, coming – on the way back, it was a very small boat, and it was very hot, and me and the rest of my family were on this very – in the inside of the boat. And it was just like being in a – on a cork, carried by the water. And my brother started first, and then it just sort of spread like the plague.*

Chris: *Oh terrible.*

Rachel: *It was ghastly.*

B

David: *Okay? Another difference is the number of the house…*

Bridget: *Yes.*

David: *In Picture A it's thirty; in Picture B it's thirteen…*

Bridget: *– is thirty. Oh!*

David: *Oh, okay.*

Bridget: *Oh. Do you think– ?*

David: *Doesn't matter. Thirty in Picture A and thirteen…*

Bridget: *Thirteen in picture B. And this number's different.*

David: *What number?*

Bridget: *The phone number of Paul Smith and Sons.*

David: *Oh yeah. So, the phone number of Paul Smith and Sons is – what? – in Picture A – is six three one nine oh. Six three one nine oh in Picture A…*

Bridget: *Mmm.*

David: *And six three three nine oh in Picture B.*

Bridget: *Okay.*

David: *Okay. How many have we got? That's three.*

Bridget: *Three. How many do we have to have? Seven. Mm.*

David: *How about the television – is that on? Yes. Oh no, the television is on, is it? – in the first picture–*

Bridget: *Yes, it is!*

David: *… and it's not on in the – in Picture B… that's – what have we got?*

Bridget: *The television is on in Picture A but off in Picture B.*

David: *Okay. Right. Anything else? Oh yes, the man's carrying an umbrella.*

Bridget: *Okay.*
David: *So what shall we put? The man…*

If you look carefully through the transcriptions, you should be able to find examples of the following features:

- evidence of real-time composing, e.g. unfinished utterances, back-tracking, repetition, use of *erm… er…*
- linking devices and signal words that mark stages in the discourse, e.g. in the Sea Journey account, *in fact, but*, and six occurrences of *and*. In the puzzle, words like *right, so*, often start a new exchange.
- follow-up words, e.g. *Yeah, Oh, Mm, Okay*, which acknowledge that the message has been understood.
- final evaluation, e.g. Chris: *Oh terrible*. Rachel: *It was ghastly*. Stories and anecdotes, both written and spoken, normally end with an evaluative comment, and such pairs of adjectives are typical.
- phrases with no subjects, e.g. *Not on a long journey, no*. Other common examples are: *Doesn't matter. Don't know… Makes me think…*
- questions without verbs, e.g. *Okay? What number? How about the television? Anything else?* Other questions that occur later in the same interaction include: *Of what? What? All right?* In the complete game interaction, of the twenty utterances that function as questions, there are ten with no verb. In written language, these would be considered ungrammatical, but in spoken language, like phrases with no subjects, they are perfectly normal and acceptable.
- lexical phrases that seem to be whole units, e.g. *in fact, on the way back, me and the rest of my family, spread like the plague.*

Some lexical phrases like *in fact, of course, spread like the plague*, are fixed phrases which rarely change. Some allow variation: *on the way back / here*. Others like *How about the…? Do you think…?* can be completed in many ways.[5]

The important thing about lexical phrases is that they come mid way between lexis and grammar. Often learners will naturally acquire such phrases as fixed chunks, then realise later how they are made up. They are commonly stored in the mind as whole units. When speaking spontaneously, we compose in real time and often resort to lexical phrases, rather than building complete sentences word by word.[6] It follows that we should not expect students to speak in full sentences when doing tasks in small groups. This would be rather like trying to speak written English – something even native speakers would find very difficult.

While not advocating that students should be explicitly taught features such as back-tracking and half-completed utterances, they should have chances to listen to, use and study them given their need to be able to understand spontaneous speech. They should also learn to recognise useful lexical phrases. We are showing them that even fluent speakers do not speak in whole perfectly-formed grammatical sentences; and that it doesn't matter if they don't either. In the classroom, there is also a tendency to ask learners to be verbally explicit about things that are already shared knowledge. This is unnatural language behaviour. Where both speakers can see each other, there is sometimes no need to be verbally explicit – they understand each other by looks and gestures. In our classes, we need to set realistic standards that are attainable and reproduce normal conditions of language use.[7]

2.3.2 Planned language

It is vital that tasks should expose learners to spontaneous language in appropriate circumstances, and allow them to use it, since most will need to cope with it in real life. However, it is also vital to offer learners opportunities to 'upgrade' their task language to a version suitable for presenting in public and reflect on the changes that need to be made. Research into planned language shows that this is likely to be lexically richer and syntactically more complex. (We have more time to think of better words, and organise our ideas more coherently.[8]) For example, if Rachel had to retell her story to a larger audience in a more formal setting, her planned version would probably sound more like this:

Rachel: *I'm quite a good sailor normally. But this time, I was with my family and we were on a very small boat and it was like being on a cork on the water. We were all sitting inside the cabin and it was really hot. My brother started being seasick first and then it just spread like the plague. It was ghastly.*

In private circumstances, then, with one or two friends, you are likely to talk spontaneously, exploring ideas and ways of getting your message across. Your listeners will recall the content of what you say, but the way you said it is unlikely to stay in their minds – it is ephemeral.

On the other hand, if you are speaking to a larger audience, or writing for someone other than a close friend or family member, it is natural to plan what you are going to say or write. Also, if what you write is going to be published, or what you say will be recorded on audio or video (in other words, made permanent in some way), you will spend even longer thinking about it, trying to make it perfect. So the more public, or more permanent, the circumstances of communication are, the more likely we are to aim at a clear, accurate and well-organised presentation.

The distinction between the two extremes of spontaneous and planned language is summarised below:

Private (or equal status)	Public (or high status)
spontaneous	planned
exploratory	final draft
ephemeral	permanent

Learners need opportunities to use the whole range of language between these two extremes. The three components of the task cycle cater for this need (see Chapter 4).

2.3.3 Predicting language forms

Although it may be possible, with experience, to predict some of the forms that may occur in closed tasks, in more open tasks, it is virtually impossible to do so.

Much of the language used in closed tasks will be transactional in nature; aimed at getting things done, like borrowing, buying, or following instructions. Some well-rehearsed formulae, e.g. *Can I have a...? What about the ...?* may be sufficient for learners' basic needs (and all they can hope for if they are on a two-week survival course) but most will want to do far more with language than this. Matching tasks and games like 'Spot the difference' are also fairly predictable in terms of the basic language needed. *Has the woman/man in your picture got a ...?*

Is there a ... in your picture? are typical questions if the speakers cannot see each other's pictures.

However, the interactional side of closed tasks is rarely so predictable. In real life, all kinds of social talk will occur, some relevant to the transaction, like discussing rules, and some quite peripheral, like gossip or personal anecdotes. This interactional language is nevertheless important for establishing social relations in and outside the classroom, and, as we said earlier, should be encouraged.

Once the task or any single element of it is slightly more open, it becomes harder to predict which grammatical structures will occur naturally and with any frequency. As we saw in the last section, spontaneous language use is a far cry from the carefully constructed textbook dialogues of former years, where a whole conversation was made up almost entirely of two or three distinct grammatical structures. From the task objectives, you may be able to predict broad areas of language use, e.g. whether speakers will be talking about the past, present or future, but there are surprises, even then. The best way to make such a prediction is to record several pairs of fluent speakers doing the task (see Chapter 6) and play back the recordings several times, observing what they have in common.

I tried this for the first time in the early 1980s when I was working in Singapore. I was planning a lesson on the topic of giving advice to holiday travellers. It was just before the mid-year break, and I asked someone who knew Thailand well to give advice to a colleague who was about to go there for the first time on holiday. I set a time limit and recorded their conversation. I expected the standard advice-giving phrases such as *If I were you, I'd..., What about...?, Why don't you...?* and talk about future plans. But when I played back the recording, I found that not one of those standard phrases was used, and most of the interaction was in the past, mingled with the present: *Well, when I went to Bangkok last I stayed at the Grace Hotel, and that was good value, though a bit noisy. [...] And another good place was Chaeng Mai. [...] You get this bus – well it's more like a jeep thing – right up into the hill villages... Oh, and the thing to do is...*

Since then, I have listened carefully to many English speakers giving advice and have observed that we rarely use the standard phrases that appear in language coursebooks for this kind of situation. Why then should we predict our learners will?

Can we, then, go any way towards identifying the language our students need for particular tasks? The only safe way is to listen to them planning and doing the tasks and find out what meanings they want to convey. These will depend largely on the type of task and the learners themselves. As individuals with different experiences and opinions, they will probably have different things to say. They might also use different approaches to topics and tasks, especially the problem-solving type. They could well be at different stages of language development, too.

It is better, therefore, to let learners do the task first, using their own linguistic resources, and then study the language that fluent or native speakers typically use in the task situation. The final part of the task framework builds on this principle (see Chapters 6 and 7).

2.4 Learning from tasks

Learners who are not used to TBL may not at first realise what its advantages are and take some time to understand what is required of them and be persuaded of the benefits (see 9.2).

Here, for example, are some comments from secondary level students aged around 15 who have just started doing some speaking tasks for the first time.[9]

> To work in group is good because everybody help. We talk, try to be the best, correct the mistakes

> The group working is good I'm with friends I like. We talk and sometimes I make a mistake My friend correct

> Working in group is good. I have fun. we discuss something . we do things together. I like it.

> It's fun you talk about something. You learn new things. You are with your good friends .

> I like group work but sometimes my friend talk all the time and not let me talk, than I change group but sometimes same happens

Source
Research carried out at Eyuboğlu High School, Istanbul, Turkey with elementary learners by Köksal, Aysegül (1993)

From the learner's position, doing a task in pairs or groups has a number of advantages. Bearing them in mind will also guide you in your role as facilitator of learning.

- It gives learners confidence to try out whatever language they know, or think they know, in the relative privacy of a pair or small group, without fear of being wrong or of being corrected in front of the class.
- It gives learners experience of spontaneous interaction, which involves composing what they want to say in real time, formulating phrases and units of meaning, while listening to what is being said.
- It gives learners a chance to benefit from noticing how others express similar meanings. Research shows they are more likely to provide corrective feedback to each other (when encouraged to do so) than adopt each other's errors.[10]
- It gives all learners chances to practise negotiating turns to speak, initiating as well as responding to questions, and reacting to other's contributions (whereas in teacher-led interaction, they only have a responding role).
- It engages learners in using language purposefully and co-operatively, concentrating on building meaning, not just using language for display purposes.
- It makes learners participate in a complete interaction, not just one-off sentences. Negotiating openings and closings, new stages or changes of direction are their responsibility. It is likely that discourse skills such as these can only be acquired through interaction.

- It gives learners more chances to try out communication strategies like checking understanding, paraphrasing to get round an unknown word, reformulating other people's ideas, and supplying words and phrases for other speakers.
- It helps learners gradually gain confidence as they find they can rely on co-operation with their fellow students to achieve the goals of the tasks mainly through use of the target language.

2.5 Summary

We first defined what we mean by task: a goal-oriented communicative activity with a specific outcome, where the emphasis is on exchanging meanings not producing specific language forms. We showed how skills practice forms an integral part of achieving task goals. We saw how tasks could be grouped into six types. We made a distinction between closed and open tasks and then considered a variety of starting points for tasks.

From task design we turned to language use in tasks. By analysing transcripts of fluent speakers carrying out tasks, we were able to identify typical features of spontaneous spoken language. We made the point that learners are more familiar with the features of written language, and often feel that they should speak in perfect sentences. But even native speakers talking in real time back-track, hesitate, and compose in short chunks making use of common lexical phrases. We suggested learners should be aware of these features, and also of how planned discourse (spoken or written) may differ.

We then asked how far it was possible to predict language forms that might be used in tasks. Except in closed tasks, we argued that such predictions were unlikely to be accurate, or relevant to learners and the meanings they might wish to convey.

Finally we summarised the learning opportunities that tasks offer.

Material appraisal

1 Classifying tasks

Prabhu classified the tasks that he used in secondary school classes in Bangalore into three categories[11]:

1) Information-gap activities involving a transfer of given information from one person to another, one form to another, or one place to another.

2) Reasoning-gap activities involving the discovery of new information through inference, deduction, practical reasoning, or a perception of relationships or patterns.

3) Opinion-gap activities involving the identification and expression of personal preference or attitude in response to a given situation.

Look through the tasks in Focus 2, or select six tasks of different types from Appendix A, and examine how they would fit into Prabhu's system.

2 Closed and open tasks – see Focus 2

a) Which two tasks have the most specific goals?

b) Which two tasks allow the participants most freedom in terms of what they could choose to talk about?

c) With elementary learners in mind, decide which are the three easiest tasks. Then put them in rank order, with the easiest one first. Which task (preceded by an introduction or demonstration) might be suitable for near beginners?

Observation

3 **Lexis**

    a) Collect as many lexical phrases from spontaneous talk as you can in a week (the language doesn't matter) then compare your list with someone else's.

    b) Look up the following words in a good learner's dictionary, and see how many fixed expressions, lexical phrases or common collocations (e.g. *hard luck*) you can find (either in the examples, or as separate expressions) for each one.

    way   thing(s)   say   hard

4 **Predicting task language**

Choose a task from Appendix A you could use with your learners. Adapt it if necessary. List the language forms and lexical phrases that might be used. Ask two pairs of fluent speakers to do the task (set a time limit of 2–3 minutes) while you record them. They should not hear each other or see your lists.

Play back the tape and see how many of the items on your list were actually used by both pairs you recorded. Write down any other language forms or lexical phrases they used more than twice.

Transcribe the best recording. Keep this data for Chapter 7.

Further reading

For further ideas for tasks, see:
J Hadfield 1987 and 1990, *Communication Games*, Nelson
A Maley and A Duff, 1990, *Drama Techniques in Language Learning*, CUP
N S Prabhu, 1987, *Second Language Pedagogy*, OUP
A Wright, D Betteridge and M Buckby, 1984, *Games for Language Learning*, CUP.
See also G Ramsey, 1987, *Images* and other books in the Longman Skills series.

Notes

1 S Abdullah, 1993.

2 An excellent account of handling project work in secondary school classes is in R Ribé and N Vidal, 1993.

3 Research indicating the value of planning time and the possible effects of additional constraints can be found in P Skehan and P Foster 1996 in J and D Willis (eds), 1996.

4 J and D Willis, 1989, Level 3 Unit 20 p. 138T, and 1988, Level 1 Unit 5 p. 120T.

5 For more on lexical phrases (multi-word units) see M Lewis, 1993 and J M Sinclair, 1991, pp. 109–112.

6 A very readable introduction to the idea of how we compose in chunks is to be found in A Pawley and F Syder in J C Richards and R Schmidt (eds), 1983.

7 The findings from the analysis of these small samples of spoken language are borne out by far larger studies, such as those reported in R Carter and M McCarthy, 1995. See also M McCarthy and R Carter, 1995.

8 This has also been borne out by research by E Ochs, 1979 and T Givon, 1979, who found that native speakers in different situations (public/private, rehearsed/unrehearsed, familiar topic/unfamiliar topic) use language that is more syntactic/less syntactic. See also M Bygate, P Foster in J and D Willis (eds), 1996.

9 A Koksal, 1993, who was working with Turkish learners in Istanbul.

10 P Lightbrown and N Spada, 1993, p. 115.

11 Categories abridged from N S Prabhu, 1987, pp. 46–47.

Components of the TBL framework

Pre-task

Introduction to topic and task

Teacher explores the topic with the class, highlights useful words and phrases, helps students understand task instructions and prepare. Students may hear a recording of others doing a similar task.

Task cycle

Task	**Planning**	**Report**
Students do the task, in pairs or small groups. Teacher monitors from a distance.	Students prepare to report to the whole class (orally or in writing) how they did the task, what they decided or discovered.	Some groups present their reports to the class, or exchange written reports, and compare results.

Students may now hear a recording of others doing a similar task and compare how they all did it.

Language focus

Analysis	**Practice**
Students examine and discuss specific features of the text or transcript of the recording.	Teacher conducts practice of new words, phrases and patterns occurring in the data, either during or after the analysis.

Discussion Points

(a) Which points in the task framework provide students with exposure to the target language in use? What are the precise sources of exposure?

(b) The pre-task phase prepares students to do the task. Select a task from Focus 2 or Appendix A. Think of three things the teacher might do and three things the learners might do during the pre-task phase of the task you have chosen.

(c) The task-planning-report components of the task cycle will obviously always come in that order. At which stages in the task cycle might students benefit most from correction?

(d) The language focus phase will almost always come after the task cycle. Why do you think this is?

3

The TBL framework: overview and pre-task phase

This chapter is the first of three that will illustrate the basic procedures of the three phases in the TBL framework.

It starts with an overview which shows how the phases in the framework and their components link together. It then examines the roles of the teacher and illustrates how teachers might operate the framework with two sample lesson outlines.

It then turns to the pre-task phase. It shows the kind of preparation that may need to be done beforehand, and identifies the steps involved in setting up a task. It goes on to illustrate a range of preliminary activities that can be used in class to introduce the topic and prepare learners for the task itself.

Finally it considers alternative ways of setting up tasks to enhance and vary learner talk, and offers solutions to a range of common problems that teachers sometimes face when managing learners in pairs and groups.

More ways to use the framework with tasks based on spoken and written text will be found in Chapters 5 and 6.

3.1 General overview

Task-based learning is not just about getting learners to do one task and then another task and then another. If that were the case, learners would probably become quite expert at doing tasks and resourceful with their language, but they would almost certainly gain fluency at the expense of accuracy.[1] Teachers often notice that learners reach a 'plateau': they get so far with their English, then stop improving. For the task to promote constant learning and improvement, we should see it as just one component in a larger framework, as shown in Focus 3 and more fully in Appendix B.

The framework consists of three phases: pre-task, task cycle and language focus.

The pre-task phase introduces the class to the topic and the task, activating topic-related words and phrases.

The task cycle offers learners the chance to use whatever language they already know in order to carry out the task, and then to improve that language, under teacher guidance, while planning their reports of the task. Feedback from the teacher comes when they want it most, at the planning stage, and after the report. Exposure to language in use can be provided at different points, depending on the type of task. Either before or during the task cycle, students might listen to recordings of other people doing the task, or read a text connected with the task topic, and relate this to their own experience of doing the task. So the TBL framework so far provides the three basic conditions for language learning – exposure, use and motivation. Within the framework, there is a natural progression from the holistic to the specific. The task cycle offers learners a holistic experience of language in use.

The last phase in the framework, language focus, allows a closer study of some of the specific features naturally occurring in the language used during the task cycle. By this point, the learners will have already worked with the language and processed it for meaning, so they are ready to focus on the specific language forms that carry that meaning. Thus the study of these forms is clearly contextualised through the task itself. This final phase, which includes analysis and practice components, fulfils the fourth desirable extra condition for learning – explicit study of language form.

Language learners need both variety and security. A wide range of topics, texts and task types gives learners variety. A framework such as this, with its three distinct phases, also gives them a sense of security. For example, once they know that there will always be a language focus phase after the task cycle, they will begin to worry less about new language they meet during the task cycle because they know they will have a chance to explore it later.

As you will see, the teaching techniques required for task-based learning are not very different from those of ordinary mainstream language teaching. The differences lie in the ordering and weighting of activities and in the fact that there is a greater amount of student activity, and less direct, up-front teaching.

3.1.1 Teacher roles in the framework

In TBL lessons, the teacher is generally a 'facilitator', always keeping the key conditions for learning in mind. Facilitating learning involves balancing the amount of exposure and use of language, and ensuring they are both of suitable quality (see 1.3.1–1.3.2).

In a TBL framework, most of the emphasis is on learners doing things, often in pairs or groups, using language to achieve the task outcomes and guided by the teacher. The teacher is involved in setting tasks up, ensuring that learners understand and get on with them, and drawing them to a close. Although learners do tasks independently, the teacher still has overall control and the power to stop everything if necessary.

The part the teacher plays during each component of the task framework also varies according to its aim. At the end of the framework, where the focus turns to language form, the teacher acts as 'language guide', for example.

In a broader sense, the teacher is also the course guide, explaining to learners the overall objectives of the course and how the components of the task framework can achieve these. A summing up of what they have achieved during a lesson, or after a series of lessons, can help learners' motivation.

The links between each task and the other components in the task cycle will also need to be made explicit. Learners will be experiencing English throughout the whole task cycle. However, as the lesson outlines accompanying the next section will show, it is only at the end, when useful language from the now familiar task, recordings and texts can be identified and focused on, that specific language objectives will become clear to students (see Chapter 6).

3.1.2 The framework and lesson planning

The components within each phase of the framework provide a naturally flowing sequence, each one preparing the ground for the next. Read Lesson Outlines 1 and 2 in Appendix C. They are based on the recorded tasks we analysed in Chapter 2. They illustrate two different types of task at two distinct levels.

You will notice several differences. The first outline is for a revision lesson, so has a very short pre-task phase and the recording (giving some solutions) is played after the task. The second outline introduces a new topic, so has a long pre-task phase with the recording played before the task, to give students an idea of what they are to do.

3.1.3 The flexibility of the framework

There are many ways in which the components within the framework can be weighted differently and adapted to suit learners' needs. For example, initially, with insecure false beginners, you may feel the report component is not appropriate. However, with learners who are confident and fluent but very inaccurate, you might want to spend more time on this component, with both an oral and a written report. And sometimes students may like to repeat the task itself with another partner at the end of the language focus phase.

If the topic is familiar and the tasks are short, there may be room for two task cycles within one lesson (e.g. listing followed by ranking). If the topic is new or unfamiliar, or if the task is longer or more complex (e.g. comparing or problem solving), the framework can be split between two lessons. A language analysis activity could, for example, be prepared for homework, and reviewed during the next lesson. Even the task cycle could be split, and the report component finalised and presented the following lesson. This would give learners more time to reflect and work out how to express themselves, thus providing an even richer learning opportunity.

There are many different ways to conduct the pre-task phase, too. It is to this which we now turn.

3.2 The pre-task phase

The pre-task phase will usually be the shortest stage in the framework. It could last between two and twenty minutes, depending on the learners' degree of familiarity with the topic and the type of task. If there is a pre-task recording to set the scene, it could take slightly longer.

3.2.1 Advance preparation

If you are planning to do a task from a coursebook or resource book, then much of the advance preparation will have been done for you. A good textbook will have ideas for introducing the topic and task, and will include preparatory activities for learners to do. You may perhaps feel you want to fine-tune the introductory plan suggested in the Teacher's Book to suit your own class, but that should not take too long. Once the topic is clear, if the instructions for the task are clearly set out in the Student's Book, learners can be encouraged to read them, plan individually how best to tackle the task, and get straight on with it without further explanation from you.

If you are designing your own task, or planning to supplement what is in the coursebook, there will be a certain amount of preparation to do beforehand, for example, finding suitable pictures, working out vocabulary-building ideas, or perhaps making a one- or two-minute recording of some fluent speakers doing the task. If it is the second or third task on a particular topic, there will be less preparation, since students will by this time have sufficient vocabulary to manage, and the pre-task phase can be much shorter.

Preparing your own tasks for the first time may seem to involve a lot of preliminary work, but you can always use them again with different classes. And once the preparation is done, you will find during the task cycle that it will be the students who are doing most of the work rather than you, the teacher.

Once students are used to task-based learning, they can work independently without much teacher intervention, which takes the pressure off you. There is normally very little marking to do after the lesson is over, since you will be helping them to edit and improve their own work as they plan their written reports in class, with the support of the group.

Let's look at what we need to do in class to set up a task successfully.

3.2.2 Introducing the topic

First of all you will need to help learners define the topic area. For example, topics such as families, school or work, are familiar to most people and should not be difficult for them to understand. There may possibly be a need to clarify, in the case of families, for example, the concept of a nuclear family as opposed to an extended family.

However, students may, especially if they come from other cultures, hold different views on what some topics are about. For example, I was once teaching a group of young adults a unit on holiday plans. I was hoping to encourage them to talk about travelling. All the students from one particular country insisted that during their two weeks' annual holidays they stayed at home and watched television. The concept of going on holiday was alien to them. It transpired they sometimes travelled on business or to visit relatives, but only a few very rich people travelled on holiday. So I had to spend time discussing with the class the concept of travel for pleasure, and change the task focus, before continuing.

3.2.3 Identifying topic language

The second step is to help students recall and activate words and phrases that will be useful both during the task and outside the classroom. You may also need to introduce a few vital topic-related words and phrases that students are unlikely to know. Usually these are introduced and illustrated in the textbook.

In any class you are likely to have some learners who know more of the target language than others. If they are children, some may have had private lessons, or may have travelled to where the language is spoken. Some are just better at remembering than others; some try, some don't. If they are adults, they will have had different language-learning experiences, different kinds of input, and will reveal different areas of expertise and weakness.

It is often difficult to gauge in advance how much topic-related language individual learners will know. The point of the introductory focus on topic and language is not to teach large amounts of new language, and certainly not to teach one particular grammatical structure, but to boost students' confidence in handling the task, and give them something to fall back on if necessary. You will often be surprised, however, at the words and phrases your learners as a class already know and can use. You won't find this out unless you give them a chance to show you, which is what the pre-task activities aim to do.

Encourage learners to pool topic-related words and phrases they know already. You could do this as a teacher-led brainstorming activity. As students think of words and phrases, write them on up one side of the board, talking about them as you write. Later, during the task, if someone gets stuck, others will often co-operate and help them out. They can all refer to the words on the board.

If the task involves reading and talking about a text, you could pick out words and phrases that are vital for a general understanding of main themes. While doing this, you could also note other less vital but still useful words and phrases that you may like to highlight later, at the language focus phase.

In 2.3.3 we drew attention to the usefulness of studying recordings of fluent speakers doing similar tasks (see 6.2 for more detail). Sometimes textbooks have transcripts of recordings you could use. In either case, make a list of a few useful words and phrases.

| 3.2.4 Pre-task language activities | Pre-task activities to explore topic language should actively involve all learners, give them relevant exposure, and, above all, create interest in doing a task on this topic. |

Pre-task activities to explore topic language should actively involve all learners, give them relevant exposure, and, above all, create interest in doing a task on this topic.

There are sometimes problems with direct pre-teaching of a list of useful words and phrases. Students who don't know them will want to spend some time writing them down and practising them, while others who know them already will be bored and feel they are wasting time.

Below is a selection of pre-task activities which rehearse topic language in a stimulating way. You will doubtless be able to think of many others.

In one lesson, one or two of these pre-tasks will probably be enough. Make sure learners know why they are doing them and how they will help them with the main task. Most could be started off as class activities and then continued in groups or pairs, with the teacher circulating.

The italics show sample instructions you might actually give your students.

Classifying words and phrases

On the board, write jumbled-up words and phrases connected with the topic and task. Talk about them as you write. (This will provide good exposure.)

T: *Read through the words and phrases and classify them in different ways, for example, cheap – expensive/hot – cold. How many categories can you think of in two minutes?*

Odd one out

Write sets of related words and phrases on the board, inserting one item in each set that doesn't fit, e.g. *a blue shirt, black trousers, a long dress, a smart tie.*

T: *Say the phrases to your partner and discuss which is the odd one out and why. Then make up some more sets for another pair to do.*

Matching phrases to pictures

You need a set of pictures related to your topic – some can be quite detailed – and two or three phrases or captions for each picture (including, if you like, one that doesn't fit). Mix all the phrases or captions up and write them on the board in a jumbled list.

T: *Which phrases/captions go with each picture? (There may be some left over that don't fit.) Write your own captions for any two pictures. Can your partner tell which pictures they are for?*

Memory challenge

This is the same as the matching activity, only you take the pictures down after one or two minutes, and students must match the phrases or captions to the pictures from memory. It is better not to number the pictures. Then students will have to specify verbally which picture they mean by describing it, which of course stimulates more language use.

Brainstorming and mind-maps

Write the main topic word(s) in the centre of the board. If you have a picture related to your topic, show the class. Encourage students to call out other words and phrases, and ask whereabouts on the board you should write them. Some ideas for classification will develop.

T: *What do you think of when you hear these words and/or see these pictures?*

Thinking of questions to ask

T: *Write four questions you might ask if you were doing a survey on TV viewing, interviewing someone to teach in your college, etc. Exchange questions with another pair and then classify them all.*

Teacher recounting a similar experience

T: *I'm going to tell you about a silly accident I once had. Listen and see whether anything like it has ever happened to you.*

After the learners have done a pre-task or two (or even while they are doing them), write up other useful words and phrases they have produced, especially ones that learners have contributed themselves.

3.2.5 Giving task instructions	The third step in the pre-task phase is to ensure that all learners understand what the task involves, what its goals are and what outcome is required. They will want to know how they should begin, exactly what each person should do, how much time they have and what will happen once they have finished.

Textbook instructions have usually been piloted with students, so they should be clear. If it is a task you have designed yourself, however, or one you have adapted from another source, write down the instructions before the lesson and try them out on a colleague. What seems clear to you may not be clear to an outsider. If your colleague is unsure about what to do, you can clarify the instructions and write a final version to use in class.

The main problem in language classrooms is often actually getting students to talk. In 2.2.2 I suggested that the more specific the goal, and hence the instructions, the more likely students are to feel secure about doing the task. Try to make the goal as specific as possible, by using numbers for example, *Find seven differences/Give two reasons*.

At first, students who are not used to task-based learning may have difficulties in understanding what to do. But as we have seen, there is a fairly limited number of task types. And once learners get used to the procedures of these, they will begin to recognise what the task requires. You will hear comments like: *Oh, it's another 'Spot the difference' task. Now I see. OK, you are A, so you start. You ask me first, OK?*

Many teachers simply read out the textbook instructions and/or give an explanation. If done in the target language, this certainly gives useful exposure, since students have to listen carefully to make sure they understand.

There are, however, alternative ways to ensure that students know how to do the task, and these provide different kinds of learning opportunities.

Students read the instructions by themselves

If your textbook has instructions which are specific enough, ask your students to read and follow them on their own. This trains them to be independent, and is in itself a useful reading skill. They can always ask you if they get stuck.

T: *Get into pairs/groups. Read the instruction on your cards/on page … On your own, spend two or three minutes thinking about what you want to say, and then begin the task. You will have about five minutes to do the task. If there is anything you really don't understand, ask each other, then me.*

Teacher demonstrates the task with a good student

Ask a good student to do the task with you, or just the first part if it is a problem-solving task or a game. Alternatively, ask a pair of good students to do a similar task together while the others watch. You may need to talk to the chosen student(s) about this before the lesson to give them time to think about it.

T: *I'm going to ask Anna to do (part of) this task with me, while you watch. Listen for two things that …*

Teacher plays audio or video recording of fluent speakers doing the task

This works well with experience-sharing tasks and comparing tasks based on learners' own input. It could be better, however, to let the learners do the task their own way first and then hear the recording afterwards, especially if the recording will give the solutions away (see 6.2.2).

T: *Listen to/Watch these people doing the same task that you will be doing later. Note down three things they find out about … Which person thinks …?*

Teacher shows the class what previous students have achieved

T: *These are descriptions of teachers written by last year's class. Pass them round and read three of them to find out … For your task, you will be talking about teachers you remember, then writing about one of your partner's teachers.*

Whether you choose spoken or written instructions, and with or without a demonstration, remember that instruction-giving is a truly communicative use of the target language. It provides valuable exposure and a chance for learners to grapple with meaning and so should be considered another learning opportunity. Resist the temptation to revert to the student's first language unless there is a major breakdown in communication.

3.2.6 Allowing preparation time

Allowing a few minutes for learners to prepare themselves individually for certain tasks has been shown to result in language use that is richer in terms of complexity and variety of syntax, breadth of vocabulary, and in fluency and naturalness.[2]

Sometimes, however, you may want to give learners a chance to practise speaking entirely spontaneously, as they would have to in many real-life situations. In this case, omit the preparation time; get them to read the instructions and go straight into the task.

If the task calls for preparation, how much time should you allow? It depends partly on the familiarity of the topic and partly on the cognitive demands of the task. A puzzle or problem-solving task, or a creative one, would be more demanding for most students than an experience-sharing one. The more complex the task, and the more unfamiliar the topic, the longer you should allow. For elementary learners with a short task on a familiar topic, two minutes may be enough. For a more complex task on a less familiar topic, learners may benefit from as long as ten minutes.

During the preparation time, learners will be able to plan how to tackle the task, think of what to say and how to say it. Interestingly, in the research quoted above, the groups of learners who were given specific language guidance at this stage actually performed less accurately than those who prepared on their own. It could be that in striving to incorporate the language guidance into what they already knew, they overstretched their linguistic resources, and were not able to pay enough attention to other features.

Once the preparation time is over, students begin the task cycle proper. Its three components: task, planning and report will all be described in detail in Chapter 4.

3.3 Managing learner talk

Before describing the task cycle, let us consider some aspects of learner talk, and then pre-empt some of the problems that may face teachers managing group- and pairwork.

3.3.1 Patterns of interaction and turn-taking

No matter what type of task it is, there will be different ways of setting it up. You will need to decide which way you prefer in the pre-task phase. The way the task is set up will directly influence the amount and quality of talk generated. Here are some typical interaction patterns:
- individual students carrying out a task on their own;
- individual students circulating, talking to different students;

- students doing a task singly, then exchanging ideas in pairs;
- students in pairs (as equals, or with one student leading);
- students in groups (with or without a chairperson);
- teacher working with groups or pairs in turn;
- teacher working with the whole class.

Each way will give rise to different patterns of turn-taking. The teacher working with the whole class is common in early tasks for real beginners; listening tasks can be done with the whole class and many require only minimal responses. The teacher talks in the target language while the learners listen and grapple with meaning (see Chapter 8).

In the patterns listed above which involve group- and pairwork, one person can be formally designated to lead the discussion and ensure that each person gets an equal chance to contribute. In other cases, speakers within a group or pair have equal rights, and can take turns to speak or choose simply to listen. They can ask questions, as well as answer, and are free to interrupt or change the direction of the talk. This is important, as we saw in 1.4.2.

Logically, pairwork allows more individual student talk in a given time than groupwork can, unless everyone talks together! It is harder for a shy or lazy student to avoid talking or 'switch off' in a pair, where both students have to concentrate. Sometimes it may be better to put two shy students together, and see how they get on. They may talk more if uninhibited by better students.

The same task can, then, be set up in different ways, resulting in different turn-taking patterns within the group or pair. As an example, see Task 8 in Focus 2. There are three totally different ways of setting this up. Consider the different learning opportunities each one offers, the probable lengths of speaking turns and the amount of clarification likely in each. The task could be done:

a) in groups, knowing that one person will, after ten minutes, be sent as 'ambassador' to another group, to explain what their own group has decided, and to compare outcomes. The 'ambassador' might or might not be designated in advance.

b) with one student chairing a group discussion, to ensure all members have a chance to express an opinion. Another student is asked to take formal minutes, in order to report the group's decisions to the class.

c) with each student beginning it in advance, for homework. In class, they explain their decisions to a partner, and reach a consensus, justifying their ranking. Two pairs then exchange views and reach a final consensus.

3.3.2 Mixed level classes

Teachers who have mixed level classes find that the same tasks can be done quite adequately by learners at different developmental stages. People of different abilities naturally find their own level and ways of coping. In mixed level pairs or groups, weaker students can benefit by hearing what better students say, and better students too, improve, through having to paraphrase, and explain.

However, varying groupings is probably a good idea as it stops students paired with slow learners becoming frustrated. The frequency with which you change groups around depends on the age, status, needs and feelings of the learners themselves.

If some pairs or groups finish the task or planning stage long before the others, first check they have not done so by missing something out! They could join up with another pair who have finished, and tell each other what they did, or ask each other to check their writing. Alternatively, they could write a list of phrases they and the other students might find useful.

3.3.3 Talkative students

Some students perceive tasks purely as 'vehicles for self-expression' and so dominate in any group or pair situation.[3] The effect is heightened if other students are shy or fail to understand the purpose of the task, and do not really know how to contribute. (Once the group realise that someone's contributions are off the point, it is likely that they will begin to ignore or block that person.)

Try asking a talkative student to be the group chairperson, whose job it is to make sure everyone else gets equal chances to talk (see b in 3.3.1). If you notice some students hardly talking at all, use pair- rather than groupwork for a spell.

Some teachers have tried using groupwork self-assessment or appraisal sheets such as those in Appendix D. Used a few times each term, they help students become more aware of how they participate in groups and of the effects of their own typical turn-taking patterns. At a very elementary level, these sheets could be translated into the mother tongue.[4]

Another sensitisation procedure is to use recordings. One teacher who felt that the boys dominated over the girls recorded groups working together, and got them to listen to the tape afterwards to see if this was true.[5] They counted the speaking turns the boys and girls had. They also noted whether boys interrupted girls more, or vice versa. It turned out in this case that there was one very talkative boy, but otherwise the interaction was fairly equal. Both students and teacher benefited from the insights they gained through doing this.[6]

3.3.4 Controlling large classes

Big classes may be a problem. Logically, though, the larger the class, the greater the need for small group or pairwork, to give learners more chance to practise speaking. I have seen quite successful pairwork in classes of 80, but it is not easy and it is certainly not possible to monitor them all. It depends a lot on age, motivation and understanding and acceptance of common goals as well as general levels of discipline.

Learning to speak a language often involves higher levels of noise than is usual in other lessons. Also, in rooms with thin walls or no walls at all, you will have to be considerate of your neighbours. Try some short tasks done in whispers. Decide on a signal which means that students should lower their voices, and another which means they should stop altogether until there is total silence, then start off again in a whisper.

Some teachers find that text-based tasks work best, since they are quieter and easier to control. Choose tasks that make greater use of writing as a form of communication or teacher-led tasks, with short intervals of quiet pairwork. It may be the noise level has risen simply because you have let a task go on too long. Always give a time limit and never wait for everyone to finish. Next time, your students will remember you stick to your time limits and work harder.

And if you feel you are losing control – don't panic. You can always stop the task and ask every pair to write down silently in English three things they have found out or decided so far. Go round and monitor. Noise and discipline are problems you can involve learners in helping to solve.

3.3.5 Balancing target language and mother tongue

When task-based learning is being tried out for the first time, explain to students that if they want to communicate in the target language, they need to practise. Discuss how people learn, the conditions for learning, how speaking can help them learn, and explain why you are asking them to try to talk, even if it is to each other. Make sure they realise that doing a task, no matter how weak their language, is a learning opportunity, a chance to practise in the privacy of their small group or pair, before having to talk in public in front of the whole class, or even in real life.

In some countries, students are very obedient and will stick to the target language if they are told why. In other countries, other forms of persuasion might be needed. But even if only half the task is done in the target language, this still results in 50 per cent more target language being spoken than if no tasks were done, i.e. if the interaction pattern was teacher to individual student.

Banning mother-tongue use altogether may not be advisable. A study carried out recently in Turkish secondary school classes with 12-year-olds revealed that in circumstances when the mother tongue was totally banned in group talk, the resulting interaction tended to be shorter, more stilted and less natural.[7] Many weaker students gave up after a very short time. If learners realise they are using the target language to communicate, they will still use their mother tongue on occasions, but they will use it in a way which is systematic, supportive and relevant to the task goals. The learners in the study, for example, used Turkish to find out how to say words they didn't know; to fill gaps (phrases equivalent to *in other words, Well, erm …*) and to hold the floor. They also used it to explain something complex so that others in the group, or the teacher, could help them express it in English. The message is clear: by allowing such use of mother tongue, you are in fact allowing students to generate more opportunities for use of the target language, not fewer. In bilingual situations outside the classroom, such language switching is quite natural.

Some teachers introduce rules on mother-tongue use from the start. For example, the mother tongue can only be spoken:
- if a student has a question to ask the teacher that they cannot explain in English;
- if the teacher asks the class how they would say a word or phrase in their language, to check that it has been understood correctly;
- if the teacher needs to explain something quickly;
- if students are comparing target language with mother-tongue use;
- if students are doing tasks involving translation or summary of a target language text.

Some teachers involve their students in the rule-making process, and together they draw up a set of guidelines that the whole class agrees on. These can be renegotiated as learners progress.[8] (And in fact the process of drawing up such a list would make an excellent communicative task, with a very real outcome!)

If you feel students are still using mother tongue when they could be using the target language, try to find out the reason. With adolescents, they may just feel silly interacting in a strange language. You might try giving them a choice of topics and tasks. If that doesn't work, concentrate for a spell on listening and reading with text-based tasks that give good exposure (see Chapter 5) until they have more confidence in their linguistic ability. After an agreed time, gradually re-introduce very simple tasks that require more spoken language.

Perhaps the tasks you are setting are too difficult. Try setting some simple ones (like Bingo or 'Spot the difference') until students have got used to interacting in the target language. Praise and encourage. Once they can manage simple tasks mainly in the target language, set a slightly more complex one as a challenge. Point out to them how much English they have been using.

Teaching them useful procedural language sometimes helps, e.g. whole phrases like *Sorry, what did you say?*, *Wait a minute*, *Can you start?*, *Your turn* and so on. Introduce these one or two at a time, as they are needed.

Some teachers have found it useful to time the amount of target language spoken in the class each lesson. Tell students how many minutes they managed. Then you could start setting targets, say three minutes with no mother tongue (except that allowed by the guidelines). Gradually increase the target time. You could also introduce some competition; peer pressure can be quite strong in such cases.

You will probably find that because the planning and report stages in the task cycle need doing in the target language, this has a wash-back effect on the task itself. And, with encouragement, students gradually use more and more target language, so that even over a term, mother-tongue use decreases noticeably.

Coping with problems and experimenting with solutions is an ongoing part of any teacher's job. It is rarely easy to implement change, and the proverb 'If at first you don't succeed, try, try again' certainly applies here. But there are solutions to be found. Talking to other teachers about how they cope in their classes can help. Ask if you can sit in on some lessons. Similarly if you find solutions that work for you, then pass them on to other colleagues and exchange ideas. Chapter 9 gives more advice about implementing task-based learning.

3.4 Summary

The first part of this chapter contained an overview of the three phases of the task-based framework: pre-task, task cycle and language focus. We saw how the task cycle encourages a holistic use of language, often supported by further exposure in the form of a text and/or a task recording. Learners then study specific aspects of that language in detail in the language focus phase, with activities that involve analysis and practice. We examined the roles of the teacher and saw how the framework can be used as a basis for lesson planning, and how components can be weighted differently according to learners' needs.

The second part of the chapter introduced the pre-task phase of the framework. In this phase, learners need an introduction to the topic, and ways to help them recall useful words and phrases and learn vital new ones that will help them cope with the task and the text or recording. To achieve familiarity with the topic lexis, a range of short pre-task activities was suggested. We then explored different ways of helping students to understand task instructions, and discussed the effects of preparation time. The value of exposure to the target language was underlined.

The final part of the chapter described alternative ways of setting up tasks, varying patterns of interaction and turn-taking. It suggested solutions to typical problems that teachers often face concerning pair- and groupwork. We suggested that learners be asked to help draw up guidelines for groupwork and class management. The balance of mother tongue and target language was also examined.

Having looked in detail at the pre-task phase, the next chapter takes us on to the main task cycle.

Material appraisal

1 Look at Lesson Outline 1 in Appendix C. How would you change the pre-task phase if:
   a) the class was partly made up of students who had recently joined and had not done the first three units?
   b) you intended to split them into A/B pairs, where they could not see each other's picture?

2 Look at a resource book or a coursebook which contains some tasks (in the TBL sense, see 2.1.1–2.1.2).
   a) What pre-task activities do they suggest? What language help do they give? Would you need to adapt this for your classes?
   b) How clear are the task instructions in the rubrics of the Student's Book? Could you ask your students to read and follow them on their own, without you reading them out loud first? If so, try doing this in class. (You may need to explain to students why you are asking them to do this.)

Planning

3 Look back at the pre-task activities in 3.2.4.
   a) Think of suitable topics for your classes that you could use with each one.
   b) Work with a colleague. Select a topic and task. Choose two or three pre-task activities to try out together by planning then doing them yourselves.

4 Look at the tasks on the topic of 'Families' in Focus 2.
   a) Which one could you use as a pre-task, in order to discover how much elementary learners know already?
   b) How might you introduce the topic of 'Teachers you remember best' if you want to lead on to a survey to discover whether most teachers are remembered for positive or negative reasons?

Observation

5 Record some group work and listen to the recording to discover:
   • when your learners use their mother tongue (see 3.3.5);
   • whether they help each other with words they don't know;
   • how often they correct each other or self-correct;
   • whether some learners dominate or interrupt more.

Further reading

For more on teaching and learning vocabulary, of relevance to the pre-task phase, see:
N and D Schmitt, 1995, who summarise clearly on pages 133–137 eleven principles for teachers to follow.
P Nation, 1990, examines the underlying principles of vocabulary acquisition and illustrates a range of practical teaching techniques – an excellent overview.

Notes

1 P Skehan in J and D Willis (eds), 1996.
2 P Foster in J and D Willis (eds), 1996.
3 J Gore, 1995.
4 For other ideas for self-assessment checklists see R Ribé and N Vidal, 1993.
5 G Alban, 1992.
6 M Bygate, 1987.
7 J Eldridge, 1994.
8 A Littlejohn, 1983.

Components of the Task Cycle

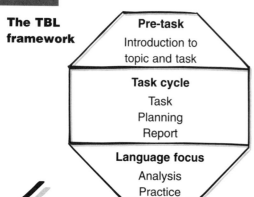

Pre-task
Introduction to topic and task

Task cycle
Task
Planning
Report

Language focus
Analysis
Practice

Look at the three components of the task cycle. During which component(s)

- will students be communicating in a private setting/a more public setting? How might this affect the kind of language they use?
- might students find a dictionary most useful?
- will you, the teacher, be most active?
- is teacher correction most likely to be effective/least likely to be effective?

Task cycle

Task	**Planning**	**Report**
Students do the task, in pairs or small groups.	Students prepare to report to the whole class (orally or in writing) how they did the task, what they decided or discovered.	Teacher selects some groups to present their reports of the task to the class, orally or in writing.
Teacher monitors and encourages; stops the task when most pairs have finished; comments briefly on content.	Teacher acts as linguistic adviser, giving feedback; helping students to correct, rephrase, rehearse and/or draft a written report.	Teacher acts as chairperson, linking the contributions, summing up.
		Teacher gives feedback on content and form, if wished.

The task cycle may be based on a reading text or listening text. It may be followed by students hearing a recording of others doing the same task. These both give additional and related exposure.

Audiences for reports (Add your ideas for others.)

Oral presentations may be:

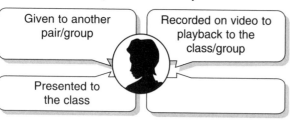

Given to another pair/group

Recorded on video to playback to the class/group

Presented to the class

Written presentations may be:

Passed round or displayed for others to read

Made into a class newspaper for another class

Shown on OHP transparency

Tasks with written outcomes

- In Focus 2, two tasks have written outcomes – 6 and 9. Choose one, and discuss briefly how you might use the TBL framework (pre-task and task cycle) to plan your lesson.

  Which component in the task cycle might need to be longer, or be divided into two stages?

- Look for tasks in Appendix A that would naturally lead into written presentations. Select three and discuss who the audience(s) could possibly be.

4 The TBL framework: the task cycle

> This chapter covers the second phase in the task-based learning framework – the task cycle. It describes in detail the three components of the task cycle, task, planning and report, and examines the role of the teacher in each. It emphasises the importance of writing in the learning process and shows how the stages of the task cycle can be adapted to different teaching situations.

4.1 The task stage

In Chapter 1, we considered various reasons why many learners left school or college without learning how to communicate in the target language. We emphasised that both exposure to and use of the target language are vital to its acquisition. We saw that output, i.e. use of language, is likely to help stimulate intake, i.e. acquisition of new forms. We saw in 1.3.3, that learners' confidence grows when they realise they can do something without the teacher's direct support. The task stage is therefore a vital opportunity for all learners to use whatever language they can muster, working simultaneously, in pairs or small groups, to achieve the goals of the task (see 2.1.2).

4.1.1 The teacher as monitor

If you are not used to TBL, the hardest thing to do at first is to stop teaching during the task stage and just monitor. You need to have the self-control and courage to stand back and let the learners get on with the task on their own. Resist the temptation to go round and help (or should we say interfere?), for example, by correcting pronunciation or suggesting better ways of doing the task. Observe and encourage from a slight distance. If the mother tongue crops up in one group too often, quietly go over and suggest an English rendering. If one pair is hopelessly stuck, help them out, but then withdraw again.

Try not to stand too close to groups. If you do, they will tend to ask you for words they don't know, rather than trying to think of another way of expressing their meaning themselves. We must ask ourselves if providing information now helps them learn to communicate on their own. There are other times later in the task cycle when correction and language support are more valuable, and more likely to be remembered.

After working hard to set the scene in the introduction phase, the teacher's monitoring role during the task stage is less active, and should now be:

- to make sure that all pairs or groups are doing the right task and are clear about the objectives;
- to encourage all students to take part, no matter how weak their language is;
- to be forgiving about errors of form (remember how positively parents react to their young children's attempts to use new words and phrases);
- to interrupt and help out only if there is a major communication breakdown;
- to notice which students seem to do more talking and controlling, and if anyone seems to be left out (next time you might change these groupings, or give specific roles within groups to even out the interaction);
- to notice if and when any pairs or groups switch to mother tongue, and, later perhaps, to find out why;
- to act as time keeper.

Timing is important. Tasks can take from one minute to ten or more, depending on the type of task and its complexity. Set a time limit that is too short rather than too long – it is easier to extend it than to stop students before the limit is up. It is better to stop before anyone gets bored, even if some pairs have not finished. Give a one-minute warning before the end of the task.

Immediately after the task, it is a good idea to take up briefly one or two points of interest you heard while monitoring, and to comment positively on the way students have done the task. It is vital not to comment in detail or to summarise their outcomes or findings, because those will constitute the content and aim of the next two components, planning and report, which learners will also do for themselves.

4.2 After the task

After your brief comments on how the task went, the lesson will probably proceed smoothly into the planning and report stages, where students prepare to tell the class about their findings. These components are the focus of 4.3 and 4.4 below. But first, we should consider why there is a need for the task to be followed up in this way.

4.2.1 Why tasks are not enough

The task component, as we have seen, helps students to develop fluency in the target language and strategies for communication. To achieve the goals of the task, their main focus is on getting their meaning across, rather than on the form of the language itself. So there could be problems such as those listed below, if tasks are the sole means of language development.

- Some learners revert to mother tongue when things get difficult or if the group feels impatient.
- Some individuals develop excellent communication strategies, e.g. miming and using gestures, but get by using just odd words and phrases and let others supply the more challenging language they need.
- Some learners tend to get caught up in trying to find the right word, and don't worry over much about how it fits into the discourse.
- There is naturally more concern for use of lexis and lexical chunks than for grammar and grammatical accuracy.

Through tasks, students may well become better communicators and learn new words and phrases from each other, but how far does the task situation stretch their language development and help with internalisation of grammar? In psycholinguistic terms, how far does this type of 'output' help 'intake'? To avoid the risk of learners achieving fluency at the expense of accuracy and to spur on language development, another stage is needed after the task itself. This is supplied by the report stage, where learners naturally strive for accuracy and fluency together and weaker students can get additional support.

4.2.2 Creating a need for accuracy

After completing the task in small groups, there is usually a natural curiosity among students to discover how others achieved the same objectives. The report stage is when groups report briefly in spoken or written form to the whole class on some aspect of their task, such as who won the game, how their group solved the problem, or two or three things they found out from each other. In doing this, students find themselves in a situation where they will be talking or writing for a more public audience.

In Chapter 2, we considered the differences between spontaneous and planned language, and saw that the language used in public is normally planned, final and permanent. For this public stage, students will naturally want to use their best language and avoid making mistakes that others might notice. They will feel the need to organise clearly what they want to say, use appropriate language and check that it is correct. They may try to find new wordings to express their meaning more exactly. They will be working towards a polished final draft which will normally be:

- presented orally, while the class takes notes of relevant points; or
- written down and displayed or circulated for others to read;

or, on occasions, it may be:

- recorded on audio cassette to be played back later; or
- recorded on video to be shown later.

The more public and permanent the presentation, the longer students will want for the planning stage. It is already quite daunting to stand up and speak in front of the class, but students preparing to be recorded will want far longer to perfect their work than groups who are not. If they are writing a letter for an outside audience, say for publication in a newspaper, they will happily do several drafts to make it good enough.

The report stage, then, gives students a natural stimulus to upgrade and improve their language. It presents a very real linguistic challenge – to communicate clearly and in accurate language appropriate to the circumstances.

Students cannot get by just tacking words and phrases together in an improvised fashion, as they could when they were speaking in real time. In planning their report, they have time to create anew, experiment with language and compose with the support of their group, teacher, dictionaries and grammar books. And it is this process that is likely to drive their language development forward and give them new insights into language use.

If students know at the beginning of the task cycle that they will be called upon to present their findings at the report stage, they are also more likely to think harder about their use of language during the task. They may also attempt to use more complex language, and try to be more accurate.[1]

4.3 The planning stage

This section deals with the planning stage, which comes after the task and before the report, forming the central part of the task cycle.

It describes how to help learners plan their reports effectively and maximise their learning opportunities. It takes us back to the classroom situation we reached in 4.1.1 where most students have just completed the task, and you have commented on one or two interesting things you heard while walking round, observing from a distance.

4.3.1 Setting up the planning stage

After you have stopped the task, what you need to do is:

1   Explain, if you haven't already, that you will want someone from each pair or group to report their findings to the class. If you tell students this before they start the task, it may motivate them to take it more seriously.

2   Be very clear about the purpose of the report (see table opposite), i.e. what kind of information students are going to look or listen for in each other's reports and what they will then do with the information.

3   If the report is for an outside audience, explain who it's for and what students can hope to achieve through their writing.

4   Be clear about what form the report will take. Explain what facilities students can use (e.g. oral presentation with/without OHP, with written notes or a full script, or in written form for display).

5   Make sure students know what resources they have at their disposal – dictionaries, grammar books, other resource books. And, of course, you will be on hand to help, too. With types of task that lead into writing, you could assemble a wall display of previous students' work – sample written reports on similar topics – to give your students a clear idea of what they are aiming at.

6   Tell students how long their presentation should be. If it is an oral one, set a short time limit (a fairly fluent learner can say or read a hundred words in half a minute). With a written report, suggest the number of words, lines or paragraphs. Be very specific about what they should include.

7   Set them a time limit. Tell them you'll come round to help.

8   If you have observed that it is the same students who tend to do all the work, give specific roles to students within the pairs or groups. For example, ask the habitual non-participator to be the writer and the active student to be the 'dictionary person' (see also 3.3.1).

Purposes for reports

These often depend on the type of task (see Appendix A).

Here are some examples.

Listing	**Comparing**	**Experience sharing**	**Creative**
Students can: • hear/read other pairs' lists and consolidate their own to see how many items they get altogether; • vote on the most comprehensive list.	Students can: • see how many have done the task the same way, or have things in common with the presenter; • find out how many agree/disagree with the content of the report and why.	Students can: • note points of interest and compare them later; • write questions to ask speakers; • set quiz questions as a memory challenge; • keep a record of main points or themes mentioned for a review or classification later; • select one experience to summarise or react to in writing.	Students can: • say what they most enjoyed in the other groups' work; • write a review of another group's product for them to read.

Ordering, sorting	**Problem solving**
Students can: • publicly justify their priorities to persuade each other.	Students can: • compare (and list) strategies for solving the problem; • justify/evaluate solutions; • vote on the best/cheapest solution; • recommend one solution.

4.3.2 The teacher as language adviser

During the planning stage, the teacher's main role is that of language adviser, helping students shape their meanings and express more exactly what they want to say. Here are some guidelines which apply to the planning of both oral and written presentations.

- Go round quickly at the beginning to check all students know what they are supposed to be doing, and why. If you have a large class and cannot help all groups in one planning session, decide which ones you will concentrate on, and make a mental note to help others next time.
- Unless one group is doing nothing, it is a good general rule to wait until you are asked before you offer help. Then you know you are responding to the learners' needs rather than your own interpretation of them. It is always worth bearing in mind that learners will learn best if they work

things out for themselves, rather than simply being told. The planning stage is a good opportunity to encourage learner independence.

- Comment on good points and creative use of language.
- If you are asked for advice, suggest positive ways learners could improve their work at a general level, e.g. *That's good. You might like to add a sentence signalling what you are going to talk/write about in this section – it may help the listener/reader to follow your ideas better.*
- If learners ask to be corrected, point out errors selectively – most important are those which obscure the meaning. Ask them to explain what they mean, and explore various options together; then finally suggest alternative wordings. Other errors you may want to point out are obvious ones that you feel other students may notice (and possibly comment on, though this is very rare) at the report stage.
- For other errors of form, try to get learners to correct themselves (you could just put a dot under a wrong preposition or verb ending). Don't be too pedantic and jump on strange wordings. It's more important to encourage experimentation than to penalise it.
- Make sure learners know how to use dictionaries for encoding, i.e. not just to check spellings and find words and meanings, but to look closely at the examples of how to use the new word, notice the verbs or nouns it collocates with and the grammar it goes with. This will help them write better themselves. Monolingual dictionaries may help most here. The Longman Activator and the Collins Cobuild dictionaries, for example, have been especially designed to help students use new words. You may need to devote some lessons to dictionary training.
- Encourage students to help each other, and to 'edit' drafts of each other's work, or to listen to each other rehearsing.
- Make sure they know who is to be the spokesperson or final-draft writer for the group well before the end of planning time.
- Remind them occasionally how much time they have left. If, at your original time limit, most students are still working well and fruitfully, you could consider postponing the report stage until the beginning of the next lesson. The advantage of this is that they may continue thinking about it and rehearsing it mentally until then. Such mental practice is, in fact, one of the strategies that successful learners use.

Stop the planning stage once most pairs or groups have more or less finished, then get students ready to make their presentations. This is the report stage.

4.4 The report stage

This section deals with the report stage– the natural conclusion of the task cycle. In itself it probably presents slightly less of a learning opportunity than the planning stage. But without the incentive of the report, the learning process of planning, drafting and rehearsing would not happen.

Depending on the level of the class and type of task, a report might last as little as 20–30 seconds or up to two minutes. So if you have twenty students in your class, producing one report per pair, you can calculate the time you will need. It will probably not be feasible or advisable to let every pair report in full.

Their reports will not resemble native-speaker language; there are bound to be strange wordings and grammatical errors. What is of vital importance is to acknowledge that students are offering them as the best they can achieve at that moment, given the linguistic resources and time available.

Always be encouraging. It is extremely important not to devalue their achievements, for example by commenting or even thinking negatively (this may well show on your face and in your body language). Instead, focus on all the things they are getting right! Notice and comment on the areas in which they are showing improvement. Above all, take what they say and write seriously; respond and react to it. Positive reactions will increase their motivation, their self-esteem, and spur them on to greater efforts next time.

4.4.1 The teacher as chairperson

During the report stage, the main role of the teacher is that of chairperson, to introduce the presentations, to set a purpose for listening, to nominate who speaks next and to sum up at the end. Some guidelines follow, the basic principles of which apply to handling all types of presentations.

Oral presentations

- Make sure there is a clear purpose for listening (see page 57) and that everyone knows what it is and what they will do with the information after the report. Some specific examples follow.

  Example 1: *You've all found out how many girls/women and boys/men your partner's family has. You are now going to tell the class. Everyone should listen to each report and write down the numbers for each family. We can then add up the totals to do a class survey.*

  Example 2: *You are now going to tell the class the story you've planned. Everyone should listen and at the end of each story I'll give you a minute to write the thing about it you remember best.*

- Make a mental note of points that will be useful for your summing up while listening to the presentations. If you are expected to give language feedback, note down good expressions as well as phrases or patterns that need clarifying or correction. Do not interrupt or correct during the presentations; this could be discouraging.
- Keep an eye on the time. If you have a large class you could ask some groups to report this time, and others after the next task (without, of course, telling them at the planning stage which groups you will be selecting).
- Stop the report stage early if it becomes repetitive. But first ask the pairs who have not reported if they have anything different or special to add.
- Allow time for a summing up at the end.

Written presentations

Handling these differs only in the initial organisation. You will need to make decisions on the following before starting the report stage:
- Will you want students to remain seated while they read each other's work? If so, you will need to work out an efficient way of passing their writing round the class.
- Can students get up and display their writing on the wall, then walk round and read each other's?

- Do you want to keep the writing anonymous for any reason? If so, ensure each group/pair adds a number or letter code to their work. The readers can note these down for the pieces they have read and you can refer to specific pieces by their code.
- Even if the writing has been done for an audience outside the class, e.g. for another class (see 4.5.4 below), students should still have a chance to read what others have written. It is useful exposure and they could learn a lot.
- Purposes should initially focus on content, but could well have a linguistic focus too. Specific examples of purposes for reading written presentations follow.

> Example 3: *Read at least ten of the descriptions of teachers. Take down the numbers/names of the ones you read. For each, note whether the description gives a positive or a negative image of that person.*

> Example 4: *Make a list of the similarities you find while reading about other people's experiences of school. Write down the name/number of the piece that you think is most memorable, and be ready to say why.*

As your students read, you could join in with them, and make notes to use in your summing up.

Audio and video presentations

Here you will also have organisational decisions to take on the following:
- Will you record all the reports, or just a few each time? And will the recording be during the oral presentation, or will students record it in their groups to play back to the class?
- Could you get students to make the recording in their own time and bring it to class?
- Do you want to play back every recording, or just some?
- Will the whole class hear/watch or just the people who recorded? (Some people are very self-conscious about being watched on video.)
- What purpose will you set for listening/viewing? Students often pick on errors rather than good points during these presentations. Giving guidelines for their feedback, e.g. *Write down two or three good points/useful phrases you hear. Suggest one way to improve it*, will help to ensure they have other, positive, reasons for viewing and listening.[2]

Summing up and giving feedback

When summing up after all types of presentations, it is important (and natural) to react first to the content of the reports.

> Example 1: *OK, so let's see. Are there more men than women in all our families put together? How close are the numbers – nearly equal? Who was the person with eight sisters and no brothers? Who had the most men/women in their family?*

> Example 2: *What interesting stories! Some were quite strange, especially yours, (Pedro)! Which story did you like best? Let's see which things some of you remembered about that one.*

The question of language feedback in the report stage is controversial. In some classes, students will expect feedback on the quality of the language they have used, even though you will have commented on it at the planning stage. Even if you believe that students actually learn very little from this, to frustrate this expectation may lead to a feeling of demotivation. Some people argue that while correction is unlikely to produce short-term benefits, it may well have a beneficial destabilising effect on a learner's fossilised system, and help keep other learners' minds open to alternative ways of expressing themselves.[3] But public correction needs to be handled very carefully because it could also seriously undermine learners' confidence.

Make sure you give feedback tactfully and positively. Give examples of good expressions you have heard, or ones students have used for the first time, and mention other good points. When correcting (anonymously if possible) you may like to say or write the phrase but leave a gap where the mistake occurred. Ask students to suggest suitable ways of completing the phrase.

With written reports, you may want to postpone detailed language feedback until after you have had a closer look at students' work. When you do this, make sure you also tick some good bits, as well as advising on weak areas.

With audio and video presentations, it is important to find out what students think they have learnt and how they think they have benefited (or otherwise) from being recorded. Occasionally, with some classes, you could ask them to react privately by writing a note to you as an informal evaluation.

End the report phase on a positive note. It is important to acknowledge the effort students put into the presentations, as well as showing a keen interest in what they have said or written.

4.5 Writing in the task cycle

This section examines how writing helps learners, and begins by looking in greater depth at the processes involved in planning or drafting a piece of writing.

4.5.1 Meeting learners' needs

In real life, only a small proportion of the population do anything more than write personal letters and fill out forms, even in their first language. Most students need to write a foreign language only for examination purposes producing, for instance, essays, letters and summaries. A few need to write as part of their jobs, and those going on to further education in the target language will obviously need practice in academic writing. It's worth finding out what your students need or want to be able to write, then you can tailor some of their tasks and subsequent writing to suit their needs.

Some learners, especially those not taking written examinations, may benefit more from additional exposure and language-focused tasks. Remember that many people learn a language well without ever having written anything.

However, language students need to write for other reasons. It is well known that writing is in itself a learning process. It often helps people to clarify ideas and to create new ones. (I've learnt a lot through writing this book.) For learners this process challenges their current language system. Composing in the target language often demands a 'restructuring' of language form; it forces learners to examine aspects of their current grammatical knowledge and adapt and exploit it so that it will carry the meanings they wish to express.

In a task-based approach, writing constitutes a natural part of the cycle. Several kinds of writing are involved. Sometimes it is used for private notes, to help students remember what was said or read; sometimes for drafting and creating often in collaboration with others; sometimes for public consumption at a report stage.

4.5.2 Planning what to write

Below are a number of stages most people go through when writing something important or difficult. They may not occur exactly in this order:

- think what to say / what not to say;
- discuss with someone how to approach the task;
- jot down some notes and ideas;
- write it out roughly to get more ideas;
- explain to someone what you've got to write;
- read the original item / reflect on the circumstances that led you to write;
- show someone your near-final draft and ask for comments;
- prune it back and tidy it up;
- think about layout and format – typed or word processed?;
- evaluate the feedback you've had and decide what to change;
- write a final draft;
- read it though to check for omissions and spellings.

Even if you only go through half of these steps, it is still clear that writing is a lengthy process. It is not always easy to express in writing what we mean. But as we have seen, the process can promote learning and thus it is worth learners spending time on it. One interesting consideration is that only four of the stages above actually involve writing (as opposed to thinking, talking, etc. about it).

These stages (once ordered for teaching purposes) can also help with drafting a piece of writing in the classroom. Many of them are likely to happen naturally in the task-based cycle if the purpose of the writing and the audience are made clear.

4.5.3 Doing a written task

In some cases the end product of the task cycle must be a polished written document. It could take the form of a letter, a story ending or a list of recommendations, depending on the agreed outcome of the task. This end product will first be introduced orally or through reading in the pre-task phase, then discussed as an integral part of the task stage, drafted collaboratively at the planning stage and finalised for the report stage.

If the writing is to be read by most of the class at the report stage, it counts as a public document and must therefore be well written. The planning stage for a written report may well be longer than that needed for an oral presentation, and the pre-task phase and task cycle may look like this:

Pre-task
Discuss topic and situation.
Teacher sets written task,
which could be based on a reading text.

Task cycle
Task
Students discuss task orally in pairs or groups, to decide content.
Planning 1
Pairs draft notes, discuss outline, write first draft. Exchange drafts with another pair and ask them to suggest improvements.
Planning 2
Redraft, check, improve, make final checks. Final draft ready for audience.
Report
Pieces of writing read by all, for a set purpose. Class discussion of findings. Summing up.

A similar amount of preparation, plus some rehearsal time, will be required if students are making a video recording.

4.5.4 Writing for a wider audience

In real life, we only write in order to communicate something to someone. Foreign language writing is often done for display, so that it can be graded rather than for any real communicative purpose. In the task above, the audience was the rest of the class.

To make a change, to give students a real sense of purpose and to raise motivation, it is sometimes possible to think of other audiences that might benefit by reading something your students have written. Could your class actually 'publish' something for other classes to read or listen to, or even for wider distribution outside school, possibly by email?

With computers and word-processing packages available in many schools and colleges, it is now easy to produce very professional-looking work.

Here are some projects that have been carried out successfully by teachers I know in different countries. Obviously not all would be suitable for your own teaching environment. In some cases parents took a great pride in these 'publications' even though they did not understand the target language.

There are some more ideas in Appendix A (see Type 6: Creative tasks).

What students wrote:	Who for:
• a guide book to the village / town;	
• brochures about local activities / amenities / sports / walks, etc.;	tourists, visitors
• a brief history of the school / village (from interviews with older residents);	visitors, parents
• a class / school / college newspaper / magazine;	other classes or students in
• letters and recordings;	another school, sometimes
• surveys on school / local attitudes;	overseas
• a diary of a holiday course.	parents, friends at home

4.6 ESL and one-to-one: task cycle adaptations

We have already seen how the type of task can influence the nature of the cycle. Writing tasks and reports being recorded need longer planning stages, for example. The task cycle will also vary depending on the teaching situation where it is used. In 3.1.3 we saw how the reporting stage could be omitted at first with beginners. This section gives other examples of such adaptations.

If you are teaching English in Britain, Australia, the USA or any second language situation – your learners will probably have many opportunities for informal, private talk outside lessons, which is similar to doing tasks in them. They may already be quite confident speaking English in small group settings. What they will need is more emphasis and time on the planning and reporting stages, to help them see where and how their English can be improved. If they are really quite confident, set higher standards. Get them to take turns to record their reports to play back to the class – anything that will raise the linguistic challenge.

In one-to-one lessons, there is no class to act as audience for a 'public' report. So how can you stimulate a natural need for accuracy?

One way is to ask students to prepare their report which they then record on audio cassette for homework. They bring it to the next session, and play it to you. Listen right through the first time, and give a positive overall appraisal, then play it through again, to give detailed feedback. Comment on the good bits, and select one or two areas for improvement each time. After this, they can erase and re-record it in their own time if they wish.

Students then keep the cassette with all their reports on. At the end of term, they can select the two or three best ones for you to listen to again.

Another way is to have one session a week where all one-to-one students meet and report to each other about something they've discussed in their lessons. Or they could play each other the recordings they have made.

Occasionally you could ask students to record themselves giving mini-presentations on video, with an audience in mind. This makes them work really hard and become aware of language areas they need to improve.

4.7 Summary

In this chapter, we have described the complete second phase of the task-based framework. So altogether we have covered:

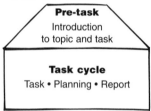

In moving from one component to the next, we are placing different linguistic demands on students, but they are demands which reflect natural language use.

In the task stage students gain fluency and confidence in themselves as communicators. But because it is a 'private' situation, where meaning is paramount, and communication is real-time, there is often little concern for grammatical accuracy.

The planning stage gives learners the time and support they need to prepare for the linguistic challenge of going public. Composing with the support of their group and the teacher, they have time to experiment with language and check on grammar. This is the process that drives their language development forward.

The report stage gives students a natural stimulus to upgrade and improve their language. It encourages them to think about form as well as meaning; accuracy as well as fluency and to use their prestige version of the target language. It allows other students to hear or read what they have done, which provides useful exposure.

We saw how the teacher's role changes with each stage of the cycle. By monitoring the task, teachers encourage learners to work independently to achieve the set goals. By giving language support at the planning stage, teachers help learners organise their conclusions into a form suitable for presentation in public. And by chairing the reports, teachers facilitate public use of language.

We then examined the importance of writing in language learning and showed how different kinds are practised naturally at different stages of the task cycle. We suggested that written tasks needed a longer planning stage and put forward a strategy for encouraging learners to write for a wider audience.

Finally, we looked at ways of adapting the task cycle to different teaching situations.

However, the task framework is not yet complete. In order to fulfil all the optimum conditions for learning, the element of language-focused instruction is still lacking and we will deal with this in Chapter 7. In the next two chapters, however, we will analyse tasks and the materials they can be based on in more detail.

Reflection

1 How far, and in what ways, do the pre-task phase and task cycle now fulfil the four optimum conditions for language learning as outlined in Chapter 1? You might like to complete this table, marking each on a scale from 1 to 5:

		Exposure	Use	Motivation	Instruction
Pre-task					
	Task				
Task cycle	Planning				
	Report				

2 If you put a language practice stage before the task stage, what effect might this have on the way students perceive and carry out the task?
3 Think of a class you have observed or taught recently.
   a) Appraise the balance between opportunities for private, small-group talk and more public, sustained talk.
   b) What opportunities were students given to use a prestige version of the target language? Were they given sufficient planning time? At what stages?
4 Look at the 'Purposes for Reports' table on page 57. Think of tasks you are familiar with (or go through the tasks in Appendix A) and see if you can add some more purposes to the table.
5 Think of two ways you might encourage students to write quickly, spontaneously and without worrying about form, in order to increase their confidence and facility in writing.
6 Look at the tasks in Appendix A or find some in a resource book, and select two or three that you could adapt as suitable writing tasks for students you know. What pre-task activities might you do?
7 Find some suggestions for writing activities in a textbook you know. Evaluate them by deciding which of the optimum conditions for learning they fulfil. How would you adapt them to fit a task-based cycle as described here (see also 9.4.2)?

Further reading

For more ideas for writing tasks and games, see C and J Hadfield, 1992.
For detailed guidance on handling the process of writing, try R White and V Arndt, 1994/5.

Notes

1 P Skehan and P Foster (in preparation).
2 For more on this see R Cooper, 1993.
3 P Skehan, 1994.

Exposure to language

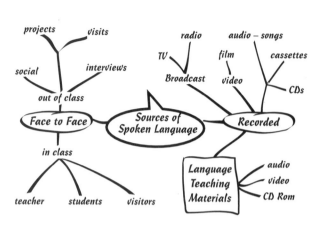

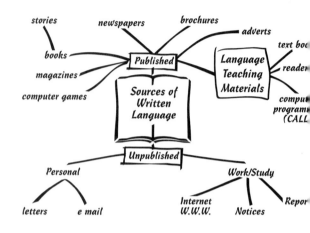

Text A

Below are the headline and opening lines of a newspaper story.

What questions come to mind when you have read this opening? Write down seven.

How many do you think will be answered in the full story?

The Guardian

The boy who came out from the cold

A schoolboy who spent the night trapped in a butcher's cold store after being locked in accidentally ...

Finally, read the whole text on page 106.
How many of your questions were answered?

Discussion Points

(a) After looking at the mind-maps at the top of this page, draw your own mind-map of sources of written or spoken texts that you could tap.

(b) First, do the tasks based on texts A and B. Think of two Pre-task activities for texts A and B above.

(c) Can you suggest a second task for text A or B that would encourage the class to read the complete text for a second or third time?

Text B

One sentence has been missed out of the Spiders story below and written underneath. Can you find where it fits best?

Phobias make life a misery for thousands. A new organisation called 'Triumph Over Phobia' (TOP) has been formed by a pioneering group of volunteers to help people cure their phobias. Here is one success story.

Spiders

One woman was so afraid of spiders she could not be left in a house alone. If she saw one she would climb on the table and not be able to get down until somebody came into the room and removed it.

During her first TOP meeting, she noticed doodles on a page which resembled spiders and she suddenly recoiled in horror.

She was eventually persuaded to look at photographs of spiders in books, then leave the pages open in a room so she saw them each time she walked in. Her husband began to move the position of the book and change the page so she saw a different one each time.

After three weeks she was given a plastic spider at a TOP meeting and took it home. She later agreed to take the real spider home and gave it the name Bernard.

Two and a half months after first going to the group her phobia had gone.

The Daily Telegraph

Lost sentence:
"One of the group took a real spider in a jar to the next meeting, where it was gradually moved nearer to the sufferer."

5 Text-based tasks

> This chapter will illustrate some basic ways to design communicative tasks based on reading and listening texts or video extracts.
>
> It begins by focusing on issues concerning the selection of suitable texts from available sources, and discusses whether we should grade texts or tasks. It explores the strategies involved in reading and listening, and looks at typical text patterns and the importance of recognising them. It then illustrates six different task designs which aim to encourage natural reading and listening strategies. Finally, it illustrates how texts can be presented in the task-based framework, and shows what teacher and learners do at each stage.

5.1 Defining text-based tasks

Chapter 2 offered a range of starting points for tasks. In this chapter, we shall look more closely at one of them: texts.

From now on I shall be using the word 'text' in a general sense to mean a continuous piece of spoken or written language. Texts in this sense will include recordings of spoken language and extracts from video, in addition to the printed word. There may be suitable texts or recordings in your course materials, or you may need to supplement these by choosing extracts from other sources (see Focus 5). The texts themselves will increase learners' exposure to the target language in use.

Text-based tasks require learners to process the text for meaning in order to achieve the goals of the task. This will involve reading, listening or viewing with some kind of communicative purpose, and may well involve talking about the text and perhaps writing notes.

Such tasks may lead into a reading or listening activity (see Task A in Focus 5: *The boy who came out from the cold*), or can arise out of the text itself (see Task B: *Spiders*). Sometimes one text will give rise to three different tasks, one before the main reading or listening phase, one during, and one after.

5.2 Selecting and balancing exposure

For this section, think of a particular language course you are currently teaching, have recently taught, or once attended. Keep this course in mind as you read.

We saw in 1.3.1 that exposure to the target language is absolutely vital. Learners can only learn through trying to make sense out of the language they experience. So the quality of the exposure, i.e. to a well-balanced range of text types and topics, is crucial.

5.2.1 Coursebooks and students' needs

Because of the impoverished and restricted language found in some coursebooks, many teachers are aware of the need to use supplementary materials. But these must be chosen with due regard both for the language and the learner. For example, a course supplemented entirely by authentic texts taken from front-page stories in quality newspapers would most benefit a learner who was planning to take up journalism, but learners wishing for a broader, more general experience of English would need a greater variety of written and spoken texts.

We must make sure, then, that we look at each course we teach as a whole. By the end of it, what experience of the language will learners have had? We need to appraise, as objectively as possible, the overall balance of the language samples that the course exposes learners to. How far are they representative of their language needs?

We need to be aware of learners' possible end-of-course objectives and to think how they could continue their language learning independently after the course. This can help us familiarise them with appropriate sources, e.g. listening to BBC World Service, watching Euro-News, or listening and talking to target language speakers.

Some up-to-date coursebooks try to take account of all these things, though in different proportions. Many use authentic reading materials, audio cassettes, and some even have video components. All this is useful exposure, and should be assessed, together with the classroom language that the course materials are likely to generate, to see how far the total exposure meets the learners' needs.

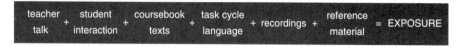

teacher talk + student interaction + coursebook texts + task cycle language + recordings + reference material = EXPOSURE

Nearly everyone is likely to need a basic command of the most frequent words, phrases, structures and text patterns (see 5.3.3). Most learners also have their favourite topics or specialist areas. These may involve the teacher in supplementing the exposure provided by the coursebook. For example, if students want to chat to people they meet while abroad, they will need exposure to typical spontaneous interaction in English. This is the most difficult kind of language to record and harness for classroom use. It is nevertheless very important and ways of providing exposure to it will be given in Chapter 6.

In what other ways might their exposure need supplementing? Does the course help learners to make the most of outside sources? Might they feel more motivated if they could sometimes choose their own texts for class use? These and other questions relating to the learner's short and longer term aims need to be asked.

5.2.2 Sources of useful material

In Focus 5, I have tried to summarise the various types of exposure available for language learners.

Spoken language

I have distinguished between sources of real-time face-to-face language, and recorded or broadcast sources.

Face-to-face communication, where the learners have direct contact with the people they are listening to, can be one-to-one, in a small group, or as part of a larger audience. Face-to-face talk is often easier to understand because learners have recourse to paralinguistic features like gestures and facial expressions, which give clues to meaning. In a one-to-one situation they are also likely to be able to control the flow of language to suit their level of understanding. This naturally modified input may be easier to acquire from (see 1.3.1).

Many of the face-to-face situations in Focus 5 could be recorded by learners (see Chapter 6).[1]

Recorded communication would normally be professionally made programmes, for radio or TV or for audio cassette, compact disc, video or film. Some sources, like the BBC World Service, are aware their audiences are not native speakers of English, and adapt the language they use in a natural way, just as one adapts in real life when speaking to a stranger who has difficulties understanding. Extracts from such sources can be termed 'authentic', because they have not been produced with a specific language-teaching purpose in mind, but mainly to communicate, inform and/or entertain.

However, materials that are especially written and scripted for language-teaching purposes to include certain functions or structures cannot be called authentic. Such materials are unlikely to be representative of natural language use, and may even make understanding more difficult (see 1.3.1).

Written language

The diagram in Focus 5 distinguishes between published and unpublished sources. A good coursebook should contain a variety of texts from published sources. For adults, these can be supplemented by extracts on topical issues from magazines, advice leaflets and newspapers (news cuttings can be also used in conjunction with recorded extracts from radio or TV news bulletins). For children, they can be supplemented by stories, activity books and reference books. Encourage extensive reading for pleasure. Sometimes a class library of short stories, magazines, children's story books and comics will help.

Unpublished sources include letters from pen-friends and data collected by students doing specialist project work. International links or twinning arrangements with schools and colleges in more than one country encourage information exchanges of all kinds between classes of similar-age learners.[2]

Advances in computer technology mean that the Internet is also becoming a useful resource. A whole range of text types is available; much of the material being spontaneous, unedited, and available without charge.[3] Some pairs of schools and colleges in different countries have established electronic mail (email) links to exchange information, or just pen-friend letters. Other institutions are exploring it for sources of up-to-date specialist information (e.g. medical 'bulletin boards') to download and print out for their ESP classes.

Material from all these sources can be made available for student use outside class time through a self-access centre or an open learning system, where texts and recordings are carefully classified and labelled.

5.2.3 Selection criteria for material

Here are some criteria that should be kept in mind; they are, however inextricably intertwined. Selecting a piece of material will involve considering all of them, and is often a delicate balancing act.

- **Exploitability:** Choose a piece of material that lends itself to classroom exploitation, i.e. to an engaging task, or series of tasks, that will probably sustain students' interest over a length of time (see 5.4).
- **Topic:** Variety is important – it is impossible to please every member of the class every time. However, an engaging task, with the right degree of challenge, will more than make up for a seemingly dull topic. An element of surprise or originality helps.
- **Length/chunk-ability:** Choose a short piece, or a longer one that has obvious 'pause' points, i.e. can be split into sections with a task set on each. This is far more productive in class than a long piece, even if it is more challenging, linguistically.

  With listening, length is also important. One minute of BBC World Service Radio contains around 200 words of running text, so a four-minute video extract could produce a text 800 words long, which is well over two pages of an average book.[4]

  We saw in Chapter 1 that quality of exposure is more likely to lead to effective learning than quantity. A short quality text, made more memorable by a satisfying task, is more likely to stick in learners' minds and provide a richer learning experience than a long, less engaging one. Ideally, we should aim at a mix of short and 'chunkable' longer texts.[5]
- **Linguistic complexity:** Try choosing occasional items where the language itself seems difficult but the general message is predictable and the genre is familiar, e.g. weather forecasts, sports reports. A simple task can be set that can be successfully achieved without the need to understand every idea.
- **Accessibility:** Is the text culturally accessible or will students need additional background knowledge to appreciate it? With Business English or other professional areas, students may need to know specific information, e.g. the type of organisation or its approach.
- **Copyright:** Check that you are not breaking copyright laws by copying and using the material in class, or by storing it afterwards.

If only one or two of the criteria above present a problem in a particular text, it should still be possible and indeed rewarding to design an initial task that makes it accessible to students.

5.2.4 Grading the text or the task?

In daily life, we process text in different ways, depending on our purpose. This is also the case when we read, listen or view in a foreign language. Sometimes we can find out what we want to know without being able to understand anywhere near the whole text. And occasionally, though we do understand every word, message and meaning are not clear.

With TV and video, the visual information combined with our knowledge of the world often helps us to predict the content and, with the help of some key words, to make sense of a fairly complex piece. Conversely, following apparently simple written instructions, e.g. to set a video recorder, is often difficult even in our first language, because we don't have the technical knowledge the writer expected.

In the classroom, the teacher may well have to supply some of the relevant background knowledge beforehand, and, without giving too much away, ensure that the key words or concepts will be recognised by learners. This could happen in the pre-task phase (see 3.2.3). Task 3b) based on the *Spiders* text, on page 84, attempts to do this.

Let us briefly consider what linguistic features might make a text problematic for a reader who wants to gain an in-depth understanding of it.

Several types of readability studies exist, but these are based mainly on sentence and word length. They conclude that the longer sentences and words are, the harder the text is to understand fully.[6] However, there is some doubt that such studies are sufficient as an indicator. Many children can read the word 'elephant' long before they can manage more common, shorter words. Other factors which are likely to cause difficulty are:

- unknown words and phrases[7];
- common words used with metaphorical or less common meanings (students recognise the word, but don't realise it is being used in a different sense);
- complex phrase or clause structure. In English, for example, the noun group in journalistic and academic text can cause problems.

Some written texts are difficult to understand simply because they are badly written and consistently confound the reader's expectations. Perhaps they are badly signalled, or ambiguous. They may omit things that are necessary, or use uncommon words for effect. In other words, the weakness may not be that of the reader but that of the writer.

Even if the text in itself is linguistically difficult, the pedagogic level still depends on the extent to which its meaning has to be interpreted by the reader, and on the reader's prior knowledge of both the topic and genre of text.

Grading a text by attempting to assess its level makes no pedagogic sense, then, unless one knows the purpose for which the information is to be used. Text comprehensibility and task purpose are inseparable. The task defines the purpose for which the text needs to be understood.

The text selection criteria we considered in 5.2.3 above are also relevant when grading texts.

As a general rule, if the text is linguistically dense or complex, set an easy task, and follow it with others that encourage learners to focus on different aspects. If the text is easy, you can set more challenging tasks, for example understanding implications or inferences. It is more realistic to grade the tasks rather than the text.

5.3 Reading and listening strategies

This section examines the ways in which language learners read, and compares them with common strategies in mother-tongue reading. Listening requires different processing abilities from reading, even though there may be linguistic features in common. We then consider the importance of recognising natural patterns in text. These will give us some principles upon which to base task design, and help us to generate fresh ideas for tasks.

5.3.1 Reading

Unless learners are given a specific purpose for reading, they tend to see the text as a learning device and read one word at a time. When they come to a word they don't know, they stop to think about it or look it up. Often learners sub-vocalise, i.e. read the words in their heads. This gives them time to think about the phrasing and pronunciation, but means they read very slowly, and often fail to interpret the whole meaning.

'I understand all the words but I don't know what the writer is getting at' is a common complaint from learners reading a second language.[8] They will need to read the text two or three times to get even an approximate sense. All this takes time and many less motivated learners give up.

Motivated learners do seem to absorb a lot of language by reading very thoroughly. But to become efficient readers, they need to develop a more versatile range of reading habits. When listening to spoken language, words are already grouped together in phrases, with the message-bearing words stressed; in written text, such clues are missing. Readers need to work out which words belong together and form units of meaning – a 'phrasing' or 'chunking' process; they also need to recognise the key words and phrases.

Reading for meaning should become a priority, and they need to get used to the idea of sometimes reading for partial or approximate comprehension, rather than aiming at perfect understanding each time. We saw in Chapter 1 that people who tolerate ambiguity tend to be better language learners. Perhaps the same goes for toleration of approximate understanding.

As far as possible, the tasks set should encourage the kinds of language-processing behaviours students will need after their course, for example, reading for specific information. Reading word by word is unlikely to be among them.

Teachers sometimes read out loud while learners follow the words in their books. This may help learners initially with relating sounds to symbols, and phrasing and chunking, but in the long run, it may encourage inefficient reading habits. Silent reading for a specific purpose is far faster, more selective – there is no need to read every line or paragraph – and gives learners practice in recognising meaning units for themselves.

How do we normally read in our own language? When reading a newspaper, for example, we rarely start at line one and read every word in every line until the end. We flick through the pages (sometimes even back to front!), dipping into the text in the middle if something catches our attention. We look at the pictures or diagrams and try to make sense of them by reading selectively. (I would bet a lot of money that you have already done the same with this book!) Finally, we choose the bits that suit our own specific purpose and read those in depth. If we are really keen, and have time, we might finally read the whole paper. And sometimes we might tell someone about what we are reading – summarising one aspect and very likely giving an evaluation of it. Talking about text is a common pastime.

5.3.2 Listening

Listening to lectures or the radio and viewing TV or video are slightly different from reading in that they have to be done in real time and in sequence. If you don't catch something first time, you can't go back or stop and ponder over it without missing the next bit (unless you are watching a video or listening to a tape).

This can be a problem in lessons. When listening to recordings in class, some learners panic, get left behind and give up. After a few times, they stop trying. This is bad news, because they are cutting themselves off from a vast source of exposure.

Carefully designed tasks on well-chosen texts can prevent this happening. Just as we encourage learners to speak and experiment with ways of saying what they mean, no matter what mistakes they make, we should also be encouraging them to listen, predict and make guesses about meanings without penalising wrong ones. Just as, when appropriate, we accept approximate renderings of meaning, we should also accept approximate interpretations of meaning. Rather than correcting a misinterpretation, we should find ways of giving learners an incentive to listen to or read the text again, and work at improving their comprehension for themselves. This is what a good task, or series of tasks, aims to do.

But learners should also be encouraged to make do with a very approximate understanding, and train themselves to keep listening for key words and other clues to meaning and direction. This is far more useful in the long run than becoming dependent on artificially slow clear speech. Overcoming the difficulties of coping with natural input at the beginning is largely a matter of task design.

5.3.3 Awareness of patterns in text

One strategy that helps learners find their way through a reading text, or, if listening, to pick up the thread of an argument after getting lost, is recognising particular patterns and the words or phrases that signal them.

Just as sentences have a range of typical patterns, so do stretches of language above the level of the sentence. These are sometimes called higher-order patterns or macro-structures in discourse and can have explicit linguistic markers.

Learners need to be able to recognise and exploit these patterns to improve their reading and listening comprehension and to help them organise text clearly and logically. Examples of six of these patterns follow.

Situation – problem – solution – evaluation

I read recently about a traffic problem in a village high street. The report began with a description of the street (situation), then explained that speeding cars had caused accidents resulting in severe injuries (problem). It proposed that a set of traffic-calming measures be installed (solution), stating that this would be comparatively cheap and had proved effective elsewhere (evaluation). This is a common text pattern.

Sometimes, however, it can be more complex. If the first solution proposed (e.g. to build a by-pass) is no good, the evaluation will be negative (too costly, uses valuable land) and another solution will be put forward, followed by another evaluation. So then we have: situation – problem – solution 1 – evaluation (negative) – solution 2 – evaluation (positive). The problem or solution can also be elaborated on, for example, by explaining causes, reasons, procedures.

In written English, the problem is often signalled by *but*. In spoken English, it may be signalled by expressions like *The thing is … Trouble was …* and the solution by *So what he did was, he … .*

Sequential

Stories, anecdotes and descriptions of processes often follow a sequential pattern. In spoken English this is typically signalled by a series of *and thens*. Written or planned text tends to contain a wider variety of time phrases to signal sequential patterns, such as *eventually, after three weeks, later*. With a process, you might find *First, then,* and *finally*. In spoken language, you may hear *Well, the first thing is…/What usually happens next is…* but sometimes, explicit signals are omitted, and must be inferred.

General – specific

Often a general concept will be illustrated by an example, or a general word, like 'traffic', followed by a more specific item, like 'speeding cars'. Although Rachel's account of her rough sea journey (see 2.3.1) might have seemed fairly unstructured, a closer look shows a consistent patterning. She points out that in general she's a good traveller – it was on this specific occasion she was ill. She describes the journey first, then gives specific details of the conditions in the boat. She mentions her family in general before focusing specifically on her brother.

Topic – elaboration

When writing, we introduce a new topic or new angle on an old topic by using titles and headings, or stating the next main theme or argument.

When talking, we often announce the topic before giving more details. Two examples from the 'Spot the differences' interaction in 2.3.1 are:

David: *How about the television? Is that on or off?*
David: *So, the sign… What shall we say for that?*

Main facts – supporting details

Newspaper reports typically begin with a paragraph that gives most of the main facts of the story, often in one sentence, for example, *A mother and her three daughters died yesterday when fire swept through their house in Greater Manchester.*

The subsequent paragraphs then flesh out the details: the ages of the children, how the fire started, rescue attempts and so on. This is the pattern followed in the *Cold store* report on page 106.

Hypothesis – evidence – conclusion

This pattern is commonly used when reporting research. For example, a recent project set out to investigate a possible link between unemployment levels and the rise in crime. The report began with the hypothesis that poverty and boredom due to unemployment drive young people to criminal activities. It continued by presenting evidence from various sources. It ended with the conclusion that there was indeed a link, and that the government should act accordingly.

However, texts rarely follow just one of these patterns. The *Spiders* text has situation – problem – solution as a higher-order pattern within which a sequential pattern describes the steps of the solution.

Awareness of these patterns can help learners a lot. For example, if they have just had a lapse of concentration in a lecture and suddenly hear the words *Now, one possible solution might be to…* they know they have missed at least the end of a description of a problem, and can guess that this solution will get a negative evaluation. They also know that they should listen for details of another solution. If learners can predict where the text is leading, and identify what they have missed, at least they can ask someone afterwards.

Awareness of these patterns can also help us as teachers and materials writers. If we start by identifying the predominant patterns in each text, we can design better tasks. Recognising the main parts of the higher-order pattern is useful when dividing a text, for example. And if we can devise tasks that highlight patterns, students will certainly find this helpful both when completing set tasks, and when reading or listening independently.

5.4 Designing text-based tasks

All text-based tasks aim to encourage natural and efficient reading/listening/ viewing strategies, focusing initially on retrieval of sufficient relevant meaning for the purpose of the task. This will entail both holistic processing, i.e. gaining an overall impression, and picking up detailed linguistic clues: a combination of what are commonly called 'top-down' and 'bottom-up' processes.

Later, in the language focus phase of the TBL framework, learners will examine the language forms in the text and look in detail at the use and meaning of lexical items that they have noticed (see Chapter 7).

There is a range of task designs that can be applied to texts. In this section we shall illustrate six and give examples of ways to adapt them.

Designs for text-based tasks

Prediction tasks	• from headline and early text
	• from selected parts of text
	• from pictures or video with/without words or sound track
Jumbles	• jumbled sections of text
	• jumbled key points of a summary
	• jumbled pictures from a series
Restoration tasks	• identifying words/phrases/sentences omitted from or added to a text
Jigsaw/split information tasks	• Each student in a group reads/hears a different part of a whole text or researches an

	angle of a theme. These are then combined to form a whole.
Comparison tasks	• two accounts of the same incident/event • a diagram/picture to compare with a written account/description
Memory challenge tasks	• After a single brief exposure to the text, students list/describe/write quiz questions about what they can remember to show other pairs.

You will no doubt already be familiar with some of these tasks; many are to be found in good textbooks, and some are similar to those in Chapter 2.

Sometimes you may need to use two, or even three different types of task consecutively. If the first requires only a rapid processing of the text, students will naturally want a second chance to understand more of it. If one task is particularly challenging (like the 'lost sentence' one for *Spiders* in Focus 5), you may want an easier one to familiarise students with the text first.

Task designs can also be combined, for example, prediction based on sequencing jumbled pictures in the *Spiders* tasks 3b), c) and d) on page 84.

In the final event you need to select or design tasks that motivate your students: that make them want to read, hear and learn from the available exposure, and that encourage them to develop a variety of effective reading and listening strategies. Sometimes you will need to copy and cut up a text. Sometimes retyping is necessary. However, your efforts are likely to be rewarded. The level of student engagement and quality of learning stimulated by such preparation are usually quite evident. With the task designs suggested below, students usually want to read the text, or listen again, or solve the problem and complete the task to their satisfaction. And this is ultimately what counts. If they have enjoyed tackling the text because of your tasks, they are more likely to read, listen and watch videos on their own in future. Each task successfully completed is a step on the road to learner independence.

I will now give more detail for each task design, then highlight the type of text they work especially well with.

5.4.1 Prediction tasks

Students predict or attempt to reconstruct the content on the basis of given clues from part of the text, without having read, heard or seen the whole.

a Predicting news stories

Task A in Focus 5 (based on the *Cold store* story) asked you to do this from the headline and first lines. So, having written your seven questions, ask yourself if they are all likely to be answered in the full report. Revise them if necessary. Finally, read the rest of the text on page 106 to see how many of your questions were answered. Most people find around four.

Now reflect on how you read the report. Did you read it word for word? Were there bits you skipped? How did you manage to pick so many questions that were answered in the text without actually reading it first? Your knowledge of the genre of news stories probably helped. Factual reporting means the article has to reveal more information about the 'schoolboy', e.g. his age, which gives your predictions a basis. This process has implications for learning. You were probably quite keen to read the full text to see how many of your questions were answered, i.e. you had a very specific purpose, and one you were involved in creating – they were your own questions (compare this with reading a text followed by comprehension questions set by a teacher). If you also had to check your partner's questions, you probably read the text twice, focusing on slightly different parts and skipping what was familiar. When reading through the other task designs in this section, choose a second task that would give learners a new reason for reading the *Cold store* (and *Spiders*) texts again, more thoroughly, for meaning.

Notice how many of the main facts were given in those first few lines. This text illustrates one of the patterns listed in 5.3.3: Main facts – supporting details. This is what makes it so suitable for a prediction task.

To make it easier, you could give a few more lines from the first paragraph, or supply dictionary definitions of key words, or do a pre-task brainstorming activity on ways of keeping warm in a very cold place.

b *Predicting problem solutions, story endings, poem themes*

Using a text with a situation – problem – solution – evaluation pattern (see page 73), you could:
- let students read / hear / watch only the parts which give the situation and problem, and let pairs work out two or three alternative solutions of their own, then evaluate another pair's solutions. When they have presented their best solutions to each other during a report phase, ask the class to predict which solutions are mentioned in the original text. They finally read / hear / watch the whole piece and compare and evaluate.

Using a sequential text (see page 74), you could:
- give students most of it and ask them to write an ending.
- give the ending, and ask them to write the beginning. Giving them a few carefully chosen words from the text (not all key words, and not all nouns!) may make it easier.
- get them to hear / read a video / an illustrated children's story / a series of instructions without seeing the pictures, and then ask them to suggest ideas for visuals.
- or, with the same sources, show them the video images (no sound) / pictures / diagrams first, and get them to guess what the text will say at each stage.

Using a poem, you could:
- write lines on the board, one at a time, not necessarily in order. After each line, ask what the poem could be about. Accept everyone's ideas, giving no indication as to which ideas are closest to the original. If students get too frustrated, give them a line containing more clues. Stop when they get near the actual theme and let them read the whole poem. This is fun to do as a whole class exercise.
- give the first few lines, and maybe the last line, and ask students in pairs to describe the circumstances behind the poem as they imagine them.

Make sure students don't feel they have failed if they predict something entirely different from the original text. Sometimes their ideas are even better; they are often equally interesting and viable.

NB: Prediction tasks are difficult to present in a coursebook, because some students will have read ahead and know what is coming.

Be sure to give enough clues! Only a headline or title to predict from allows students very little to work on. It encourages random, unmotivated guesses, which are often over in a few seconds, and bear little resemblance to the target text. There is little or no linguistic challenge. It is far better to give a range of clues that provide this and look intriguing.

5.4.2 Jumbles

Learners are presented with sections or parts of a complete text, but in the wrong order. They have to read or hear each part and decide in which order they would be best. Sequencing often requires quite deep linguistic processing of parts of the text, and an appreciation of the coherence of the whole meaning.

The text pattern that lends itself most obviously to this type of task is the sequential one.

- Where an account of a process/a set of instructions/a narrative is accompanied by diagrams/pictures, you could jumble either the text or the visuals. This involves matching text to visuals (see page 84).
- With listening or viewing materials (which are difficult to play in the wrong order), you could use a jumbled summary of the content or a jumbled list of main points (perhaps minus the ending) instead.[9]

Using texts that follow a general – specific pattern or a topic – elaboration pattern (see page 74), you could:

- split up the general/topic statements from the accompanying specific elaboration statements and jumble them. You might need to leave the first and last paragraph intact, to give students sufficient context.
- jumble headlines from short 'News in brief' items and ask students to read the items and select the headline that fits best. To make this more challenging, add two or three extra headlines on similar themes. Since headlines often use words with several alternative meanings, a dictionary exercise could be set at the pre-task phase to help students predict these.

Using a poem, you could:

- either mix up whole verses, or lines within verses.

NB: Jumbles can be frustrating if texts are divided into too many sections. Before you finalise the task for class use, try it out on someone who has not read or heard the text.

Jumbles are rarely suitable for newspaper reports as events are seldom written in sequence.

Always give students credit for arriving at a possible ordering, even if this is not the original order.

5.4.3 Restoration tasks

Students replace words or phrases that have been omitted from a text, or identify an extra sentence or paragraph that has been put in.

The aim here is for the student to restore the text to its original state. Although the omissions or additions are normally selected by the teacher, there is no reason why groups of students should not make their own, and give them to other groups. This could make an excellent class revision exercise, with each group working on a familiar text.

a *Omissions*

Omitting words/phrases from a written text, you could:
- put them into a box above the text (preferably with one or two extra words/phrases, so that students cannot do the restoration without thinking) and ask students to find where they fit. Leave gaps.
- make an even more challenging task by omitting some carefully selected phrases and retyping the text closing up the gaps. This way, a far more detailed reading will be required. Such a task is best preceded by one that gives students a general idea of what the text is about.

The choice of words to omit depends on the aims of the task. For example, some of the new words that students may not know could be removed or blacked out completely. Ask students to summarise the story with the words missing. This will prove they do not have to understand every word to do the task. Another way would be to remove phrases crucial to the story line, leaving gaps. On the basis of what they've read, learners speculate which phrase could be in each gap.

Omitting a single sentence, you could:
- put it underneath the text and close up the gap. If you have picked a good sentence, students will have to read quite carefully to find where it fits best (see Task B in Focus 5).

b *Additions*

Adding an extra sentence to the original text, you could:
- ask students to spot the stranger. It will need to be fairly well disguised, for example, by containing some of the same lexis as the text, but should not make sense in the context. For example, in the *Cold store* text on page 106, you could add the sentence *Even the butcher himself was freezing cold* in the middle of paragraph three.

Adding another text of a similar length on a similar topic but from a different genre, you could:
- merge the two for students to read and separate the paragraphs into the two original texts. For example, this could be done by finding a text about spiders from a children's encyclopaedia, splitting it into four or five short sections and inserting it into the *Spiders* text. (You would obviously need to retype the merged texts.) This task would be more suitable for higher-level students.

c *Tabularised information*

Using a separate table/flow chart/diagram summarising the main points of the text or programme extract, you could:
- omit some points (and jumble them below) or add a specific number of extra points. Students begin by discussing the points, and trying to identify which fit where, or which might not fit. They then read/listen/watch to confirm their predictions.

5.4.4 Jigsaw tasks

The aim is for students to make a whole from different parts, each part being held by a different person or taken from a different source.

Students read/listen to/view their section, and report to the others what it contains. They then discuss how it all fits together. The final product is either the reassembled text or a new piece containing the synthesised information written by the group or presented orally.

Using a text with a situation – problem – solution – evaluation pattern (see page 73), you could:

- split it into four or more sections (depending on how many solutions are offered and evaluated, and how these are organised within the text), to make a small-scale task.
- make such tasks into large-scale projects, for example, to produce a report on a specific aspect of a country by compiling information from different sources such as interviews, reference books, travel brochures and TV documentaries (for more ideas see Appendix A, Type 6: Creative tasks).

Using a recording you could:

- do a split listening task, where the whole class hears the same recording, but different groups must listen for different information or to a different person. Then they are asked to pool what they can remember and summarise the content, having been given a set number of points to include. (This makes them sift and evaluate the points they have retrieved.) The same technique can also be used for quick dictation of a whole text or conversation.

Using a video, you could:

- do a split viewing task, where half the class turn their backs to the video, while the other half view normally. They would then pool and summarise the information as above.

For students to complete all jigsaw tasks to their satisfaction and bring them to the standard needed for the report phase, they will need to read/hear/view the sources several times after the initial task is completed. They may then have a natural desire to read or hear each other's sources, too, to check their information. This naturally increases their exposure and experience of language.

5.4.5 Comparison tasks

These are similar to the tasks described in Chapter 2.3.1 and Appendix A Type 3. Instead of spotting the differences between two pictures, learners compare two (or more) similar texts to spot factual or attitudinal differences, or to find points in common.

Using different accounts of the same incident/different descriptions of the same picture or person, you could:

- ask students to read about each others' experiences of school to find and list points that they have in common.

Using a single event covered by different media, e.g. a news story and a broadcast recording or the same news story from two different newspapers, you could:

- ask students to list the points in common or spot the differences.

Using a report/review of a video extract, you could:

- incorporate two pieces of false or additional information that were not in the original extract. Students then compare the report/review with the extract itself.

5.4.6 Memory challenge tasks

Speed is of the essence here. These tasks are based on the fact that different people will notice and remember different things from a text they have read fast (set a time limit!), or from a recorded extract they have heard or watched only once. You may, when doing them, decide to cut right down on the pre-task phase, because you will get a greater divergence of impressions if students do it 'cold' the first time.

After a single, brief exposure to the text, depending on the content, you could ask pairs to do one of these things:

- list a specific number of ideas/things they remembered best (and why). When reporting these, they find out how many people chose the same ones, and why.
- describe in as much detail as possible one place/person mentioned/ shown in the extract.
- write three (or more) quiz questions about the text that they are sure they can answer correctly. They then ask other pairs their questions.
- with TV adverts on video, list the images on screen, in the right order, and then link them with what they can recall of the text.

After the report phase, (so long as the teacher does not give away the correct answers) the class will naturally want to read, see, or hear the piece again, perhaps several times, to see who remembered the best, and whose first impressions were the most accurate (or strangest).

5.5 Planning a text-based task lesson

The task framework can be used flexibly as a planning tool to enable students to get the most benefits from text-based tasks.

When using texts of any kind, the pre-task phase may involve a quick study of the title or a small extract, or words and phrases from them. The task cycle may take a bit longer, depending on the length of the text or recording. The balance can also be changed slightly; there may be less emphasis on the planning and reporting components, to give more time for the reading and listening. There may be two or even three task cycles arising out of one text, each giving different insights into its meaning.

A sample outline for a lesson beginning with a prediction task follows. Note what teacher and learners do at each stage. Each phase begins with general instructions and is followed by a section of a specific lesson plan based on the *Cold store* text on page 106.

Sample lesson outline for text-based tasks

Pre-task

Teacher introduces topic, source of text, its original purpose, characters, and other relevant information to set scene and activate learners' prior knowledge, using background material if suitable.

Tell class about the coldest day you remember.
Ask: *What's the coldest you have ever been? Where? Why?*
Brainstorm on words/phrases expressing cold, including *cold store/freezer.*
Brainstorm on ways to keep warm.

Task cycle

Task 1

Teacher sets up initial task for students to do in pairs, e.g. prediction task based on extract from text/video programme.
Teacher helps with meanings of key words and phrases if asked.
Pairs discuss predictions.

Write headline and first lines (up to *accidentally*) on board.
Ask pairs to write down five questions they'd like answers to.

Planning and report 1

Students plan brief oral report for whole class, to compare predictions.
Teacher encourages but does not reveal whose predictions are closest.

> Pairs tell each other the questions they thought of. Discuss possible answers.
> Let pairs now write seven questions they are sure will be answered in the story.

First full exposure

Students read whole text/hear or view recorded material once or twice, to see how close predictions were.
Teacher chairs general feedback on content. (Avoid detailed explanation at this point – students may resolve own problems during the second task.)

> Pairs read whole *Cold store* story to find how many of their questions were answered.
> Ask how many got 7/7, 6/7, 5/7, etc.

Task 2

Teacher sets second task of different type, e.g. memory challenge. Without reading/hearing/viewing again, pairs list specific number of points, events, etc. in order they were mentioned or happened, or pairs prepare list of quiz questions for other pairs to answer from memory.

> Either
> Memory challenge: Pairs turn texts over. List six or seven things that happened in chronological order. Start from *At the end of the afternoon's work in the butcher's shop, Peter went into the cold store.*
> Or
> Memory challenge: Pairs prepare six or seven quiz questions to give another pair to answer from memory.

Planning and report 2

Pairs tell/ask other pairs, exchange lists or report to whole class.
Teacher encourages but does not reveal solutions.

> Either
> Pairs read each other's lists and complete their own.
> Or
> Pairs answer each other's questions and see how many they get right.

Second full exposure

All students read/hear/view again, once or twice, to check what they have written, and see which pairs remembered most. General feedback.

> Either
> Pairs read text again, to check facts and find anything else that could go in list.
> Or
> Pairs read text again, to check answers they got wrong.

> Writing task: Plan and write a summary of the story consisting of exactly 60 words.

Not all cycles will be precisely the same since they depend on the type of task.
    Once the task is set up, the role of the teacher is very much that of facilitator, encouraging students to process the text for themselves, and to help each other understand it sufficiently to do the task. It is the learners who should be doing all the work. At the end of the last report stage, the teacher can chair a summing-

up or evaluation session, before focusing on language.

The next and final phase in the task framework is language focus, with analysis and practice components, which give learners chances to take a closer look at the language forms in the text. These components will be described in Chapter 7.

5.6 Summary

The task designs described in the main section of this chapter complement the tasks described in Chapter 2. The aim of these two chapters has been to provide a wide repertoire of task types and designs. The examples in this chapter are based on written or spoken texts, and require learners to apply their real-world knowledge and experience to assign meaning to what they see, hear or read.

Tasks based on text motivate learners to read or listen for a particular purpose. Each time they do so, they interact with the text in a slightly different way, and retrieve different kinds of meanings according to the task goals. This process offers a variety of learning opportunities, and it is essential that the texts chosen form altogether a representative sample of the target language the students will later need.

We saw in Chapter 1 that exposure is vital for language learning. Its overall quality and quantity must be carefully appraised. The language contained in some textbooks fails to offer a fair sample of the target language as a whole. To help counteract this, and to broaden students' experience of language, this chapter has offered an overview of possible sources of suitable written and spoken material and listed criteria for its selection. It has presented some common text patterns, and given guidelines for the design of a range of text-based tasks, all of which should motivate learners to read and listen and employ a range of strategies in doing so. The final section illustrates how the task-based framework can help in the planning of text-based lessons, and clarifies what teachers and learners do at each stage.

Material appraisal

1 **Appraising language exposure – see 5.2.1**
Choose a coursebook that might be suitable for students you know. Go through it quickly to appraise the amount and range of language, both written and spoken, which it contains. Does it offer learners a relevant balance of language experience? What kinds of language and types of texts are lacking?

2 **Appraising external sources of exposure – see 5.2.2**
Even if you are not in a place where the target language is commonly used, think how many possible sources you/your learners have available.

3 **Grading tasks – see 5.2.3, 5.2.4**
Here are four tasks based on the *Spiders* text in Focus 5. Which would provide the easiest route to understanding the text and finding out how the woman was cured: a), b), c) or d)? Which might be the least effective task in providing learning opportunities? Why?

Read the Introduction about the TOP group and the first paragraph only of the text. Then either:
a) Together think of three ways the TOP group could help this woman. Exchange ideas with other pairs. Select four ideas you think might appear in the text, then read the text to see if you guessed correctly.

a living spider in a jar

a toy spider

afraid of spiders

drawings of spiders on a note-pad

pictures of spiders in a book

or

b) In pairs, look carefully at the five pictures, and read the captions. The pictures show the stages in which the woman was cured of her phobia about spiders. What order do you think they should be in?

or

c) The same task as b) above, but without captions to the pictures.

or

d) The same task as b) above, but with captions using words and phrases from the text (i.e. 'doodles' instead of 'drawings').

4 Reading strategies – see 5.3.1

Find some written texts either in a textbook or other sources, and see what kinds of tasks you could use from this chapter that would encourage learners to read for meaning. If possible, try them out in class and observe the kind of strategies students use to do the tasks.

5 a) Try to observe people reading, in and out of class. Do they read in a linear fashion?

b) Interview some good language learners in a class you know. Ask them to think about how they read and to tell you in a later session. What advice would they give to other learners who want to improve their reading?

6 Listening strategies – see 5.3.2

a) Examine the listening materials used in conjunction with a course you know. How would the balance suit students you know?

b) Find an extract of spontaneous speech with a transcript, and devise two tasks you could use to encourage students to listen with involvement. Try them out in class, and get learners' feedback.

7 Task design – see 5.4

If you can get permission to use them in class, record some TV advertisements, preferably ones that students may not know, in the target language. Satellite channels are good for this. Would one be useful for memory challenge tasks? Which ones? Would one be useful for split viewing or predicting?

8 Try out two or three different text-based task cycles with one class. You may need to add some language-focused work afterwards (see Chapter 7). After each task, get students to reflect on what they did and write some feedback for you. They could either complete sentences like:

I found this task (easy/boring/hard/interesting).

I talked (a lot / a bit / not as much as I wanted to).

or you could ask them to write three things they liked about the lesson or two suggestions for improvements.

9 Look through resource books (three good ones are: R Holme, 1991 *Talking Texts* Longman; A Duff and A Maley, 1990 *Literature* OUP; Bassnett, S McGuire and P Grundy, 1993 *Language through literature* Longman) and observe the range of texts and tasks they suggest. How many fall into the task categories offered in this chapter and Appendix A?

Can you find any additional types of task that would motivate your learners to process texts purposefully?

Further reading

For the range of text types available and for ways of exploiting them for teaching language, see G Cook, 1989.

For more on teaching, see F Grellet, 1981, C Nuttall, 1996, J Richards, 1990, Chapter 5 or C Wallace, 1992.

For more on listening, see A Alderson and T Lynch, 1988, and J Richards, 1990, Chapter 3.

For an excellent summary of task types suitable for literary texts called 'Ten generative procedures for developing language activities', see A Duff and A Maley, 1991, pp. 157–65.

Notes

1 See M Legutke and H Thomas, 1991 on a secondary school in Germany who used their local airport as a rich source of language data.

2 Classes could exchange written materials, audio and perhaps even short video recordings on any variety of local and international topics. Language teaching magazines often have a 'wanted' column for pen-friends / school links.

3 The Internet address: http:/lwww.les.aston.ac.uk/ext ling.html will give you a menu to start exploring what is available for language teachers.

4 Other criteria for the selection of video material should include visual interest / appeal; for example, if the screen only shows 'talking heads', there is very little to exploit on the visual side, other than personal expression, lip and body movements, etc. See M Allan, 1982, p. 22.

5 This is not to say that long texts or whole programmes are not useful exposure. They are, if they are moderately comprehensible. Reading and viewing for pleasure can, however, be done out of class. Here we are thinking of making the most of limited classroom time, which is often expensive for the student.

6 D Crystal, 1992, p. 372 describes American research which has produced a formula for calculating the 'fog index' of a text.

7 More than one unknown word in twenty is likely to render a text frustratingly difficult (P Meara, 1993).

8 When you were at school, do you remember reading a foreign language text out loud in your best pronunciation? And then realising at the end that you had hardly any idea of what it meant?

9 Actually making the summary of the video extract or listening text, and deciding how to jumble it would have to be done beforehand. Perhaps this could be set as a task for a higher level class to do in groups, trying the jumbled versions out on each other afterwards.

Recordings in the TBL framework

A The two framework diagrams show that recordings can be played either after or before students do the task. With what sorts of task (give some examples) would you use the first? What about the second? Why?

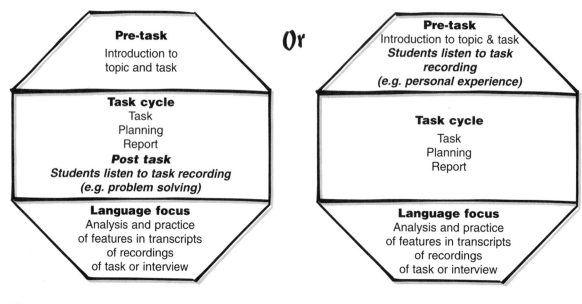

Pre-task
Introduction to topic and task

Task cycle
Task
Planning
Report
Post task
Students listen to task recording
(e.g. problem solving)

Language focus
Analysis and practice of features in transcripts of recordings of task or interview

Or

Pre-task
Introduction to topic & task
Students listen to task recording
(e.g. personal experience)

Task cycle
Task
Planning
Report

Language focus
Analysis and practice of features in transcripts of recordings of task or interview

B

What kinds of spoken interaction

- do your learners normally hear?
- will they need to understand?
- do they want to take part in?

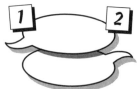

For what reasons might they need exposure to

- clearly spoken planned monologue?
- spontaneous real-time interaction?

C How can you increase learners' exposure to spontaneous interactive talk? There are two ideas below. First read them and then think of

- two tasks that you could record for a class you know,
- two topics that your learners may like to interview people about,
- another idea for increasing their exposure to spontaneous speech.

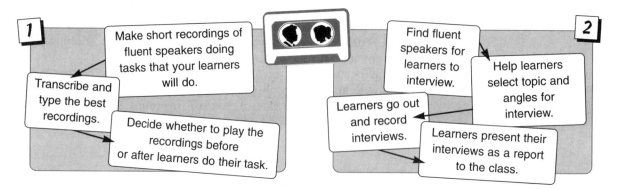

1

Make short recordings of fluent speakers doing tasks that your learners will do.

Transcribe and type the best recordings.

Decide whether to play the recordings before or after learners do their task.

2

Find fluent speakers for learners to interview.

Help learners select topic and angles for interview.

Learners go out and record interviews.

Learners present their interviews as a report to the class.

6 Exposure to spontaneous speech using recordings

> We begin by assessing what exposure to spontaneous speech the TBL framework as described so far offers the learner. We then turn our attention to ways of enriching this experience: firstly, and most importantly, through providing recordings of tasks that students will be doing themselves, and secondly by helping them collect their own data by recording interviews with target language speakers.
>
> Practical advice and tips for making recordings are given, as are guidelines on when and how to use them within the TBL framework. Studying the accompanying transcripts will help learners understand and participate better in real-time target language interactions, both in and outside lessons. It will also give them insights into the grammar of the spoken language, a topic taken up in detail in Chapter 7.

6.1 Spontaneous speech in the TBL framework

In 5.2.1 we acknowledged that spontaneous speech and spoken interaction in the target language are important sources of exposure for learners. We also pointed out that this is the most difficult type of language to bring into the classroom for teaching purposes. Exposure to it does occur naturally in the TBL framework, as we have already described, and we will briefly summarise where and how.

The pre-task phase (see 3.2) gives learners exposure to topic-related talk, probably mainly from the teacher. Contrary to prejudices about 'teacher talking time', this can be very useful. Most learners want to know what the lesson will be about, so should be trying fairly hard to understand what the teacher is discussing with them. As we saw in 1.3.1, it is this grappling with meaning that helps input become intake.

During the task cycle, learners listen to each other, both while doing the task and reporting. It is likely that there will be some social talk, and hopefully some or most of the planning talk will be in the target language. If the task is based on a text from an audio or video recording, this does, of course, provide valuable extra exposure. Otherwise, during the pre-task phase and task cycle, most of the exposure to spoken interaction is teacher and learner talk. Is this enough?

6.1.1 Why learners need more speech exposure

Apart from teacher-led conversations, typical samples of real-time interaction are generally all too rarely heard in the language classroom. Textbooks contain mainly written language; cassettes mainly carefully edited spoken language, a lot of which is scripted. Some of this will be planned monologue. Some courses contain interviews with native or fluent speakers, but even interview interaction, though useful, is fairly controlled and sometimes semi-scripted, to ensure that particular language structures are used. This kind of interaction is very different from the hurly burly of real-time conversation, where we are constantly composing what we want to say next while still listening to what is being said, and all the time waiting for a suitable opportunity to say it.

Can we realistically expect our learners to shed their inhibitions and take part in real-time conversations in the target language, without having had experience of them? What they need are the kinds of words and phrases that sustain the interaction and link their ideas together without sounding blunt and awkward. They need to know the words and phrases typically used for introducing new ideas, bringing a conversation back to a previous point and so on. (Phrases like *So anyway…, What I did was, I…* would rarely appear in written form.)

As we pointed out in 2.3.1, one reason why many learners find it so difficult to talk could be that they're trying to do so in perfect sentences: the style of planned or written language. Exposing them to spoken language shows them instead how to gain time by using semi-prefabricated chunks and familiar phrases as they search for the particular words vital to their message.

Having made out a case for enriching learners' exposure to spontaneous spoken language beyond teacher and learner talk, we must consider where we can find material that is comprehensible. It is well known that conversational talk in a foreign language can be very difficult to understand.

6.1.2 Providing speech exposure

One practical solution is to make your own recordings, with transcripts, of fluent target language speakers doing the same tasks as the students. This will give students exposure to accessible samples of real-time talk that is immediately relevant to their learning situations. Look out for textbooks that provide such task recordings, with transcripts.

Secondly, if you are in an environment where fluent speakers of the target language are easily accessible, it might be possible to get groups of learners to record interviews to bring back into the classroom. By fluent speakers, I do not mean they must be native speakers. In many cases it is more appropriate that they are not. It is quite likely that your students will be using their English with non-native speakers. Initially, too, they will find a local variety of English easier to understand than a non-local variety. With ESP groups, you may be able to make professional contacts with target language speakers in local companies (see 6.4).

A third solution is to exploit the recorded interviews in textbooks and resource books. Some are more formal than others, and the turn-taking routines are different from casual conversation: it is always the interviewer who controls the conversation. But as samples of another type of spoken interaction, they are still useful.

Finally, you can help by bringing the learners into contact with native speakers of the target language. We described how this could be done in 5.2.2.

6.2 Using task recordings

One bonus for the teacher is that tasks can be quite short, so recordings of them are manageable in class. Longer recordings can be split into smaller stages when being played back.

6.2.1 The benefits of task recordings

For learners, listening to recordings of fluent speakers doing their tasks has many advantages.

- They have a reason for listening. Since they will be doing a similar task (or have just done one) they will want to hear how others got on.
- They know what the task goals are, so they have a fairly clear idea of the kinds of meanings that might be expressed. Task recordings tend to provide input that is broadly comprehensible.
- They get used to listening for specific things and not understanding everything. This is good practice for real-life situations.
- They hear how speakers negotiate opening moves, sustain the interaction, evaluate progress, and bring things to a close.
- They get used to features like false starts, overtalk, and interruptions. They will gain confidence in their ability to handle natural talk and begin to enjoy the colloquial feel of it.
- They can clarify meanings and examine the typical features of spoken language in more detail by studying the accompanying transcripts.

Although learners will not spend their lives outside the classroom doing tasks, the language used in this kind of interaction replicates a great many of the features of natural talk. Once used to a task-based approach, most learners find using task recordings with transcripts a satisfying and motivating learning experience.

Feedback from secondary school students who have been listening to task recordings either before or after doing their own tasks.

I think it helps me because I understand the passage and I get examples that I couldn't find, So it is very good to listen it once and then discuss it.

I think it helps me a lot to listen to People on the tape before I do it my Self. Because Sometimes I don't understand What to do Sometimes it gives me ideas of what to do

I think it's very good for us because, before we do The project, we listen to the tape recorder, so we do the project very easily. Sometimes, we don't understand it; wit the tape recoder, we understand it more easy. It's very helpful.

Listening to someone in the tape-recorder disscussing about something helps me because Sometimes explanation isn't enough to under stand clearly, but when I listen to the tape - recorder I can easily understand what we will do. It is also help me to get better my Pronounciation.

6.2.2 Pre- or post- task listening?

Closed tasks

If the task consists of a problem or a puzzle to solve, or is a listing or ordering and sorting task, where there are correct or possible alternative answers, it would obviously be foolish to play the whole recording first. Once students hear the solution, or get to know one set of answers, there is no longer a purpose for them to do the task.

In this case, they would do the task first, then hear the recording afterwards. They can compare the strategies speakers used in the recording with their own strategies. They may notice words and phrases they could have used themselves. They should find the recording reasonably easy to understand, and will be able to guess the meanings of many words that are unfamiliar. They will be able to predict fairly accurately the direction the conversation will take.

Occasionally there might be a good reason for splitting the recording up. You may, for example, want to play just the first part of a problem-solving recording before students begin the task, to give them an idea of how to get started.

Open tasks

If, however, the task consists of comparing personal experiences, then it might be quite useful for students to listen before they do it. In this case there is no solution – just a range of different experiences. The recording can usually be introduced and played as part of the pre-task phase (see 3.2). Alternatively, if the recording itself seems rather difficult, you might get students to do the task first and then listen to the recording. You will need to weigh up the pros and cons, and decide which way will give the best learning opportunities and the most satisfaction.

By listening first to recordings of one or two pairs doing a similar task, students will get a clearer idea of what they are expected to do, and how. They may get more ideas about what to say themselves, and of the general shape of the interaction. It may also help them recall useful words and phrases.

We have, then, two basic cycles, depending on the type of task. The two framework diagrams in Focus 6 set out these alternatives.

Notice that the language focus at the end of the framework can be based wholly or partly on the transcripts of the recordings students have already heard and processed for meaning (see Chapter 7 and Lesson Outlines 1 and 2 in Appendix C).

6.2.3 Handling task recordings

While listening to task recordings, it is important for learners to feel they are managing to understand quite a lot for themselves. As they get used to the full task framework, they will feel reassured by the fact that they can read the transcript and study the language used later.

If the pre-task phase has familiarised the class with the task topic and objectives, learners will have some expectations of the recording already. They will have even more if they have already done the task themselves. Before they listen, you should do the following.

- Introduce the speakers on the cassette.
- Make sure your students realise the speakers are doing a similar task to the one they will do or have done.
- Make sure they know that you don't expect them to understand everything. Tell them it might sound difficult to start with, but you'll play it several times.
- Make sure students know why they're listening each time you play the recording, whether it is before or after the task.
- If the recording and listening purpose are introduced clearly in the student's book, encourage students to read this for themselves. After they have worked out the instructions, ask them to explain to you what they are going to hear and listen for.
- The first time students hear the recording, make sure they have a fairly basic listening purpose. Examples follow, based on the recording about school subjects made by four adults in their mid-twenties and transcribed below (see Focus 2, Task 7).

Sample task-recording transcript

Catherine: *We've each got to say a little bit about our favourite subject at school, and which were the ones, erm, that we liked the least and for what reasons. Why don't you start?*

Caroline: *Right, well. My favourite subject was always English, I think because I liked writing stories. The least favourite was always Maths. I was awful at it. I think I, erm, didn't concentrate on some vital bits and missed out and then it just got worse and worse. I used to sit at the back and giggle quite a lot. And, er, so it was pretty disastrous, really.*

Stephen: *I liked science subjects, but I think that was because the teachers were very much better in that than in subjects like French which I really didn't like at all. I didn't mind things like Maths and English, because I could do them, but it – the languages, French, Latin, Greek, got a bit, you know – I got a bit behind, and the teachers weren't that helpful, so I didn't like those as much …*

John: *What did you dislike?*

Stephen: *Well, French …*

Collins Cobuild English Course Level 2, Section 58[a]

First hearing – listening purposes

Either T: *Listen to Catherine's group talking about who liked which subjects best. After Catherine, you'll hear Caroline first, then Stephen. So you're listening only for their favourite subjects, right?*

Or   T: *Tick the subjects on the list as you hear them mentioned. Which one is not mentioned?*

Or   T: *Each time you hear them mention a new subject, put your hand up.*

Second hearing – new listening purpose

Either ask for a little more detail or less accessible information.

T: *This time, listen for the subjects they liked least. The ones they didn't like at all. You'll hear three people this time, Caroline, Stephen and John. OK? Their least favourites. Then I'll play it again for you to check, and then you can try to catch why they didn't like them.*

For pre-task listening, some of the simpler tasks suggested in 5.4.1–5.4.6 might be suitable.

The basic objective at this stage is to encourage learners to listen selectively. Setting a different purpose each time they listen, each slightly more challenging than the last, is a way of grading the activity. This way, different parts of the exposure become clearer, until most of the interaction becomes comprehensible input.

While learners are listening, help if they get really stuck, i.e. if they don't catch vital words and phrases, but remind them they can check queries when using the transcript or in the language focus phase later. Avoid the temptation to tell them which are the right or wrong answers until the end of the cycle, unless they get very frustrated, or they may stop trying to understand.

Through using task recordings we are aiming to fulfil more of the optimum conditions of learning (see 1.3.1–1.3.4). Recordings provide a rich input of real language, of the kind students will need to use themselves. There is also a natural motivation for students to process that language. It comes from two sources – knowing they have done or will be doing the same task; and finding that they have been at least partly successful in understanding fluent speakers in a natural, holistic interaction.

6.3 Making your own task recordings

Many resource books have great ideas for tasks, but no recordings. So, you might like to try making your own. The question is, how easy is it?

Many teachers are used to writing short dialogues and recording them; recording tasks takes no longer, but it is the other way round. You set the tasks and record them first, then transcribe the speech after. The advantage is that you get naturally occurring English.

6.3.1 How to record tasks

To save time and effort, it is better to plan a series of tasks and record them in one sitting. Writing the instructions for each on a separate card works quite well. You hand the speakers a set of cards and they record one task after another until they have finished. You could ask pairs to do six tasks at a sitting. At two minutes a task, the actual recording will take twelve minutes. So allow twenty minutes, the extra being for setting up the tape recorder, testing the microphone, and for the odd query. At this rate, you could record two pairs doing six tasks in one lunch hour and still have time for a sandwich.

Some guidelines follow. You will want recordings that are reasonably short and fairly clear, with not too much overtalk or background noise. They need to be natural, rather than acted or scripted. For real beginners, agree with the speakers beforehand on how to do the task, and stress the need to keep it short and simple.

a *Who to record and where?*

- Vary the people you ask to record. As we said in 6.1.2, they do not need to be native speakers, as sometimes fluent non-native speakers are easier for students to understand. Sometimes a combination of native and non-native speakers is more appropriate. Also, some people are naturally good communicators and stick to the point. Others don't. If you ask language teachers, make sure they know you are not looking for any particular language form, so they don't distort what they say by introducing what they think are target structures.
- Start with pairs rather than groups. Recording more than two speakers nearly always makes it harder for learners to understand, unless you ask one to act as chairperson. This was done for the school subjects recording: Catherine acted as chairperson, and the other three spoke in turn.
- Record at least two pairs of speakers doing each task and choose the best recording. (It's better if the second pair doesn't listen to the first pair, especially if the task is a problem they have to solve.)
- Try to use a quiet room with curtains (and preferably a floor covering) which will absorb any echoes, and put a coat or jacket over any hard surface near the microphone. Even if the cassette recorder has a built-in microphone, you nearly always get better sound with a separate microphone placed between the speakers. Always do a short test recording first – get each person to count up to ten – and play it back to see how it sounds.

b *Instructions and timing*

- Make sure that your instructions are very specific. If tasks are too open-ended, speakers tend to ramble or digress and, when playing the recordings back in class, students lose interest.
- To help speakers feel less inhibited, do one or two short simple tasks first, for a warm-up.
- Set a time limit and encourage the speakers to keep to it. Remember that two minutes of talk will give you around 400 words of transcript (and too much for most learners to digest at once). Ask the speakers to follow the task instructions closely and to be brief – to start with, the briefer the better. Ask one of them to be the time keeper. A small clock or a stop watch on the table will help.
- One common question is: how can I record a task to practise a specific structure? The short answer is, you can't. The whole point of task-based teaching is to give learners experience of hearing and using natural rather than contrived language.

- Dividing a task into stages gives you more options when using it in class. You can also ask speakers to summarise what they have found, orally, or in written form, drafting it out loud with one person writing. Then in the lesson you can use the recording of the summary before the report stage.

Here is a sample card with recording instructions for Task 6 from Focus 2. The instructions are in three parts, plus a final part which involves drafting a written summary.

> Each of you, think of one teacher you remember well. You have one minute each to tell your partner why you remember them.
>
> When you have finished, try to find two points they had in common, e.g. did you remember them for positive or negative reasons?
>
> After one minute, one of you should summarise your findings briefly, so agree on two or three sentences to write down.

- Afterwards, ask the speakers for their opinions on the tasks – which tasks they liked best and which they didn't like, and why. This is all useful feedback. If a task doesn't seem to work after two sets of fluent speakers have tried it, don't set it for your learners to do.

c *After recording*
- Select the best task recordings to use in class. You can also select parts of recordings if necessary, or break them up into chunks if they are rather long. You may have to discard some because speakers have digressed, talked for too long, or have ideas that are too 'way out'.
- Copy the recordings you choose onto a second cassette. Give each task a title. Label the edited cassette and keep the master cassette safely.
- Transcribe the tasks you want to use in class. More advanced students might enjoy helping you with this; they will gain useful insights and learn a lot of colloquial language. Other teachers might help, too.
- Keep an index of task recordings, with tape counter numbers relating to the cassette recorders used in class. Make sure cassettes and transcripts are numbered and listed, and arranged on storage shelves so other teachers can find them easily.

6.4 Interviews recorded by learners

As noted in 6.1.2 above, it is sometimes possible to arrange for learners to interview fluent speakers, record the interviews on audio cassette, and bring them back to use as classroom data.

The topics will depend on what students are currently studying, what they are curious about, and what kind of people are available to talk to. You may, for example, find people in the same field as your ESP learners. But basically, most people are willing to talk about things the students are interested in. And students, after initially feeling a little nervous, find that they can speak enough to hold interviews, and bring back to class something unique, personal, useful and satisfying.

6.4.1 Making and using interviews

A group of twenty students, working in pairs, doing one interview per pair, could, between them, bring enough material to last for more than ten hours of classroom time. Not all need to record at the same time or on the same day. The recordings can be done as a series of mini-projects, gradually through a term.

Each interview may only have lasted a few minutes, but the subsequent planning, leading up to presentation of the interview data at the report stage, can be a lengthy and linguistically enriching process. Some regular class time can be devoted to it. Students might need help with parts of the transcription, with the drafting of a description of the interviewee, and their reactions.

During the report stage, the pair presenting the interview to the class will introduce the speaker, describe the background, play back and comment on the interview (or sections from it), hear the other students' reactions and answer their questions. This would then probably lead to some language-focused work designed by the teacher, or possibly by the recording pair. Together with initial pre-interview planning, the whole process can involve the learners in serious and intense language study, as well as opportunities to listen to and use the language for real purposes.

6.4.2 Benefits of recording interviews

- Students will most probably speak haltingly and sound like learners so it is likely that people being interviewed will adjust their speech accordingly. This should lead to input that is naturally modified to become comprehensible (see 1.2.1).
- In an interview situation, the learners are the controllers and the initiators. Once they have had a little practice, they can manipulate and direct the interview.
- Because the data 'belongs' to them, they will be keen to work at understanding and exploiting it, with the teacher's support. They usually like to present at least a part of it to the whole class.
- Gradually students build up a bank of locally recorded data which the whole class has access to and experience of. Even if all the interview recordings cannot be copied, the transcripts can.
- The process of collecting their own data increases learners' self-reliance, independence and confidence.

6.4.3 How learners can record interviews

a *Where and who to record*

When students are staying or travelling in a country where English is spoken, perhaps for a school trip or a summer school, the immediate environment offers a wealth of opportunities, from the staff and other students in the school to people they meet while doing sports, etc. More formal contacts can be made with local institutions, businesses and tourist attractions.

Students who are not in a country where English is commonly used, might still be able to find fluent speakers somewhere (see 5.2.2).

If possible, plan a staged series of interviews. Start with people students are familiar with. Then progress to people outside the school/college. Finally try to find local personalities whom students don't know, e.g. the local librarian, museum curator or fire station manager.

Encourage students to collect from their interviewees any written documentation (brochures, adverts, leaflets etc.) that could serve as background information for the class.

b *Before they start*

Check there is adequate recording equipment available. Students can be requested to supply their own, if they have Walkmans that record.

List people who might be interviewed, and order them according to status and familiarity. You may need to ask permission from heads or directors. Arrange convenient times. At a later stage students can do this for themselves. Once used to interviewing people, they often feel confident enough to stop and interview strangers, e.g. fellow travellers.

c *Preparation*

Try to find some spontaneous recorded interviews from a resource book – preferably ones that students have heard previously. Let them listen again to identify some interviewing strategies. Do interviewers simply read out a list of questions and wait for the answers? Lists of prepared questions are good for confidence, but can lead to a very jerky interview. Most students will need help with picking up and reacting to the points made by the interviewee. They will need practice in expanding and elaborating on what they have heard. If you can find a recording of an interview where this happens, so much the better.

Select interview topics that students find interesting. Try to link these with the topics in the coursebook, or resource book, then the vocabulary is more familiar. Let students practise interviewing each other on the selected topics. Then get pairs to start recording interviews, and listening to themselves as interviewers. You could also ask two good students to practise on you, while the others listen. At this stage they may feel they need to identify useful phrases and try out different strategies.

Once they are conversant with the topic they want to explore, they can prepare for their first real interview. It is usually better if students plan and carry out the interview in pairs, taking turns to ask the questions. Get both students to record at the same time, each with their own cassette recorder and microphone, in case one does not work, or is inaudible. There is always one person in the class who forgets to press 'record' or release the pause button! (It's sometimes me …)

Plan your teaching programme ahead, incorporating the stages shown in d) below.

d *After the interviews*

Once students have recorded their interviews, they will have lots to tell you. Get them to write down what they did and how they felt about it straight away, using the target language, either in note or diary form for personal reference, or as an informal letter to you. Either will form the basis for a planning stage.

Ask them to select two or three short sections to transcribe. Give them an approximate word limit. Two minutes' worth could be about 400 words, and will take some time to write down accurately. Tell them to leave a gap for words or phrases they can't catch, otherwise it can turn into a frustrating process. (Even native speakers find spoken language difficult to transcribe.) By asking them to select two or three sections, you are making it likely that they will listen to the whole piece several times, and will begin to notice new things about their data.

'Noticing' is a vital part of the acquisition process (see 1.2.1).

Help students plan how to present their interviews to the whole class, so the others can benefit fully from their data (see 4.3.1). Help with transcription problems if you can, but bear in mind that there are bound to be bits which are difficult or impossible to make out. Take this opportunity to decide which language features from each person's data the class could usefully focus on.

Schedule the reporting sessions. You may want to spread their presentations over several lessons. At the end of each report, do some language-focused work. Students may like to plan a visual display or write parts of their final report, or prepare background information on a wall poster or handout. Some students add photographs or drawings with captions. Allow time for an evaluation session after the last reports.

The main cycle of work will probably happen over at least four lessons, spaced apart; it also depends on the number of students taking part, and the number of interviews to report. The task-based framework can be used flexibly and expanded as needed, as the following example shows. The tasks here, of course, are the interviews. We will summarise the whole process here.

Stages in recording and using interviews

Pre-task 1	Introduction to idea of interviewing and collecting data. Decisions on selection of topic(s). Pairs/groups decide angle on topic. Think about interview planning.
Pre-task 2	Exposure to familiar interview recordings already used in class.
Language focus	Opening and closing moves, questions, techniques for reacting to what interviewer says, and for continuing topic. Useful phrases.
Rehearsal task	Students interview each other and practise recording. Evaluate their own recordings and finalise strategies for real interviews.
Main task	Students carry out and record real interviews, outside class. Write (in note form) what they did, how it went.
Planning	Students transcribe sections from recording. Prepare to present interview to class.
Report	Class hears interview, listens to commentary, reads displays/handouts, takes notes, asks questions.
Language focus	Study of transcripts. Useful phrases noted and practised. Other features collected (see Chapter 7).
Final review of reports	Sections of interviews replayed. Students summarise what they did, to remind class. Finally class votes on most interesting person interviewed.
Evaluation	Evaluation of interview recording as language-learning process.

6.4.4 Video recording a 'vox pop' programme

Brief interviews can also be done using video recorders. This is a more complex process than audio recording, but, if you have the equipment, is great fun to do and creates many opportunities for genuine use of language. It is really only possible where there are a number of target language speakers around.

'Vox pop' means 'voice of the people'. On TV News programmes, you may have seen people in the street being stopped, and asked their opinions on a particular issue. The programme is a series of short, fast interview extracts. However, to get enough material for a two-minute programme, TV crews record many more interviews than are needed, select only a few of the best and edit them together, with a voice-over commentary to introduce the programme and perhaps link the extracts.

This is probably too sophisticated for general use. As a special end-of-term project, or in a summer school, students could interview local people with a camcorder, using a simpler technique called 'in-camera editing'. They start by recording the title and introduction then record interviews in the order they want them. If any don't work, they rewind and record over them, making careful use of the counter numbers. Each group of students chooses a different topic. The final product can be introduced and shown to the class, who vote on the best programme.

See Appendix A, Type 6: Creative tasks for more ideas on who and what to record.

6.5 Summary

We began by assessing the exposure to spontaneous spoken language that the TBL framework offers so far, and making a case for providing extra exposure, by such means as recording tasks for use in class and encouraging students to go out and interview people.

However, in designing, recording and selecting tasks and planning interview situations, it is easy to get caught up in technicalities. Our overall aims should be to:

- bring a range of samples of spontaneous interaction into the classroom;
- broaden learners' experience of spoken language;
- give them opportunities to use language spontaneously themselves;
- allow them to compare their language use with that of fluent speakers in a similar situation by listening to task recordings and studying transcripts;
- give them confidence in using the new language outside the classroom by recording interviews.

By involving students in the process of recording interviews to collect language data, they are more likely to become motivated and remain so and therefore to learn more. If, working together with your students and other teachers on tasks and interviews, you can achieve this, you will have done well.

The following chapter will give you techniques for exploiting the spoken data for language focus activities. In the meantime, the tasks below are designed to help you to put some of these ideas into practice for yourself.

Material appraisal

1 Recorded materials

Find a textbook or resource book with recordings and tapescripts or transcripts. Look at the transcripts and try to decide whether they are scripted or unscripted talk. If unscripted, are they carefully planned, or do they seem entirely spontaneous? Listen to the recordings and identify typical features of spoken language. Discuss with a colleague how far these listening materials will satisfy your learners' current and future needs.

2 Coursebook exploitation of recordings

a) Select one unit and look at the accompanying recordings. What do students do with them? At what point in the lesson do they hear them? What is the rationale behind them? Is there an introductory task or listening purpose given for them? Are there any exercises or awareness-raising tasks which exploit the language used in them?

b) Could you now suggest other tasks that could be set before or during the listening stage?

3 Pre- or post-task listening – see 6.2.2

Look carefully at the types of task in Appendix A. If you had recordings for them, which would you probably play to the class before they do the task, in a pre-task phase, and which afterwards, as follow-up?

Planning

4 Record some tasks – see 6.3.1

Select two or three tasks suitable for your students. Try recording two different pairs of reasonably fluent speakers doing them. Remember to set a time limit. Compare the recordings – the way speakers achieved the task outcomes, the types of interactions and the language used. Which would be better to use with your learners? Why?

5 Preparing a transcript and planning a lesson

Having completed 4 above, select one task to try in class, and transcribe the recording. Decide whether you would play the cassette pre- or post task. Try out the task and your recording in class, following a task – planning – report cycle. Finish the lesson by letting students see the transcript and select three or four phrases to find out more about.

6 Interviews

Try interviewing someone yourself on a topic that you could use with students in class. Transcribe some extracts from the recording. Make a list of things you notice about the language from doing this. How could you use your recorded interview in class?

Observation

7 Classroom research – recording students doing tasks

Select a closed type of task for which you have a recording. Record pairs of students doing the same task and compare this with the original recording. Ask students what differences and similarities they notice.

FOCUS 7

Components of the language focus

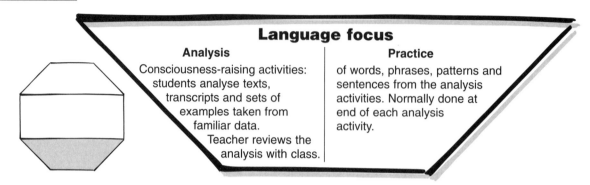

Language focus

Analysis
Consciousness-raising activities: students analyse texts, transcripts and sets of examples taken from familiar data. Teacher reviews the analysis with class.

Practice
of words, phrases, patterns and sentences from the analysis activities. Normally done at end of each analysis activity.

Select two of these language analysis activities and try them yourselves. What do you discover from doing them?

Analysis activities can start from:

Semantic concepts

Themes, notions, functions

a. Read the transcript of the conversation about school subjects on page 91. Find phrases which show positive or negative reactions to them, e.g. *so it was pretty disastrous, really.*

b. Read the cold store story on page 106 and find all the phrases referring to time, e.g. *for ten hours, After that.* How many ways can you classify them?

Words or Parts of a word

c. In the text about Romania (Lesson Outline 4, page 000) there are five phrases with the word *of.* Can you find them?

d. When do we use the word *any?* What does it mean? Study the examples collected below.
1. *You can use it to slice any kind of fruit or vegetable.*
2. *Can you buy me some flowers? Any colour will do.*
3 *Come any time you want.*
4. *Report any suspicious phone calls.*
5 *Don't leave any ladders lying about outside your house.*

Categories of meaning or use

e. The word *with* has four main categories of meaning:
1. 'together', e.g. *I went with my sister.*
2. introducing descriptions of people or things, e.g. *the house with the green door.*
3. indicating how you do something, e.g. *I paid for it with my credit card.*
4. 'because of', e.g. *metals expand with heat.*

Which category do these examples belong to?
– *the man with the white hair.*
– *she was purple with cold.*
– *I'd try to pick the lock with a bit of wire.*
– *He still lives with his parents.*
– *I can't see the TV with you sitting there.*

Practice activities

can be combined with analysis work. How many do you recognise? Can you think of any more?

repeating phrases

completing phrases

dictionary exercises, e.g. matching word to definition

recording reports

DIY (Do It Yourself) concordances

computer games

unpacking and repacking a sentence

progressive deletion from board

recording phrases

gapped transcript

Now look at the language focus sections of Lesson Outlines 1, 3 and 4 in Appendix C. Can you find examples of some of the analysis and practice activities on this page?

7 The TBL framework: language focus

> Language Focus is the last phase of the TBL framework. It follows the report stage of the task cycle (see Chapter 4) and adds an opportunity for explicit language instruction.
>
> This chapter illustrates four starting points for analysis activities, showing how they can be handled in a learner-centred way. It then exemplifies a range of practice activities. There are many ideas for designing both kinds of activities. Their purpose is to highlight specific language features from the texts or transcripts used earlier in the task cycle. They encourage students to focus their attention on forms of the language which they have already processed for meaning. Sample lesson outlines with language focus activities are given in Appendix C.

7.1 From meaning to form

Within the TBL framework, tasks and texts combine to give students a rich exposure to language and also opportunities to use it themselves. Throughout the task cycle, the emphasis has been on students understanding and expressing meanings in order to achieve task outcomes and report their findings. But in Chapter 1, where we summarised the conditions for language learning, we saw that, in addition to exposure, use and motivation, learners also benefit from instruction focused on language form. This will not necessarily be teacher-led, though the teacher will introduce the activities, be on hand to help while students do them and review them at the end.

7.1.1 Analysis and practice

Most of the activities in this chapter entail an element of analysis. Their aim is to get students to identify and think about particular features of language form and language use in their own time and at their own level. This will help them to recognise these features when they meet them again, both inside and outside class, and will lead to a deeper understanding of their meanings and uses. A certain amount of form-focused practice, integrated with analysis activities, may also help students pronounce and memorise useful phrases and common patterns and also give them confidence to try out new combinations and to generate some of their own.

7.2 Language analysis activities

These are sometimes called consciousness-raising activities, language awareness activities or even meta-communicative tasks, i.e. tasks that focus explicitly on language form and use.

Analysis activities should not consist of decontextualised presentation and practice of language items in isolation. Because they follow the task cycle, they involve learners in a study of the language forms that were actually used or needed during the cycle. So they are already familiar with the meanings expressed, and now have the chance to study the forms which realise those meanings.

If there are not sufficient examples of a particular language feature in the task cycle text or transcript, extra ones can be assembled from previously read texts or transcripts of earlier recordings. Invented examples can be used as a last resort, but unfamiliar examples out of context are often less meaningful to the learner, and the use of the target item will be less clear. Beware of introducing examples which are not typical of natural language. It is better to collect examples that have actually occurred in sources familiar to students, or look some up in a good learner's monolingual or semi-bilingual dictionary.[1]

Let us suppose that you want to focus on the uses of *in* after doing the *Cold store* text in 7.3. You could try using the following concordance analysis, which includes examples from texts and transcripts presented in Chapter 5 and Lesson Outlines 3, 4 and 5 in Appendix C. The instruction would be:

Circle the phrases with *in*, e.g. *trapped in a butcher's cold store*. Which refer to place and which to time? How many are left over? How could you classify those?

1	spent the night trapped **in** a butcher's cold store after being
2	after being locked **in** accidentally, ran on the spot for
3	aged 15, was locked **in** the store in a Stratford-upon Avon
4	Peter, who lives **in** Banbury Road, Stratford, said: 'I
5	she could not be left **in** a house alone. If she saw one she
6	she suddenly recoiled **in** horror. She was eventually
7	photographs of spiders **in** books, then leave the pages open in
8	leave the pages open **in** a room so she saw them each time
9	each time she walked **in**. Her husband began to move the
10	took a real spider **in** a jar to the next meeting, where it
11	economic development. **In** an interview he discussed aspects
12	played a prominent part **in** Romania's transition to a market
13	one of the key figures **in** Romania's process of economic
14	trade was excellent **in** the first months of the year and up
15	increased 20 percent **in** the first half (of this year)
16	were very much better **in** that than in subjects like French
17	better in that than **in** subjects like French which I really

As can be seen from the examples on the previous page and those in Focus 7, analysis activities aim to promote:

- observation through identification
- critical investigation of linguistic features.

There are always specific goals to stimulate purposeful analysis. The process of identifying where phrases begin and end in the examples requires some linguistic analysis and draws attention to the structure of typical phrases and sentences. The process of investigating different aspects of *in* gives new insights into its meanings and uses.

Analysis activities give learners time to systematise and build on the grammar they know already, to make and test hypotheses about the grammar and to increase their repertoire of useful lexical items. Learners can ask the teacher individual questions and go on to investigate other features that they notice. The important thing is, they are all working at their own level and at their own pace, and making discoveries that are meaningful to them. Although focusing initially on the same specific analysis goal, individual learners will probably each have gained slightly different insights into how language works, depending on what they knew already. Thereafter, with constant exposure and opportunities to use language, they will be more likely to notice further examples, and discover how and when to use them for themselves.

Before presenting a range of analysis activities, let us first examine how the teacher should handle the language focus phase.

7.2.1 Setting up analysis activities

Ensure the focus and purpose of each activity is clear. Give an example or two, and perhaps do the beginning of the activity with the whole class. If the instructions in the textbook are clear, then ask learners to read them and get on with the activity in their own time.

Make sure you have at least one good learner's dictionary available (see Note 1) for both you and your learners to refer to.

7.2.2 Monitoring analysis activities

Learners continue the analysis in pairs or individually. Now is the time to go round and see how they are getting on. Help out if they are not sure what to do, but avoid the temptation of doing it for them. Let them think for themselves. They need to test their own hypotheses and make their own discoveries. A good rule is: if in doubt, hold back. You will often find that a minute or two later, they will do for themselves what you were about to help them with. Keep an eye on weaker learners, though, and perhaps give them a bit of extra attention.

Be ready to handle individual questions. These are often about different aspects of the text altogether. Sometimes you may refer learners to a dictionary, or the reference section of a book. Sometimes a quick answer is best, in order to keep the focus on the current activity. If you don't know the answer, or need time to think about it, it is better to say, for example, *That's quite a difficult question. We could look it up in the dictionary – it might give some clearer examples.*

Remember that students will not necessarily notice the same things as you but will pick out things that are new to them and that they can fit into their own developing picture of the target language. These may be further examples of features they have focused on earlier or things that clash with a previously held conviction and make students re-examine their view of how that feature works.

You will notice that individual learners find different ways of classifying the same examples. Often there is no single right way; it depends on how the learners perceive the examples. For instance, if asked to classify the questions from the *Find seven differences* transcript (see page 31), some learners simply classify them into short questions and long questions. Even this is useful – it shows that typical questions in spoken English are often short and have no verb.

If students finish early, you can ask them to classify further e.g. the long questions, or plan a practice activity for the class to do later, e.g. gapped examples (see 7.4).

Some teachers allow low-level learners to speak to each other in their first language at the analysis stage. Learners will be quoting the examples in the target language anyway, so a certain amount of code switching (mixing of languages) is likely to occur. Many teachers, however, especially those with multilingual classes, find that sooner or later, students get quite good at talking, in an exploratory way, about the target language in the target language. This affords extra speaking practice and is definitely to be encouraged. Try to keep to the target language yourself. This gives your students a chance to acquire the expressions they need for talking about language.

7.2.3 Reviewing analysis activities

This is where you take the lead again. Once most learners have finished the activity, stop them all and go through it as a class. Ask different pairs for examples, and write them on the board. You can do this category by category, or in list form, asking students to categorise afterwards – it depends on the type of task set. For example, when reviewing the *in* analysis, you would get students to call out the phrases category by category (place then time), select typical ones to write up, ask students how they might classify the phrases left over and write those on the board, in sets. It is often useful to ask students to explain their reasons for classifying an example in a particular way. You may find that some examples fit more than one category. Discuss these cases with the class, asking them why.

When the review is complete, ask the class for further examples that they know, and add these to the categories. With the *in* analysis, you could ask for more time phrases, and more phrases with *in* showing an emotional state (*in fear, in embarrassment*). You can also focus on other useful collocations or words that occur, e.g. the word *figure* has many meanings. Do students know them? They could look them up for homework. Finally, suggest that they continue to look out for (and note down) similar examples from what they subsequently hear or read.

Most students benefit from keeping personal language notebooks. Students will find different ways of organising these. After every language analysis activity, give students time to select examples from the board to enter in their personal notebooks. If they notice similar examples in what they hear or read, they should add those to their notebooks, too. If regularly maintained, such notebooks can give students a real sense of progress. Encourage them to keep their notebooks up to date. Spend time each week letting students read out recent examples to share insights with the class.

In the course of carrying out and reviewing the analysis activities, learners will have practised saying target words and phrases and hearing them repeated in different contexts. But you may feel you want to give the class some more orchestrated practice to pull the activity together at the end, or to add some variety, or speed things up.

If, during the review stage, students are having problems with the pronunciation, intonation or stress of a particular phrase, get the class to repeat it in chorus once or twice then speed it up for fun. At the end of the review stage, you could get them to do a choral reading from the board, or, as you clean the board, do some progressive deletion (see 7.4). Such activities can be fun and often give weaker learners more confidence.

The next section describes a range of analysis activities that can be used with texts or transcripts within the TBL framework, after the task cycle.

7.3 Starting points for analysis activities

As you saw in Focus 7, there are three main starting points for analysis activities: semantic concepts (themes, notions, functions), words or parts of a word and categories of meaning or use. With spoken texts, using transcripts and recordings, you could also start from a particular phonological feature, e.g. stress within a phrase, or the pronunciation of a single sound.

This section illustrates a range of analysis activities for language focus based on the *Cold store* text. Before beginning these analysis activities, students will have completed two task cycles: a prediction task and a memory challenge task, as illustrated in the lesson outline in 5.5. By the time students have checked both tasks, they will have read the story at least three times, will be familiar with most of the meanings expressed in the text, and will now be ready to explore language form.

Although there are nine analysis activities illustrated here, you would probably select only the three or four which would best suit your learners at the time. Generally speaking, it is a good idea to begin with an activity that focuses on the words and phrases expressing meanings related to the main theme running through the text. Then tackle two or three other activities using different starting points. Some can be set for homework, and reviewed next lesson.

Notice that activities g) and i) both focus on phrases/clauses with *-ing* verbs, but from a different starting point. You would choose either one or the other, not both. In activities a) and g), some examples re-occur. But this is useful; it encourages learners to observe language from different angles – meaning and word form.

Try to select starting points that will catch the right kind of samples to stimulate a deeper investigation into grammar and meaning. For example, looking for *had* in activity e) will catch verb phrases with *had* and help students explore the use and meaning of the past perfect. Likewise, in activity h), collecting *-ed* verbs and classifying them will lead to a study of the use of the passive.

Analysis activities can be adapted for different levels of learners and made more or less challenging, for instance by increasing or limiting the range of examples. The starting points illustrated in this chapter can be applied to simpler texts. For beginners, it is often easier to start from a word or part of a word. A simple text about someone's family and a recording transcript of a family tree task will give plenty of examples of words ending in *-s* or *-'s* that even low-level learners could find and classify, e.g. *So, my husband's name is Dave. He's got two sisters, one's called Marian – she's the oldest…*

Sample Language Focus Activities

The boy who came out from the cold

A SCHOOLBOY who spent the night trapped in a butcher's cold store after being locked in accidentally, ran on the spot for ten hours to stay alive.

Peter Emerson, aged 15, was locked in the store in a Stratford upon Avon butcher's shop for 14 hours with the temperature around freezing point.

Staff arriving for work at the Wood Street shop found him yesterday morning with his teeth chattering and his face purple with cold. Still freezing, Peter immediately telephoned his parents, who had reported him missing to the police. Peter, who lives in Banbury Road,

Stratford, said: 'I help out at the shop after school and I had gone into the cold store just before closing time. I was behind a big food shelf when the door locked behind me.

'At first I thought it was someone playing a joke but when I realised it wasn't and began shouting all the staff had gone home. I tried to kick the door open and to pick the lock but it was no good.

'I was wearing only a shirt, trousers, a thin pullover and a white butcher's smock. It was bitterly cold and I realised that I might die, so I ran on the spot for about ten of the 14 hours.'

                    The Guardian

Three starting points

Semantic concepts (themes, notions, functions)

a) Find six phrases in the story which refer to the cold and its effects, e.g. *cold store, temperature around freezing point*. What similar phrases do you know?

b) Find eight phrases and words about time, e.g. *spent the night, immediately*. How many ways can you classify these? List them according to categories, e.g. those which answer the question 'When?' and those which tell you 'How long?'

c) How many phrases refer to people, e.g. *a schoolboy, his parents, someone playing a joke*?

d) How many clauses/phrases can you find that refer to a place, e.g. *ran on the spot, help out at the shop*? To practise these, choose any six and write them down but leave a gap for the preposition. Give them to your partner. Can he/she complete them from memory?

Words or parts of words

e) Find three verb phrases with *had*. Could you use a simple past tense form instead? Would it change the meaning in all three cases?

f) Find the phrase *pick the lock*. Use a dictionary to find this use of *pick*. What other interesting phrases with *pick* can you find? Choose four to teach your partner.

g) Find nine phrases/clauses with verbs ending in *-ing*, e.g. *Staff arriving for work*. How could you classify these? (How many begin a sentence? What about the others?) What meaning does *-ing* seem to have?

h) Find the verbs ending in *-ed* and divide them into two or three categories. Now find other past-tense-form verbs from the story to add to the appropriate lists.

Categories of meaning and use

i) Find phrases/clauses with verbs ending in *-ing*, which:
   • describe someone or something
   • follow *is/was/are/were*
   • follow verbs like *stop, start*

How many are left over? How could you classify them?

7.3.1 Meaning: themes, notions and functions

Inevitably, the main themes in a text or transcript are revealed in the lexis. Often the title or opening paragraph will give an indication of what these are. In the *Cold store* text, the main theme is the cold; in the *Spiders* text, it is the part that spiders play in the cure of the phobia. Sometimes, identifying the theme words and phrases will help students to notice lexical repetition and how this can form cohesive ties through the text.

There will also be other themes or notions you can trace through a passage. In the *Cold store* text, we looked at expressions referring to time, people and place. Sometimes in a business or financial text, phrases expressing the notion of increase/decrease may appear frequently. In a spoken transcript of a problem-solving task, there may be several ways of reaching agreement that would form a useful function focus. In an interview or discussion, the functions of questions would be a good choice.

Once students have identified the words and phrases in the text that echo each theme or express each notion, you can help them to add to each category, explore shades of meaning and build up lexical sets.

Activities starting from the main themes, notions and functions are excellent for broadening students' vocabulary and increasing their repertoire of lexical phrases.

7.3.2 Words or parts of words

Appendix E lists the most frequent 200 words in spoken and written English, and these can form the basis of many classroom activities. The 20–30 most common words make up a very large proportion of any text and will probably occur quite frequently in any reasonably sized one; they often appear in lexical phrases. Common words that are slightly less frequent may not occur in large numbers in any one text, so you (or your students) may have to collect examples of these from earlier texts and transcripts.[2] For words with two or more very distinct uses, like *that* or *so*, you may want to collect examples of one use at a time.

Many of these very common words are often referred to as 'grammatical' words. If you look down the frequency lists, there are very few words which give any indication of topic until you get past the 150 frequency band. A study of the form and uses of the very common words will certainly help to consolidate learners' developing picture of the grammar of the target language. So far in this chapter, we have seen activities focusing on *in*, *had*, and *pick*.

Activities focusing on parts of words, such as *-ing*, *-ed*, *-s*, /*-'s*, *-ly*, *-tion*, *-ful*, or prefixes, such as *un-*, *over-*, *multi-* may give insights into grammar, phrase/sentence structure and word formation.

Analysis tasks starting from words or parts of words can involve learners in the following:

- classification according to grammatical function (see i) on page 107) – *-ed* verbs split into past simple (*I realised*); past participle in an adjectival form (*spent the night trapped*); past participle in a passive (*was locked*)
- exploring meaning and effects of alternative choices of form (see e) on page 107)
- identifying, from a set of examples, the odd one out, or what they have in common. This can be structural, or semantic (see d) in Focus 7).
- exploring collocation (see c) in Focus 7), where students collect phrases with *of*, such as *balance of trade*.
- collecting similar examples from learners' previous knowledge or from a

dictionary (see f) on page 107)
- classification according to meaning and use (see Lesson Outline 5, Language focus 4, page 107)

7.3.3 Categories of meaning or use

Once learners have met several uses of a common word, you can assemble a number of familiar examples to build a revision activity. Start by giving the common categories of meaning or use of the word or phrase and then ask learners to match each example to a category (see e) in Focus 7 and i) on page 107). The *in* concordance analysis in 7.2 above gave the reader two categories as starting points: place and time. These two categories make good starting points for the study of any preposition. However, it is often the study of the phrases that fit neither category that proves most fruitful in terms of exploring collocation and idiom.

To prepare such activities, you can look up a word's basic categories of meaning and use in a good learner's dictionary or a reference grammar. With common words which tend to have many different meanings, you may need to be selective in your choice of categories, or conflate some to make more general categories.

7.3.4 Phonology: intonation, stress and sounds

Phonology is another area worthy of analysis, and working from recordings and transcripts can be invaluable. Learners need practice in identifying the main message-bearing words in the flow of speech. This involves recognising how spoken language is chunked, (each chunk is known as a tone unit), and hearing which word within each chunk (or tone unit) carries the main stress. This stressed word, which usually has a falling tone ⌐↘ or a fall-rise tone ↘↗ , will be the main message-bearing word, and the key to understanding the meaning of that chunk.[3] So, instead of listening for sentences, learners should get used to listening for tone units and stressed words. If they do this, they will be more able to cope with the flow of speech.

Although intonation can be acquired subconsciously while interacting in the target language during the task cycle, learners often find that specific practice in recognising tone units and key words can help their comprehension. Language-focused work on intonation and stress, then, can include exercises like the following, using the task transcript or a short section of the task recording:

- Listen again for the intonation used with each question. Where does the main stress fall? Practise saying the questions after the tape.
- Read the transcript first and mark in pencil where you think the main stress will fall in each question and discuss why. Then listen to see if you guessed correctly.
- Listen while reading the transcript and
  – mark the stressed words
  – try to identify, like this, / with slash marks / the approximate boundaries of tone units / that you hear./
  – on a second listening, decide whether the tone on the words with the main stress is falling ⌐↘ (indicating new information) or fall rise ↘↗ (indicating shared information).

For example, notice the difference in meaning between

I'm going to PARis / this APril. (= not Rome)

and

I'm going to PARis / this APril. (= not May)[4]

Exercises like these make it clear to the learner that it is the stressed words that carry the important information. Poor pronunciation of an unstressed word rarely impedes communication. So on the whole, exercises which focus on stress and intonation are more effective that those focusing on discrete sounds. If, for example, a learner confuses the sounds in *bit* and *beat* and says *Would you like a beat of cake?*, he is unlikely to be misunderstood. However, at elementary level, some emphasis on discrete sounds will be both satisfying and helpful for learners in distinguishing words that sound similar to them. Learners will never be able to imitate new sounds if they cannot hear them, and to make them practise their pronunciation until each word or phrase is perfect is both frustrating and a waste of time. Pronunciation is probably best acquired slowly through situations where meaning is paramount.[5]

To practise discrete sounds, choose words that come from a familiar spoken source, and try to make up sets of words or phrases that have sounds in common. Some examples follow.

- Which vowel sound is in all these words: *Sunday Monday company number mother young London*?
- Which sound is the odd one out: *phone post road old home love oh! go* ?
- Notice how the end of the word *mother* is said. It is a weak sound [-ə(r)] . Find in the following sentence at least four words which, if spoken, would probably contain a syllable with this weak sound:
  He's now a top grade secretary in some computer company in London.

To supplement this review of analysis activities, see Lesson Outlines 3, 4 and 5 in Appendix C, which give more examples of language focus activities and show how they can be integrated into the TBL framework.

7.4 Language practice activities

As we saw at the end of 7.2.3, practice activities can combine naturally with analysis work and are useful for consolidation and revision. We saw in Chapter 1 that practice activities on their own are unlikely to give learners deeper insights into the meaning and use of grammatical patterns, or speed up their acquisition of these patterns, but they may provide confidence and a sense of security. They may also be a good way – for some students at least – to learn typical lexical phrases.

It is best to cover a wide range of items and aim at small improvements in each, recognising that language learning is an organic process. If the language items you are focusing on are common (which they should be!), they will naturally occur again in future exposure, and, so long as learners recognise them, they will get another chance to think about and practise them then. This is the advantage of an exposure-rich classroom – common words, phrases and patterns are continually recycled. Try to explain this to students.

The practice activities summarised below can be based on features of language that have already occurred in previous texts and transcripts or on features that have just been studied in analysis activities. Some are purely oral, some require writing in preparation for an oral stage, some are mainly written. They can be done singly, in pairs or groups, as team competitions or teacher-led sessions with the whole class. Many of them could be prepared by learners as homework.

a *Repetition*

Repetition of useful phrases, or dialogue readings can be done by individuals, students in pairs, or, if led by the teacher, with the whole class in chorus or in large groups, with each group taking one part. It is fun to begin slowly and build up speed, to see how fast they can do it.

b *Listen and complete*

Teams or pairs write a list of useful phrases or sentences. One learner says half or a little more of each item. The first team or pair to complete it successfully gets a point.

Or you can play a recording and press the pause button in mid-phrase – which team or pair can continue? Don't give the answer yourself but, after several attempts, play the tape and let the class identify who was correct. (Allow four or five seconds – if no one can do it, you get the point.)

c *Gapped examples*

Learners (singly or in pairs) write out a list of five or ten useful phrases or sentences from the text or transcript, omitting one word or phrase from each one. They exchange lists with a partner or another pair, who has to complete them from memory, and keep a note of their scores. Or they can read them out to the whole class for completion. They can also be written on OHP transparencies and done with the whole class in teams.

d *Progressive deletion*

Do this whenever you have examples of language on the board after an analysis activity. It is guaranteed to liven the class up and increase concentration.

Number the examples. Call out numbers one at a time (but not in order) and ask individual learners to read each example out loud. As they read, delete a word, or even whole phrase from that example. Continue to call out the numbers, even when there are hardly any words left, and get individuals to continue to read them out as if they were still complete. You will end up with a clean board, with only the numbers left on, but you can still challenge the class to 'read' what was there.

e *Unpacking a sentence*

Choose a long sentence from a familiar written text. One from a newspaper report often works well, for example, the second sentence from the *Cold store* text in 7.3. Ask learners to write the same information in as many short, simple sentences as they can, without repeating any facts.

Or allow learners to repeat the same information, but ask them to write it in different ways. Set a time limit, of, say, five minutes, and see how many different (correct) sentences each pair can build in that time.

You can either review the exercise by getting learners to write their sentences on the board, or asking them to read them out, for you to write.

f *Repacking a sentence*

After completing the 'unpacking' exercise above, ask learners to close their books. They then have to work in pairs to pack all the information from the short sentences back into one long sentence without looking at the original text. It doesn't have to be the same as the original sentence, but it must be grammatical. Pairs can exchange and check each other's sentences.

Then ask two or three pairs of learners to write their sentences on the board or on an overhead transparency for the class to spot the grammatical differences. Explore whether these contain any shift in meaning or emphasis.[6]

g *Memory challenge*

Take a set of similar types of word, e.g. narrative verbs, from one text (or possibly two texts, to make it more of a challenge). Mix them up. Can students write the complete phrase or sentence containing each item? If you are using verbs, can students remember who or what was the subject of each and what followed it? Try identifying these, from the *Cold store* text in 7.3.

> *reported   found   spent   realised   gone   locked   telephoned   began   ran*

h *Concordances for common words*

If you don't have a computer with a concordancing facility, don't worry. In this activity, the learners themselves act as text investigators. Divide about ten familiar texts and/or transcripts among learners, so they each have one or two to investigate. Select one or two very common words from among the top 40 or so of the frequency list in Appendix E for them to find. For example, one week you could concentrate on common prepositions. Ask learners to go through their texts and write neat concordance lines for each word including the six words before and after it. These can then be assembled (on an OHP transparency, photocopy poster or the board, dictated by students) to form the basis of a classifying activity (like the one with *in* in 7.2). They can also be used for an odd-word-out activity, a cloze test, or even a memory challenge, where you ask for the source or context of the line.[7]

i *Dictionary exercises*

For the best results, use a good learner's dictionary (see Note 1). Exercises can include the following:
- matching words to definitions: students choose three words from a text or transcript to look up, and find which dictionary definition best fits each word in its context. They then explain them to each other.
- exploring collocations: give students two familiar collocations from a text or transcript, and ask them to use a dictionary to find other useful ones based on the same verb or noun, e.g. from *balance of trade* (Lesson Outline 4 in Appendix C) learners may find *dependent on foreign trade, trade fair, trade secret.*
- generating your own examples: learners look up words they are not sure how to use. They then read the examples and grammatical information in the dictionary and write two sentences with each word.

j *Personal recordings*

If learners have their own cassette recorder, or can use a self-access centre to make their own tapes, they can record the contents of their language notebooks, or any useful phrases they want to remember.

They can also record the report that their group presented to the class, play it back, listen to themselves, and then record it again with improvements.

k *Computer games*

A large number of schools and institutions now have computers, and some have CALL (Computer Assisted Language Learning) facilities. These are quickly getting more affordable and user-friendly. CALL activities are often quite good for practice purposes, especially if students work in twos or threes and use the target language to reach decisions. Many games can be used to give practice in reading and completing texts. Learners can also input their own stories or texts, and turn them into games.

7.5 Creating a pedagogic corpus

You will have noticed that the language samples used in the language focus activities in this chapter were mainly drawn from texts or recordings already familiar to you as readers. These texts and transcripts together make up a 'mini-corpus' of around 1,000 words of running text.

As language learners progress through a course, the texts they read and recordings they hear form a similar corpus of language. This corpus can be called a pedagogic corpus because it is common to all students in the class. Wherever possible, it is this language that should be used as a source for examples.

Keep copies of all the supplementary texts and task recordings you have done in a file for each class. This file of materials, together with the coursebook texts, form the class pedagogic corpus which you can use as a resource for future language focus activities, and possibly for test items.

If you have access to a computer and a concordancing programme, these materials can be made into a computer file for each class, with new texts typed in as they are used. The programme can then build an index of all the words in the corpus, giving the location and number of occurrences. It can also build a set of concordance lines for any word you wish to look at more closely. Some such programmes also link into an electronic dictionary, so students can switch between the word in their text and the dictionary entry. It also allows you, as course designer, to compare the frequency of the words in your pedagogic corpus with a standard frequency list from a research corpus, to see what words are missing or under-exemplified. Some coursebooks are now being published with CD-ROM materials, which allow students and teachers to do all of the above and more.

Whether or not you have your pedagogic corpus on computer, there is a very important principle here. Instead of a teacher 'presenting' language to learners as 'new', language analysis activities encourage learners to reflect on the language they have already experienced. A methodology which depends on teacher presentations encourages learners to rely on the teacher. It says to them, 'I am the teacher. I will explain the language system to you. Listen to me and you will learn.' A methodology based on analysis and consciousness raising says, 'Be a creative learner. You have valuable experience of the language. Examine that and you will learn from it.'

This not only makes sense in terms of motivation, it also makes sense in terms of language description. One of the biggest problems in the classroom is finding a meaningful context to illustrate samples of the language. In the texts that learners study we already have language which is contextualised, authentic and familiar to them. Why make up decontextualised examples?

It is obviously important to expose learners to a well-balanced pedagogic corpus, so as to give them as wide a range of language types and topics as they are likely to need. We discussed this in Chapters 5 and 6. You would certainly need a greater variety of texts and recordings than the 'mini-corpus' assembled here for illustrative purposes.

7.6 Summary

This chapter has illustrated a range of analysis and practice activities, focusing the learner on different aspects of language form and use. The lesson outlines 3, 4 and 5 in Appendix C show how the language focus phase leads naturally out of the task cycle. They also give further examples of analysis activities.

We stressed that the aim of such activities is not to perfect learners' production of the target language and make it automatic, but to draw their attention to the surface forms realising the meanings they have already become familiar with during the task cycle and so help them to systematise their knowledge and broaden their understanding. We also aim to ensure that they will recognise similar words, phrases and patterns in future texts and exposure, so that they can carry on learning outside the classroom and after their course.

During the language focus phase, the teacher should give students as much focused thinking time as possible. Once the purpose of the analysis activity is clear, the teacher should let learners get on with learning and making discoveries for themselves, without interference. During the teacher-led review stage, students listen to and benefit from each other's ideas on classification. It is then that you can add any points you feel students have failed to notice, or perhaps redress an imbalance by adding a few examples. You might then lead the class in two or three practice activities.

Finally you can choose whether to end the teaching cycle on a quiet, reflective note, perhaps with students writing their personal selection of useful words and phrases in their notebooks, or on a lively one, perhaps a choral practice activity. Either way should give learners a sense of security and consolidation.

This chapter brings us to the end of the three-part TBL framework. In the classroom, the next lesson might continue the same topic but introducing a different kind of task, or it could be the start of a whole new topic with a series of tasks built around it. In this book, the next chapter offers ways of adapting the task-based framework to suit beginners and low-level learners.

Material preparation

1 a) Select a small set of texts and/or transcripts to form a small pedagogic corpus suitable for your learners. If possible, enter these into a computer with a concordancing facility. If not, do some initial analysis by hand. Look for common words that occur several times.

   b) For each text, design one activity for each starting point in 7.3.

    c) Finally, try some of them out with your class.

2 a) If you have not already completed all the language analysis activities in this chapter, choose three or four and do them thoroughly. Compare your findings with those in the key in Appendix G. Try to review the activities with another teacher who has done them.

    b) Make a note of insights you have gained.

3 Look at the language focus activities in Lesson Outlines 3, 4 and 5 in Appendix C. Identify their starting points. Think of ways you might adapt one of those lessons to suit students you know.

Further reading

A good reference book giving insights into English usage is *Cobuild Students' Usage*, by B Mascull, 1996 Cobuild/HarperCollins.

To gain insights into eleven principles of vocabulary learning and to help learners keep efficient vocabulary notebooks, read the paper by N and D Schmitt in *ELT Journal*, Vol 49/2, 1995, pp. 133–43.

Notes

1 The best dictionaries use corpus-based research and take typical examples from a large corpus of language. Monolingual dictionaries give most insights into use as well as meaning. Semi-bilingual dictionaries usually have mother-tongue translations of words, but definitions and examples in the target language.

2 If you have access to a computer or word processor with a concordancing facility, it is very easy to generate sets of examples automatically. But first, of course, you have to enter the texts and transcripts into your computer.

3 In fact there are likely to be two stress-bearing words, but the significant one is normally the second, which carries the meaningful tone shift. See B Bradford *Intonation in Context*. This book follows the Brazil system, which is based on *Discourse Intonation in Language Teaching*. For teaching more advanced learners, see D Brazil, 1994.

4 For more such examples taken from Brazil's description of intonation see M Coulthard, 1985, pp. 100–19.

5 Note that it is extremely rare for adult learners, or learners starting the target language after their early teens to gain a perfect accent. It seems that only children, starting young, are able to acquire near-native pronunciation.

6 These and many other practice activities can be found in S Lindstromberg (ed), 1990.

7 For more on this, see J Willis in B Tomlinson (ed), forthcoming 1997.

FOCUS 8

Tasks for beginners

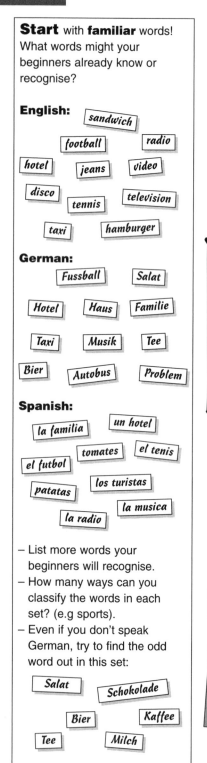

Start with **familiar** words!
What words might your beginners already know or recognise?

English:
sandwich
football
radio
hotel
jeans
video
disco
tennis
television
taxi
hamburger

German:
Fussball
Salat
Hotel
Haus
Familie
Taxi
Musik
Tee
Bier
Autobus
Problem

Spanish:
la familia
un hotel
tomates
el tenis
el futbol
los turistas
patatas
la musica
la radio

– List more words your beginners will recognise.
– How many ways can you classify the words in each set? (e.g sports).
– Even if you don't speak German, try to find the odd word out in this set:

Salat
Schokolade
Bier
Kaffee
Tee
Milch

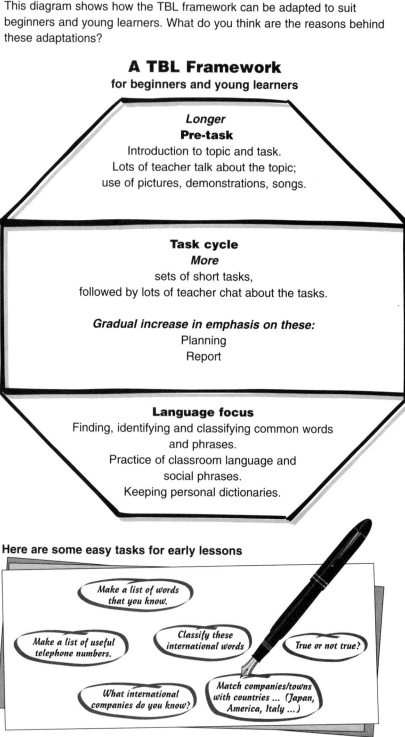

This diagram shows how the TBL framework can be adapted to suit beginners and young learners. What do you think are the reasons behind these adaptations?

A TBL Framework
for beginners and young learners

Longer
Pre-task
Introduction to topic and task.
Lots of teacher talk about the topic;
use of pictures, demonstrations, songs.

Task cycle
More
sets of short tasks,
followed by lots of teacher chat about the tasks.

Gradual increase in emphasis on these:
Planning
Report

Language focus
Finding, identifying and classifying common words and phrases.
Practice of classroom language and social phrases.
Keeping personal dictionaries.

Here are some easy tasks for early lessons

Make a list of words that you know.

Make a list of useful telephone numbers.

Classify these international words

True or not true?

What international companies do you know?

Match companies/towns with countries ... (Japan, America, Italy ...)

What other easy tasks can you think of?

8 TBL for beginners and young learners

People who travel or work in foreign language environments often begin to learn the new language by picking up useful words and phrases and only later make sense of the grammar. In a beginners' classroom we need to provide opportunities and motivation for natural language use in a supportive environment. This chapter shows how the TBL framework can be adapted to teaching beginners. It illustrates simple tasks that provide comprehensible exposure, help them build up a stock of useful words and phrases and later develop insights into the grammar. It also offers ways to help non-Roman alphabet beginners, and suggests a range of activities for younger learners. Finally, it summarises basic principles for teaching beginners and young learners successfully.

8.1 Using tasks with real beginners

A TBL approach works well with real beginners although many people are initially doubtful. This section first discusses why tasks are beneficial for beginners, then shows how the framework can be adapted to their needs.

8.1.1 Words and phrases before grammar

Many teachers feel that real beginners need to be taught some grammar before they can start to do tasks. But is this really the case? In task-based learning, students learn by doing; the learning is part of the task itself.

As we mentioned in Chapter 1, if we are visiting a foreign country where we don't speak the language, we take a dictionary or a phrase-book rather than a grammar. Initially we need words and phrases, not a knowledge of grammar. It is nearly always lack of vocabulary that prevents us from understanding. Children learn their first language by listening and finally producing approximate renderings of words and phrases. We don't expect them to start with perfectly formed grammatical sentences.

In both cases, the desire to communicate, make oneself understood, and understand other people's meanings, is paramount. Tasks provide opportunities for learners to listen to and participate in meaning-focused interactions from the very beginning, helping them to acquire the new language more naturally.

Many tasks require minimal syntax and can be achieved quite successfully by learners using just words and phrases. Tasks based on familiar words, and games such as Bingo can be used from the start. Teacher-led tasks and activities, such as 'Simon says', only require learners to understand a series of instructions – they do not need to speak at all.

Real beginners, whether travellers or classroom learners, can begin to make themselves understood by learning a lot of words together with a small stock of well-chosen formulaic phrases and sentence stems. As their experience increases, they notice typical forms and patterns in language and the grammar starts to fall into place. They begin to explore different ways of expressing more exactly what they want to mean. It is at this stage that a focus on grammar becomes useful.

8.1.2 Helping beginners learn

When teaching beginners, we need to give them a lot of exposure to the new language, and to make that exposure comprehensible. Tightly-focused tasks with familiar, clear objectives, are ideal for this.

We also need to remember that beginners may feel more vulnerable and shy when attempting to use the new language in front of other students (whose language may be better than theirs) than if they were trying to make themselves understood outside class to a native speaker. Work in pairs and small groups helps to reduce this fear.

Exposure and use were two of the optimum conditions for language learning outlined in Chapter 1. However, the affective factor is especially important when teaching beginners. A task-based approach encourages beginners because it values what learners can achieve no matter how little language they have. For beginners, the teacher's most important general priorities are:

- establishing a relaxed, anxiety-free atmosphere in the classroom;
- providing a lot of exposure that learners can make approximate sense of;
- building on what they know, but without expecting perfection;
- not forcing them to speak at first if they prefer not to;
- reassuring them of their progress, and generally boosting their confidence.

8.1.3 Adapting the framework to beginners

The TBL framework for beginners (see Focus 8) differs from the standard framework in four main ways. Firstly, there is much more weighting given to exposure. One result of this will be a longer pre-task phase and a shorter task cycle. Secondly, the cycle may well consist of sets of short tasks rather than one long one. Thirdly, because there is less emphasis put on public use of language until learners have gained confidence, the planning and report stages are either omitted or very short, with the teacher giving the first reports informally. Finally, the language focus concentrates initially on words and phrases, only gradually progressing towards grammar. For young learners, there is unlikely to be any language focus.

In the next two sections, we will illustrate the kind of tasks that can be done, and how to follow them up.

8.2 Tasks for beginners

This section suggest a series of tasks and games for the very first lessons. All are teacher led initially; some can then be continued by students working in pairs.

8.2.1 The first lesson: preparation

The principle here is to start with what learners already know. Even complete beginners in English will find there are a lot of words they can already recognise which will help boost their confidence. Many are used internationally, like *football*, *taxi* and *telephone*, and, depending on the mother tongue, there will probably be some cognates, like *psychology, university, invite*. There will be some differences in pronunciation and spelling, but the meanings should be clear.

In preparation for the first lesson, collect about twenty or thirty words from the target language which learners are likely to recognise. As well as 'international' words, there are likely to be words that have become familiar through pop songs, computers, business and other sources. Don't order or classify the words – this is what students will do themselves as their first task.

8.2.2 The first lesson: pre-task phase

The very first lesson with learners who don't know each other will probably begin with simple personal introductions and learning names. Give them some simple formulae for doing this, e.g. *I'm Ana. I'm from Malaga.* You can then get straight on with the pre-task and first tasks, which will be largely listening ones.

Sample procedures for a pre-task phase follow, based on familiar words for learners of English. As far as possible, keep to the target language, speak as naturally as possible, but using a lot of mime and demonstration. Don't be afraid of pausing now and again to allow learners some thinking time.

Write *How many words do you know?* on the board, and some of the words you have chosen. Say each of them several times as you write or do drawings for them randomly on the top of the board, for example: *'Football' – who plays football?* (Mime) *You? No? Do you? Yes? And do you watch football on television? No? Who watches football on television? You do. That's one, two, three, four of you who watch football on television. So, 'television' is another word you know,* etc.

The specific aim of this phase of teacher talk is to get learners to tune in to the target language. It provides very useful exposure which learners can make sense of, with the help of gestures and mime. They will certainly not understand everything you say, but they will be listening for meaning, and getting the general sense. The familiar words act as 'anchors'. By the time you have done around twenty words, they will be making approximate sense of words and phrases like *Yes. Do you know? That's a good one*, etc.

You may like to lead some choral pronunciation practice for some of the words as you write them up. This can make beginners feel more secure. At this stage they are converting their own pronunciation to something that sounds slightly more English, and perhaps noticing differences in spelling.

8.2.3 Tasks for the first lesson

Once students have heard all the words, and recognise their written forms, there are several kinds of simple tasks and games that they can do with them.

Classifying

This is a useful starting point for older children and adults. It involves classifying the words already on the board into categories, such as *Sport* and *Transport*. Draw a column for each category on the bottom half of the board, and say and write the category names clearly, writing an example for each category, e.g. *Sport, . . . erm, football*. To show students what to do, start by categorising a few more words with the whole class, adding them to appropriate columns. Then get learners in pairs to add words to each column. They do not need to produce formal sentences. Even if they are only saying *Tennis, er, Sport; Taxi – Transport*, they are using language for a purpose and meaning what they say. They are also getting a chance to try out the new ways of pronouncing familiar words in the privacy of their pairs.

They can then try to think of other words to add to the categories, asking about ones they are not sure of. At the end, you can use the extra words they have classified and introduce some more verbs, e.g. *play, like, wear*, to talk to students about yourself and to find out a bit more about them. Remember you are not expecting them to produce or use these words, only understand them.

Finally, count up the words focused on. It should be satisfying for learners to find a good number. In one class recently, teacher and absolute beginner students found over one hundred familiar words. This was extremely motivating.

This classifying task can be followed by a selection from the following:

Odd word out

Students make up sets of four words from one category, then add one word that is different. They say them to the whole class, who listen and pick out the odd one out, e.g. *football tennis bus golf polo*.

Memory challenge and 'Yes or No?' games

These can be played as a class, with the teacher talking about individual students, using the knowledge gained from earlier tasks, e.g. *Juan plays basketball. Yes or no?* These sentences can be written on the board. Pairs can then make up two or three similar sentences for the teacher to read to the class.

Jumbled spelling dictation

To help students learn the names of the letters, choose a familiar word, jumble the letters and dictate them for the class to write, e.g. *N, S, E, J, A*. You can mime and give them clues, e.g. *something you wear*. Students then have to work out the word and write it down or shout it out. This is a game they can continue playing in groups or pairs. Give them a minute or two to jumble the letters of their word, put their 'jumbles' on the board and see how many each pair can do in three minutes.

Sorting alphabetical letters by name

Help students group the letters according to their vowel sounds, e.g. *Put A, H, J and K in one circle, B, C, D, E and G in another.*[1]

Sorting words alphabetically

Students in pairs put each set of words into alphabetical order. They can then read them out for another pair to check.

8.2.4 Other tasks for early lessons	The tables below give an overview of some types of simple tasks. Some have already been explained in 8.2.3. Others are explained later on in this section. All these tasks can initially be done, or at least begun, with the whole class, with the teacher leading. This gives good exposure to the target language in use, and illustrates the objectives of the task or game. If necessary, two good students can then be asked to demonstrate the task. If you are able to record tasks, you could play a recording of the task being done by others (see Chapter 6). Once learners have got the idea, they can continue in groups.

Listing

Brainstorming
- words you know
- names of countries
- words from songs
- family words (*brother, sister*, etc.)

Memory games
- things you remember from a picture
- 'Yes or no' games based on pictures or personal facts

Ordering and sorting

Classifying
- international words
- international products
- well-known people
- 'Odd word out'

Sequencing
- jumbled spelling dictation
- 'What's missing?' (sets of numbers, etc)

Collecting sets ('Happy families')

Comparing

Matching
- words and actions ('Simon says')
- words and pictures with card games
- words and song lines
- countries and companies
- names and numbers

Identifying
- Listen and draw/point/do
- Bingo with numbers, colours, words, phrases

Problem solving

Puzzles
- How many triangles?

General knowledge quizzes
- 'True or not true?'

Guessing games
- Mystery objects
- Verbal hide and seek, (*Where is my key in this picture?*)

Surveys
- Make a class telephone number list
- What makes of TV/car/computer do learners have?
- Why are learners learning the target language?
- What languages can they speak already?

Memory games

Most listing tasks can be turned into memory games (See Appendix A, Type 1). Here's a variation, using a bag of familiar objects. Take the items out of the bag one at a time and put them back very quickly, talking about them as you do so. Then, in pairs, learners recall the items and write or draw them. Set a time limit.

You can do the same using a simple picture. Without showing it to the class, talk about the things or people in it first, to arouse their curiosity; then show it quickly and chat very briefly again about what is in it. Give learners thirty seconds to remember everything, then put it away. In groups they try to remember everything and tell you in English, as you go round to see which group has remembered most.

What's missing?'

Here is a version that can be played with any words that make up a sequence. Learners say a set of four or five words, omitting one, e.g. *five, six, seven, nine* or *Wednesday, Friday, Saturday* and the class (possibly in teams) shouts the missing one. (Note that even native speakers need to practise beforehand to disguise the gap.)

Bingo

Learners can draw their own bingo cards of, say, nine squares. They black out four squares, leaving five blank. (Have a card ready or draw one on the board.) You then call out two alternative numbers, colours or words from lexical sets for them to choose from and fill in the blank squares, e.g. *Write either five or fifteen. Colour a square either blue or red. Write either 'bus' or 'taxi'.* Each learner will then have a slightly different card. Then you can call the items out one at a time, or let each group do so in turn, until someone calls 'Bingo'.

Later on, try some common phrases on a single theme like travelling to class, e.g. *Write either 'walk to class' or 'cycle to school', 'come by car' or 'come by bus'*, etc. This is getting closer to a purposeful dictation exercise.

Puzzles

These can be based on a geometric drawing with shapes, sizes and colours, e.g. *How many different shapes can you find in this big square? How many small triangles? Big ones? Big blue ones?* A geometric diagram done with coloured pens 'on an overhead projector transparency is very effective for puzzles like this.

General knowledge quizzes: 'True or not true?'

These can be played using any general knowledge theme, or even mental arithmetic, e.g. *Berlin is in Germany. Six plus two is ten*, etc.

Guessing games

These can be based on pictures, flash cards, lists or real items in a container, which you do not reveal to learners until they have guessed correctly. If using single items, select them round a theme, e.g. useful things for a journey / a day's shopping. The class guesses what you have got by asking questions.

Here is an example. Before the class, put seven or eight useful items (e.g. for travelling to a business meeting in a big town) in a bag. Bring the bag into class, explain where you are going, and ask students to guess what is in it. Give plenty of clues to help them guess, e.g. *Money, yes. I've got some money, but not very much money. What else might be useful instead of money? It's small, rectangular, made of plastic…* They won't understand every word, but they will listen out for key words and should pick up some clues. If they say the word in mother tongue say it again in the target language as you search for it in your bag. Each learner then chooses any five of those items, makes a list or draws them, and they play again in pairs or fours. How many questions does it take for the others to guess?

You can play the same game next class with different things, or by adding to the descriptions, e.g. *a blue pen, a red notebook*.

Mystery objects

This is a variation on the above guessing game, but is played by feel, so you need a soft bag containing a range of items. Give pairs or groups twenty seconds to feel the contents of your bag, silently and without looking. They must then agree on the contents and how to explain them in English even if they don't know the words, e.g. they think they can feel a corkscrew (a word they are most unlikely to know) and may attempt to explain it thus: *thing for open bottle – er – wine*. Explaining is a useful communication strategy for learners to practise.

Surveys

Simple fact-finding surveys on familiar topics encourage learners to begin to interact in larger groups and to socialise. For example, finding out what months each other's birthdays are in, or what they (and/or their families) do in their spare time will help them them build up simple phrases like *watch television / play computer games*.

Tasks based on familiar songs

Songs make a welcome change. Listening, then matching words to music, words to song lines, or simply following the words written down can offer a different kind of learning opportunity. Some learners enjoy singing along and teenagers may welcome the opportunity to find out what the words of a familiar pop song mean. Songs also contain a high proportion of common phrases.

8.3 Language focus for beginners

After a set of tasks, when learners have gained some experience of the language in use, its patterns will begin to make sense. This is the time to focus on language form and the next section deals with ways of doing so.

8.3.1 Analysing recent exposure

Many of the tasks suggested above for the first lessons were based on words already familiar to students. Listening to the teacher talking about these words in the target language, showing how they can be classified, and later organising other tasks enriches learners' exposure to many more common, useful words, in phrases like *All right? So what about this one? Listen again. Is that right? I'll say them again. OK, that's it*. Their meanings too will usually be clear from the context and from the teacher's accompanying expressions and gestures. Ideally, learners will also have heard recordings of parallel tasks, and so begin to notice and gradually acquire useful words and typical phrases.

A language focus in each lesson, after the task, can serve to highlight common phrases such as the one in the transcript below. (If you cannot record tasks, try writing short summaries of some of them.)

Sample task: Which English words are now international?
Transcript of unscripted task recording:

Will: *'Pizza'?*
Helen: *'Pizza'.*
Eva: *Mhm. 'Hamburger'.*
Helen: *Mhm Mhm.*
Chris: *What about 'taxi'?*
Eva: *Oh yes, that's a good one.*
Will: *Erm...*
Helen: *'Picnic'? What about that?*
Eva: *Oh yes, that's a good one.*
Helen: *What about... 'week-end'?*
Eva: *Mhm.*
Chris: *Yes. 'Hamburger'?*
All: *Ah, we've done that one! Got that!*
Chris: *Oh, we've got that. Sorry.*
Will: *'Hotel'?...*

(J Willis, 1990, *Collins Cobuild English Course* First Lessons)

This recording could be used after a teacher-led task on international words. Students first listen to the recording to identify the international words (they could raise a hand when they hear one), which may take two or three hearings. They then listen again while reading the transcript and underline them. Once they have made sense of the transcript in its written form and processed it for meaning, they can focus on the following aspects of form:

- Underlining the responses to suggestions (e.g. *Mhm mhm. Oh yes, that's a good one.*) and classifying them according to whether they mean 'yes' or 'no'.
- Circling all the phrases with the word *that*, and practising saying some of them, either by repeating after the tape or in chorus.

8.3.2 Teaching classroom language

So far we have focused mainly on words and phrases occuring in teacher talk and task recordings. But what about meanings that individual students need to express but lack language for? How far can these be taught?

In the course of doing the tasks based on familiar words students will probably have been wanting to ask things like *How do you say/write X in English? Sorry, I don't understand. Can you say X again? What does X mean? Is this right?*, etc. These are useful classroom expressions that the teacher can 'feed in' as required, one at a time, and let learners practise. However, it is most unlikely that they will be reproduced immediately, even if they are repeated correctly in practice sessions. Learners will naturally find their own ways of expressing these meanings, and for some time will use approximate renderings. Don't worry; this is all part of the natural learning process.

Some teachers make a list of such expressions into a poster to keep on the wall of the classroom. Items are added as required, maybe two or three every lesson. These can be classified into categories such as 'asking about spelling', 'asking about meaning', positive/negative expressions, e.g. *I'm not sure, I don't know* and 'ways of starting/ending a task'. At the end of every week, the list can serve as a focus. Some expressions may initially have been learnt as unanalysed chunks but can be used later to exemplify common patterns.

8.3.3 Teaching social language

Simply chatting to students socially provides useful experience of language. It is important to expose learners to everyday social language in class. Exploit natural classroom situations by, e.g. asking why someone has arrived late, or what someone is carrying in an interesting-looking parcel. Whenever you meet a student outside class, and when it is polite to do so, speak in the target language. After some time, students will volunteer to say things in the target language themselves.

There are some formulaic phrases and simple exchanges which can be taught for various social occasions, such as greetings, introductions, saying good-bye and leaving. Also phrases like *It doesn't matter, I'm sorry I'm late. That's fine,* can be supplied as needed, and practised.

8.3.4 Moving towards grammar

Once beginners have got used to hearing the target language spoken most of the time in class, and have built up a repertoire of words and phrases they can deploy to get their basic meanings across, they will feel more confident. A wider range of tasks can then be set, and, as the exposure gets richer, their learning will begin to snowball – the more they know, the faster they can learn. It is then that a focus on grammar in context will begin to pay off.

The language-focused activities designed to help them systematise their knowledge can also draw on examples from earlier texts and tasks, as suggested in Chapter 7.

To help beginners perceive their progress, at the end of every lesson list on the board the new words, phrases and patterns highlighted in that lesson. Count them up. Make sure learners realise what a lot they have understood and done. At the end of each week, summarise again and underline the progress they have made.

8.4 Teaching non-Roman alphabet beginners

With learners who are not familiar with the Roman alphabet, or those who have not received much formal education, you will have to start more slowly. The same tasks can be done, but broken down into smaller parts.

Introduce the spoken language first. You could start off with simple introductions and name-learning games. It might at this stage be motivating to teach learners how to recognise and write each other's names. Speakers of Arabic, Chinese, and other such languages will also need practice in reading and writing from left to right.

8.4.1 Reading for non-Roman alphabet beginners

You can introduce the same kinds of tasks as were shown in 8.2.3 and 8.2.4, but based on more restricted, carefully chosen sets of words.

As before, make a list of the words they will recognise when they hear them, or ones they can learn easily, perhaps because part of the word sounds similar for most languages, as in the words *television, coffee* or *sugar*. But this time, group them according to what letter of the alphabet they begin with. You may want to separate those that start with a capital letter and introduce them later.

You will probably find that when introducing reading, learners will initially recognise written words by looking at the first letter, and judging the word length. With this in mind, pick three or four initial letters and make sets of words of different lengths. Don't worry about the choice of letters after the initial letter – this would restrict the choice too much. You might end up with a set like: *tea, television, taxi, tennis, football, family, coffee, car,* which you can use as a basis for the classification task suggested in 8.2.3 above.

You can also organise sets of words for 'Odd word out' based on this principle:
- *tea, telephone, taxi, television, table*
- *coffee, cake, Coca-Cola, computer*

Once learners have recognised the first letter, they will look further along the word for more clues. Gradually they will recognise words by their shape, instead of trying to decipher them from individual letters.

To introduce capital letters, for recognition only at this stage, you could do some classifying games with names of people or companies they have heard of, or names of towns or countries. Sequencing games can be played with the days of the week or months of the year (which all need capital letters in English).

Sets of flash cards containing words and phrases (some could have pictures on the back) are very useful for beginners working in groups, because they can be physically moved around during classification activities. Students in groups can then make up their own 'Odd word out' games without having to write anything. Matching games also encourage meaningful reading, as students try to find an appropriate picture to match a word or phrase.

Bear in mind your learners' immediate needs, too. If they have just arrived in a foreign country, you could make up a set of useful sign words, like *Parking, No smoking, Open, Closed, Exit, One Way,* etc.

Note that although reading out loud in the initial stages will help students to recognise and practise sound-symbol relations, it is essential to encourage silent reading and quick word and phrase recognition to enable them to read faster and more efficiently later on, otherwise their exposure will remain very limited.

Once your learners have met most of the letters, you can help them to learn alphabetical order, which will be vital when they begin using a dictionary.

8.4.2 Writing for non-Roman alphabet beginners

Basic handwriting books may be available locally. However, if you don't have one, it is probably best to introduce letters according to their shape and the direction of the strokes. So, for example, you may teach letters *c, o, a, d* together, then go on to *g* and *q,* while the letters *r, n, m* can be followed by *h, b,* and *p* since they have a similar initial stroke.

Learners can move on to games like Bingo, using letters instead of numbers (see 8.2.4). Students can make their own Bingo cards, choosing five out of a set of ten letters, and writing each one down as it is called out.

Following a systematic introduction of individual sets of letters, let students copy and practise reading the new words and phrases from handwritten handouts or the board at the end of every lesson. This will help their motivation and give them confidence.

Once they have listened to task recordings, they can also use the transcripts for reading practice, and be encouraged to copy down useful words and phrases.

Let students in groups play simple spelling games, e.g. each dictates one word from a recent transcript to the group, letter by letter. The group writes it down and then says whether it is spelled correctly or not. They can set each other simple spelling tasks, like dictating four or five newly introduced words, and arranging them in alphabetical order. They can write their own 'Odd word out' cards. They should now be ready for the tasks in 8.2.3.[2]

8.5 Teaching young learners

Many of the tasks and activities suggested for older learners above can be adapted for use with children. There is also a wonderful variety of games, action songs and practical creative tasks that are less suitable for adult learners.

8.5.1 Children as language learners

Young learners, up to the ages of eleven or twelve, are often less self-conscious and less anxious about beginning to learn a new language than adults are.

They are used to making sense of things without understanding everything; they often have very good memories, and are good at imitating. They enjoy playing games, and are often more used to activity-based learning than adults are. There are many familiar primary-level routines, like learning to count, story telling, action games, matching and classifying, that can be used in the language classroom. Children love playing the same games and hearing the same stories many times over, and don't get bored by repetition. Younger children do, however, have a shorter concentration span than teenagers and adults and need a greater variety of activities within one lesson to keep them interested.

Children are naturally curious, and usually respond well to a classroom that is full of colourful pictures and interesting things. Try to collect items from countries where the target language is used and display them. Talking to the children about the items on display provides useful exposure. Change the items around regularly, or bring in some new ones each week so that the children notice the changes. Choose items that the children can touch and ask you about.

The first priority must be to let children hear as much spoken language as possible. As with adult teaching, exposure is vital, and it can be made comprehensible and engaging by involving the children in tasks and activities they enjoy and want to take part in.

Although most children will be keen to join in songs and games once these become familiar, it may be much longer before some of them start speaking the target language naturally of their own accord. Don't worry if they are silent or continue to speak their mother tongue. So long as they are engaged in the activities and trying to understand the language, they will be increasing their vocabulary and beginning to acquire the language naturally. It would be unnatural and unrealistic to ban mother-tongue use altogether, and it could also cause shyer children concern. It is better to expect children to move gradually from mother-tongue use to target language use, and to encourage all attempts to do so (see 3.3.5).

8.5.2 Activities for young learners

This section offers three sets of activities, A, B and C. Each set demands a little more linguistic competence from the children. Set A does not necessarily involve the learners in any language production at all, but provide incentives for listening and trying to understand as much as possible. Set B offers exposure and minimal language use. Set C requires more language production.

A Listen-and-do activities

These include games which involve physical responses like changing places or ball throwing, where the teacher calls out names or numbers of children who then change places or try to catch the ball. There are games where children listen and do things, such as 'Simon says'. If the teacher says *Simon says 'Stand up'*, the children must obey. If the teacher simply says *Stand up* (i.e. without *Simon says*), the children must not move. If they do, they are out of the game.

Getting children to follow instruction sequences can be enjoyable especially if the end product is fun or satisfying. Making their own Bingo cards (see 8.2.4) with different colours in the squares would be a good example of this kind of activity. They can then use their cards to play Bingo. Children can follow instructions for colouring a picture, adding things to a drawing or making things out of paper or card. You can get groups of children to listen and arrange things in a certain way, e.g. build a tower out of classroom things, or order a set of pictures, leading to a story-telling session. After completing the activity, children can compare achievements, and the teacher can talk about some of them (e.g. *Who has got the highest tower?*).

Story telling

Children love listening to stories. Hearing teachers read aloud from books with pictures, and making use of mime and gestures, gives excellent exposure. Each time they hear a story, they will understand a bit more, and words and phrases from it will become more and more familiar. You can heighten their involvement by getting them to join in, e.g. they might mime all the actions they hear, which will help them to recognise the part that verbs play in a sentence. Start by reading the story slowly, while they mime, then read it again, getting faster and faster. If it is an animal story, ask them to make the right animal noise every time an animal is mentioned. Encourage them to listen and act out familiar stories while showing pictures one at a time or doing blackboard drawings.

Listening to songs

Miming the actions can be fun. *The wheels on the bus go round and round* is a good 'action song'. Most children's courses have suitable songs in them.

B Classifying

Get children to name objects, picture cards or shapes and sort them into sets and explain why, e.g. *all animals / all small squares*.

Collecting games

'Happy Families' and other games based on sets are fun and easy to set up, and can be played with a few phrases, like *Have you got…?*

Matching games

These are based on whole pictures or individual picture cards. Children match cards with words or phrases to appropriate parts of pictures or individual picture cards. They can bring or draw their own pictures or make their own picture cards.

Memory games

These can easily be adapted to suit the topic and level of the class. Use cards with words and phrases on one side and pictures on the other. Teams take turns to choose a picture and remember the words on the back.

You can also play Pelmanism, where several pairs of cards are mixed up and placed face down. Children turn one over, say what it shows, and try to pick up its pair. If they fail, they replace both cards in the same position; if they succeed, they keep the cards.

Traditional games

Those that involve formulaic phrases like *What's the time, Mister Wolf?* can be played outside in a playground.

C Puzzles

These can include making a square or a rectangle or even a house or other object out of similar sets of coloured shapes. This can be done in groups, without letting other groups see. Children then tell other groups which shapes they used, to see if others have made something similar. A further degree of challenge can be added by giving incomplete sets of shapes, so that learners have to ask for specific ones to make their object.

Verbal hide and seek

Using a big picture of a room, or a place familiar to the children, the teacher decides where in the picture to hide a small object like a key. The children guess where it is by asking, e.g. *Is it in the vase? Is it under the book on the table?*, etc.

Modelling

Following instructions written in the target language to make, for example, a village, farmyard or garage out of cardboard cartons, old plastic bottles etc. and writing signs for it, can generate a lot of talk. Children ask for things they need, and subsequently present and describe their finished product.

There are many children's courses which have more ideas for activities and games. However, these sometimes underestimate children's ability to understand and cope with language, and control too rigidly the language they are exposed to and can use. If this is the case, try to enrich their exposure with activities like the above, adapted to their circumstances.

8.5.3 Language focus for young learners

The games and ideas in this section are all designed to make children more aware of specific features of the language they have already experienced, for example, singular and plural forms and basic sentence patterns. They assume a little reading knowledge.

Matching words to pictures

Children find a picture to match the word card they select, distinguishing between singular and plural, e.g. *balloon / balloons* or *a red balloon / some red balloons*.

Sentence building

Playing with words to make sentences (silly ones, too) can be fun. You will need cards with words and phrases on. A set based on personal themes could include cards with children's names on that can be assembled to make true (or untrue) sentences about each other, e.g. *David / doesn't like / chocolate*.

For some general knowledge themes, e.g. animals, include cards with a larger variety of phrases, so children can make a range of sentences, perhaps two sensible and two silly ones, e.g. *Zebras / are / black and white. Monkeys / like eating / people.* Phrase cards help learners to acquire typical chunks of language as single units. Choosing ways of completing sentence stems, and matching sentence halves also focus attention on 'chunks'.

Stories

After reading a story a few times, learners can be given jumbled cards with sentences from the story to arrange. A second set of cards can have some sentence endings missing so they can make up their own. Children are often very creative and with some help can make up and illustrate their own variations on familiar stories for others to read.

Work based on stories can also be done with the whole class in an active way. You could write all the narrative verbs on the board, and ask the class who did what, e.g. *tasted – who tasted something? Was it Grandmother?* will focus their attention on the verb and the structure of a typical sentence.

Read a very familiar story missing out all the adjectives (write them on the board, jumbled, or make a funny noise instead of saying them). Learners have to try to remember the right word and say the whole phrase, e.g. *the brown owl, his tall tree.*

Products for display

Children also respond well to producing classroom displays, labelling pictures or models with explanations in English and writing their own stories. Even very young learners enjoy producing their own illustrated story books. Since this language is for public display, they will try hard to be clear and accurate.

8.6 Summary

In this chapter I have illustrated a range of tasks suitable for real beginners and young learners, which not only provide them with useful exposure to teacher talk, but also help them to acquire fairly rapidly a basic stock of words and phrases, and give them the opportunities and the confidence to use them.

Here is a summary of the main principles for teaching beginners and young learners that we have covered in this chapter.

- Use the target language in class as much as possible, starting mainly with words and phrases they know or can guess.
- Build on what they know and can do, rather than what they find difficult.
- Establish a friendly and co-operative classroom atmosphere so that all will feel free to contribute or to ask if they need help.
- Ensure that all activities are handled in a way that builds learners' confidence in their ability.
- Don't expect long contributions in the early stages.
- Don't over-correct and don't expect perfection. Take up learners' suggestions and rephrase encouragingly.
- Don't ban mother-tongue use but encourage attempts to use the target language.
- Ensure adult learners understand the order of the TBL framework, and realise that they will get a chance to study the grammar at the end.
- Help them to understand the rationale behind each component in the task framework and how TBL reflects and stimulates natural acquisition.

Although the tasks described in this chapter are designed for real beginners, it is clear that weak or remedial students will also benefit from them. Those who have previously failed to learn a language when taught through other methods may well find that they succeed when following a task-based approach. They need their confidence restoring, and tasks might be the ideal way to achieve this.

Planning

1   Make a list of words you think that a beginners' class of learners from a particular country would know or recognise. How many ways can you find of classifying them? Make up five sets for learners to play 'Odd word out'.

2   a) Select two or three tasks from this chapter and prepare relevant materials for them. Try them out on a colleague.

b) Record two pairs or groups of fluent speakers (these could be children) doing these tasks (see Chapter 6). Select the versions that worked best and transcribe the recordings. What language features might be useful for a language focus phase? Plan one or two analysis activities. Identify some useful phrases to form the focus of a suitable practice activity.

c) Use the task framework to help you plan the lesson and try the tasks out in class. Either record your lesson, or get someone to observe it and write a brief account of everything the learners did. Later, listen to the recording, or read the observer's notes, and reflect on how it went. Find time to discuss it later.

3   Find some coursebooks for beginners and evaluate them with a specific group of learners in mind. What approach to language learning do they take? What opportunities do learners get to try things out for themselves? Examine the quantity and quality of the exposure they would get, if the courses were taught using one of the teacher's books. Make a note of additional tasks you might like to try out.

Observation

4   If you have never taught beginners or young learners, try to find some classes you can observe. What type and balance of exposure are the learners getting to the target language? Observe the range of learning styles within the class. Follow one learner and try to see the class from his or her perspective.

Further reading

For more on using a task-based approach with young learners see *Teaching Children English* by D Vale and A Feunteun, 1995, CUP.

For ideas for using stories to provide motivating exposure for young learners see *Story as Vehicle* Multilingual Matters by E Garvie, 1989, and for a wealth of stories and activities see *Storytelling with Children* by A Wright, 1996, OUP.

Notes

1   Avoid contrasting sounds of problem letters, like *e* and *i*; or *g* and *j*. Research has shown that associating two items to contrast them can lead to long-term confusion, as both are stored together in the brain.

2   I would like to acknowledge the very great help given to me in writing this section by Corony Edwards, whose experience of handling non-Roman alphabet beginners is far more recent than my own.

Changing to task-based learning

Discussion Points

– Remind yourself of the conditions for learning
– Which conditions for learning are likely to be fulfilled by each component in the framework? E.g in the pre-task phase, students get exposure to the teacher talking about the topic, some opportunities to use the language to suggest words or to ask questions, and some instruction when new words and phrases are introduced.
– Discuss how you might explain the rationale behind TBL to a) students, b) parents, c) colleagues.

Conditions for learning

Exposure
to the target language.

Opportunities to use
the language, both spontaneously and planned.

Motivation
to listen and talk, read and write, study and reflect.

Instruction
Focus on language form

(See Chapter 1 section 3).

The TBL framework

Pre-task
Introduction to topic and task.

Task cycle
Task
Planning
Report
Students hear task recording or read text.

Language focus
Analysis and practice
Review and repeat task

Problems with learner resistance?

Which of these might your learners say? Suggest a solution for each!

How do we know if we are making progress?

Not enough grammar!

I don't like doing pairwork with people who speak my own language.

I like to be corrected more when I speak.

What about the exams?

The recordings are useful but hard to understand.

LEARNERS!
LISTEN A LOT.
READ A LOT.
SAY WHAT YOU CAN.
Don't worry about making mistakes.

With TBL, you'll find
FLUENCY LEADS TO ACCURACY.

Start a language note-book. Write in it regularly.
Record yourself talking.

Bring in texts you want to read.
Bring in things you can talk or write about.

TEACHERS!
THINK OF LESSON OUTLINES
AS FRAMEWORKS FOR LEARNING
NOT AS
PLANS FOR TEACHING

GIVE LEARNERS TIME TO LEARN!
IF IN DOUBT – HOLD BACK!
Let them learn on their own.

Remind students of their progress.
Exchange tasks and recordings with other teachers.

Add one more piece of advice to each poster.

9 Adopting TBL: some practical issues

> The aims of this chapter are to set TBL against the background of common language-teaching practice, and to address some of the issues that face the practising teacher and trainer when attempting to introduce a new approach which centres on the learner. After showing how TBL can benefit classes preparing for exams, it lists a variety of ways in which teaching materials can be geared towards TBL and finally summarises the advantages of a task-based approach.

9.1 PPP and TBL

This section will show in what ways TBL is essentially different from another very common paradigm for language teaching – that of presentation, practice and production, often known by its initials as PPP. The aim of a PPP lesson is to teach a specific language form – a grammatical structure, or the realisation of a particular function or notion.

9.1.1 The PPP paradigm

A typical PPP lesson normally proceeds like this:

> **Presentation stage**
>
> Teacher begins by presenting an item of language in a context or situation which helps to clarify its meaning.
>
> Presentation may consist of pattern sentences given by teacher, or short dialogues illustrating target items acted out by teacher, read from textbook, or heard on tape.

> **Practice stage**
>
> Students repeat target items and practise sentences or dialogues, often in chorus and/or in pairs, until they can say them correctly.
>
> Activities include pattern practice drills, matching parts of sentences, completing sentences or dialogues and asking and answering questions using pre-specified forms.

> **Production stage**
>
> Students are expected to produce in a 'free' situation language items they have just learnt, together with other previously learnt language.
>
> This 'free' situation can be a role play, a simulation activity or even a communication task such as those in this book.

So a PPP paradigm begins with the presentation and practice of a small sample of language, with the focus on a particular form. The language is tightly controlled, and the emphasis is on getting the new form correct. When the teacher asks a question, the reply is often required to conform to the target pattern. Finally, the students are given a chance to produce the new pattern in a 'free' situation. It sounds very sensible.

9.1.2 Some problems with PPP

There are, as experienced teachers are well aware, several problems with this paradigm:

- Sometimes learners manage to do the task or role play at the production stage without using the target form at all. This may be because their own developing language systems are not yet ready to cope with its use, or because they don't need the new pattern to express the meanings they want. They can, after all, use what language they like at the 'free' stage.
- Sometimes they tend to overuse the target form, and make very stilted and unnatural conversation, e.g. *What will you do tomorrow? Tomorrow I will go to my aunts' house. I will go by bus. I will see my cousins. I will play football with them.* Learners who do this are probably still 'in practice mode' – they are trying to display control of the new form rather than express their own meanings. They are not actually concerned with communication.
- PPP gives an illusion of mastery as students can often produce the required forms confidently in the classroom, but once outside, or in a later lesson, they either do not use them at all or use them incorrectly.

The PPP cycle derives from the behaviourist view of learning which rests on the principle that repetition helps to 'automate' responses, and that practice makes perfect. This research has now been largely discredited, as far as its applications to language learning go. As we showed in Chapter 1, language learning rarely happens in an additive fashion, with bits of language being learnt separately, one after another. We cannot predict and determine what students are going to learn at any given stage. Instruction does help, in the long term, but it cannot guarantee when something will be learnt. Rich and varied exposure helps language develop gradually and organically, out of the learner's own experience. Unfortunately the PPP cycle restricts the learner's experience of language by focusing on a single item. By relying on exercises that encourage habit formation, it may actually discourage learners from thinking about language and working things out for themselves.

The irony is that the goal of the final 'P' – free production – is often not achieved. How can production be 'free' if students are required to produce forms which have been specified in advance?

9.1.3 Comparing PPP and TBL

The following diagram allows us to compare a typical PPP lesson with a typical TBL one, bearing in mind the key conditions for learning.

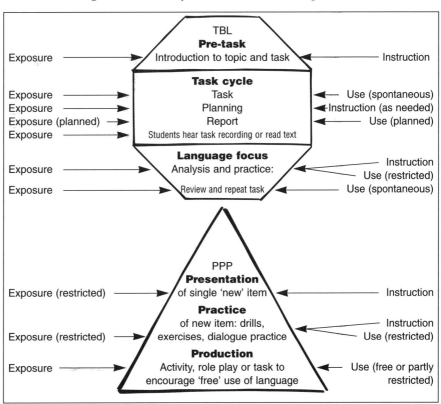

TBL, as we have explained, offers a holistic language experience where learners carry out a communication task, using the language they have learnt from previous lessons or from other sources. Only after the task cycle is learners' attention directed towards specific features of language form.

One question that many trainees ask is whether TBL is like PPP but in reverse order. At first glance, it might appear so, but the TBL framework offers far more opportunities for free language use and the linguistic content of the language focus phase is far richer.

The way students use and experience language in the task cycle is radically different.

- All three components (task, planning and report) are genuinely free of language control and learners rely on their own linguistic resources.
- The task supplies a genuine need to use language to communicate, and the other components follow on naturally from the task.
- In all three components language is used for a genuine purpose – there are outcomes to achieve for the task and the purpose of the drafting, rehearsal and practice at the planning stage is to help learners adjust their language for the report stage.
- The report allows a free exchange of ideas, summarising learners' achievements.
- The planning stage encourages learners to consider appropriateness and accuracy of language form in general, rather than the production of a single form.
- There is a genuine need to strive for accuracy and fluency as learners prepare to 'go public' for the report stage; it is not a question of either accuracy or fluency at any one point in the cycle.

The teacher's roles and approach to lesson planning are also different (see 9.1.4).

Some people may argue that all you need to do is to add planning and report components to the end of the production stage in the PPP cycle. But as we saw in 9.1.2, if production in the form of a task follows a presentation stage where one single structure is focused on, there are likely to be problems.

The TBL framework solves another general language-teaching problem – that of providing a context for grammar teaching and form-focused activities. PPP and TBL procedures are different here too.

- In a PPP cycle, with the presentation of the target language coming first, this context has to be invented. In a TBL framework, the context is already established by the task itself. By the time learners reach the language focus phase, the language is already familiar.
- The process of consciousness raising used in the TBL language focus activities encourages students to think and analyse, not simply to repeat, manipulate and apply.
- Listening and reading – both part of the TBL framework – provide a more varied exposure to natural language than examples made up to illustrate a single language item as in a PPP cycle.
- The exposure in the TBL framework will include a whole range of words, collocations, lexical phrases and patterns in addition to language forms pre-selected for focus. Students will realise there is more to language than verb tenses and new words.
- In a PPP cycle, it is the teacher who pre-selects the language to be taught. During the TBL analysis stage, learners are free to ask about any aspects of language they notice.

- A PPP cycle leads from accuracy to fluency; a TBL cycle leads from fluency to accuracy (combined with fluency).
- In TBL, all four skills – listening, speaking, reading and writing – are naturally integrated. PPP only provides a paradigm for grammar and form-focused lessons; it needs to be supplemented by skills lessons to give learners practice in listening and reading and more exposure to language.

To summarise the comparison so far, we can say that TBL begins by providing learners with a holistic experience of language and then helps them analyse this language in order to help them learn more efficiently. PPP provides discrete language items in a vacuum and then looks for some activity to practise them.

9.1.4 From PPP teaching plan to TBL learning framework

It follows from 9.1.3 that the teacher's approach to lesson planning will necessarily be different.

A PPP lesson plan typically sets out a narrowly predetermined set of objectives and procedures for the teacher, and is usually seen and discussed from the teacher's point of view. A TBL lesson outline offers a more flexible framework, enabling learners to move from language experience to language analysis.

In a PPP lesson, except during the final production stage, teachers are at centre stage, orchestrating the class. In TBL, teachers have to learn to set things up and then to hold back, intervening only when needed, and reviewing each phase at the end. The way the lesson outline is written (and the way the lesson is discussed or appraised) should reflect this.

This change of roles can be a problem for teachers switching to TBL. Many feel they are not doing their job unless they are centre stage, teaching, or giving advice. But professionalism in TBL comes from selecting and sequencing tasks, setting up optimum conditions for learning, recognising quality learning opportunities and judging when and how to intervene and when to move learners on to the next phase.

9.2 Introducing TBL

All learners, young and old, come to their first foreign language class with a set of expectations. These may be based on the kind of teaching they have had before, or on what other students have told them about language classes. A task-based approach may not immediately fit in with their views of classroom learning, so introducing TBL will not always be easy. The first time round there are bound to be some problems. But students who have experimented with TBL in many parts of the world have reported that:

- they gain confidence in speaking and interacting quite soon after beginning a task-based course;
- they enjoy the challenge of doing tasks and find many of them fun;
- they are able to talk about language itself in addition to other topics;
- they can cope with natural spontaneous speech much more easily, and tackle quite tough reading texts in an appropriate way;
- they become far more independent learners.

Teachers and trainers who have also experimented with TBL report that:

- with mixed-level classes a TBL approach works far better than a PPP one;
- learners bring their own experiences to lessons and often come up with interesting and original ideas;

- by the end of the course they are often surprised at how much their learners have achieved.

9.2.1 Helping learners adapt

To adapt to a TBL approach, learners need to understand both the principles behind it and the purpose of each component. They need to understand why it is different, and how they are likely to benefit in the long run.

At the beginning of the course it is certainly a good idea to talk to the class about the process of learning, and the rationale behind the classroom activities that will be used. You may need to do this, or get someone else to, in their mother tongue. (Although this is not necessary with very young learners, you will almost certainly have to explain to their parents.) Many schools using TBL methods prepare a written handout for their new students.

Explain that TBL might be a new experience for them, and different from other styles of teaching they know, but that if they take an active part in the lessons they will begin to improve very quickly, and learn to communicate. Their grammar will develop naturally and later on they will concentrate on accuracy as well as fluency. Remember that many will have been unsuccessful learners and will already feel nervous about starting a new class. Some will have learnt at schools where they had little chance to hear the target language spoken or to speak it themselves. However, with clear orientation, most learners will soon respond positively to TBL.

Below is a list of things you could do to help make the transition to TBL run smoothly. If you are in a monolingual situation, much of this could be done in the learners' mother tongue.

a *Find out about your learners*

Find out why they are learning the language, e.g. is it for travel, to understand TV or to talk to foreigners? Do they need it for their studies, their work or just to pass exams? What kind of topics are they interested in? Their answers will help you select suitable materials and tasks for them to do.

b *Explain how people learn languages*

Explain that people learn a language most effectively if the four conditions are met. Write these on the board and explain them (see Focus 9).

With remedial beginners, discuss why they haven't succeeded before. This is often not because they are lacking in some way, or 'not good at languages', but because all four conditions were not being met sufficiently well in their former language classrooms.

Explain that in the TBL classroom the aim is for learners to take an active part in the learning process. They must be prepared to use whatever language they have. Language learning means getting involved, experimenting, taking risks. Emphasise that errors are an inevitable part of learning and that learners will not be penalised for them. But there will be specific times when they must try to be accurate, and you as teacher will help them.

c *Introduce the TBL framework*

In advance, plan a sample task-planning-report cycle. Choose a simple task with an obvious outcome, like exchanging names and telephone numbers to assemble a class phone list. There should be a related listening or reading text before or after the task. Select some language items for the language focus component (see Chapter 7).

Show students a diagram of the TBL framework so that they will be able to identify the stages in a task cycle. Take students through this, and after they have done the task, react positively. Spend some time helping them with the planning stage, so they feel confident and able to report. Review their reports positively – list some things they did well.

At the language focus phase, use the listening transcript or reading text for analysis work, so that students can see that grammar is dealt with, and in context. After the analysis, do some practice activities, for example, choral drilling to practise pronunciation and bring the class together again. End on a positive note.

Finally, suggest that students write down new phrases and patterns they want to remember in language notebooks, and practise them. Later you could suggest ways to organise their notebooks.

After the TBL lesson, summarise what students have done, showing them how each step helped to create suitable conditions for learning. Help them to recognise that much of their learning will be subconscious, and that it may be some time before they notice any improvement.

With learners from traditional grammar-oriented backgrounds, you may need to adapt your explanation of TBL a little, to coincide with their ideas of what language teaching is about. For example: *First we'll revise/learn some new words and phrases for the topic (pre-task); Then you'll have a chance to use them, first in small groups and then with the whole class (task-planning-report). After that we'll listen to the tape/read the text, and study some of the grammar from it (language focus).* This is a somewhat distorted description of the task cycle. But when grammar-oriented students hear the learning process couched in familiar terms, they are more likely to recognise that the whole framework is purposeful.

d *Show how TBL works with their course materials*

In a later lesson, you will need to introduce students to the materials you will be using with them. This could take the form of a familiarisation session with the textbook: perhaps an overview of the whole book and then one early unit, identifying the steps of the TBL cycle as you go through it. Or you may have to explain that you will be using the textbook in a different way, omitting or adapting some parts (explain why).

Early on in the course, for each task cycle, announce the components as you start and finish each one. Be explicit about what the purpose of each step is. Students will begin to feel secure, knowing what to expect next. At the end of each unit of work, review their achievements and help them perceive their progress. Highlight what they have learnt.

Encourage learners to continue to learn outside class. To increase their exposure and extend their vocabulary, they could borrow readers or magazines, or listen to target language radio programmes or cassettes while travelling to school or work.

It is well worth asking your class for regular feedback, either on anonymous slips of paper or in the form of learner diaries that they write after each lesson or block of lessons and that you read regularly. Then you will get to know how individuals are reacting, and if there are any problems, you can negotiate possible changes before they become demotivated and give up.

There is bound to be an initial experimental period while you are getting to know a new class, when some things don't work so well. If this happens, don't panic; reflect and investigate instead. Try alternative ways. Use simpler tasks. Make sure you can explain or demonstrate the purpose for each activity. Be clear about what you expect of your learners at each phase.

Here are some comments from a group of secondary school students who had been introduced to TBL a few weeks earlier. Their teacher wanted to find out if they liked being recorded at the report stage and whether this would make them more aware of the need for accuracy.

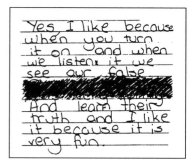

> Sometimes I like to being recorded but sometimes I don't like. While I am being recorded I don't want todo any mistake and talk with better English.

> I sometimes like and don't like because I have lots of mistakes and I don't want to record them. But sometimes I like it very much because I get very excited and I try to speak English more serious and spell so it's good, so I usually like it.

> Yes, I like because when you turn it on and when we listen it we see our false ~~██████~~ And learn their truth and I like it because it is very fun.

After an initial orientation period most learners take easily to TBL. You will soon notice the progress they make, and take pleasure in their increased confidence. However, some learners react quite strongly against TBL no matter how enthusiastic the teacher is. It is to these we now turn.

9.2.2 Countering learner resistance

Learners from certain educational backgrounds and cultures have such different classroom expectations they may well need more rigid teacher control to begin with. Students sometimes expect to be 'seen and not heard'. If they do say something, it is often a repetition of the teacher's actual words. They love choral drills and copying from the board, because these are 'safe' activities. They may wonder why your classes do not make extensive use of rote-learning techniques. They may feel they are not 'being taught' enough.

This section pinpoints the most common student problems, gives possible reasons for them, then offers solutions that have worked with many teachers.

> *Problem: 'We don't do enough grammar.'*
>
> Earlier versions of TBL tended to play down explicit grammar instruction, or ignore it altogether. Some teachers feel that practice activities are out of place in a TBL cycle and avoid them.
>
> Sometimes learners do not recognise consciousness-raising activities as a relevant substitute for being taught 'proper grammar'. They are used to the security of a teacher-led PPP cycle and being given rules (even though many of them don't work).
>
> *Possible solutions*
> - Highlight the time spent on the language focus component and do extra practice activities.
> - Summarise the main language points at the end of each session. Discuss any useful rules or guidelines.

- Ensure learners always have written transcripts of recordings to study. This gives a feeling of security.
- Include some choral repetition of short sections of the tape, and rote-learning of parts they find useful.
- Ensure students keep language notebooks. Encourage them to add extra examples from out-of-class reading. Check the notebooks regularly, and show an interest in them.
- Set relevant exercises from a student grammar book for homework or self-access time. Go over them in class.

Problem: 'We'd like to be corrected more when we speak.'

Learners coming from a teacher-centred class are used to a constant focus on accuracy, and may not realise that correction is likely to be more effective at some times than at others.

Possible solutions
- Make clear the distinction between exploratory talk at the task stage and planned talk at the report stage.
- Encourage learners to correct each other at the planning stage.
- Hold a 'language clinic' after some report stages. Write corrected versions of common errors on a wall poster.
- Individual learners who are keen to perfect their spoken language may record themselves doing tasks or presenting reports. Encourage them to listen carefully to their recordings and write down any bits they are not sure about to check later.

Problem: 'We've been doing this course for some time and don't feel we're making progress.'

Progress in a language is often imperceptible to learners, because so much is acquired subconsciously. New language has to be assimilated and internalised before it becomes available for use (see Chapter 1 Statement 3).

Students used to a grammar-oriented PPP style think they are making progress because they are covering a lot of grammar very explicitly. But although they seem to master a grammar point at the time of learning it, they often find later they can't use it.

Possible solutions
- Help students to keep records of items covered in their language notebooks. They should also keep vocabulary books. Every few weeks, hold a 'review' day: students review their language notebooks at home and produce a test to give each other in class. Each team can take responsibility for one text or unit.
- Have a 'repeat task' day. Get students to repeat, with different partners, some of the tasks they have recently done or parallel ones. (Warn them in advance which tasks you might ask them to do, then they will revise useful lexis, etc.)
- Ask an outsider to visit the class once or twice a term. The outsider doesn't need to be a teacher – just a good speaker of the language. The visit may work better if you do not remain in the class. The outsider, who knows about the topics and tasks your students have covered, can

talk to students, set repeat tasks, be interviewed by your class and report to them informally on their progress.

- Record pairwork regularly (say every six weeks). This allows you to assess long-term progress, but requires organisation and time to play back material.[1]

Problem: 'We find the recordings of natural speech hard to understand.'

As we saw in Chapter 2, spontaneous spoken English is very different from written English and from dramatised, idealised dialogues recorded by actors in a studio.

Possible solutions

- Explain that it is likely to be hard at first. But it will get easier, and enable them to understand more when they meet speakers of the target language, and to do better in listening and oral exams.
- Break the recording up into shorter sections. Find a simple thing for students to listen for each time.
- Let students follow the transcript and listen at the same time. Ask them to underline each important message-bearing word, and then to identify and practise useful phrases.
- Set cloze tests on the transcripts so learners have to listen again to identify the missing words or phrases. (They can make these tests for each other by blacking out the words on a copy of the transcript.)
- Encourage them to listen to target language speakers outside class.

Problem: 'We don't like doing pairwork with people who speak our own language.'

It feels unnatural to start with and they are afraid of picking up bad habits from fellow students. There may also be students they don't like being paired with.

Possible solutions

- Establish the target language as the main means of communication in your lessons, and this feeling of unnaturalness will wear off after a while.
- Research suggests that learners learn a lot from each other even if they do share a first language. This has been borne out by student feedback.
- Make sure learners change partners fairly regularly. They will learn different things from different people.

9.3 Assessment and TBL

Another very common worry often voiced by students new to TBL is 'What about the exams?' Many students and teachers worry that a TBL approach will undermine students' chances of success in exams, especially if these put more emphasis on grammar and accuracy than on ability to communicate appropriately. Exams – school exams, university entrance exams or external public exams – are often the student's main motive for studying a language. Anything not directly connected with them is felt to be a waste of time. If their exams do not test oral communication, students wonder about the relevance of taking part in oral tasks.

9.3.1 How TBL can help with exams

Language exams set out to test students' knowledge of the language, and ability to perform in it. So how can TBL help students to do well?

The TBL framework, together with a balanced selection of texts and tasks, aims to give students enough breadth of language experience and practice in language use, to attain both the knowledge and the skills required in most kinds of exams. Rich experience of the language in use will help learners to 'get the feel' of what sounds or looks right, making them more likely to pick or supply a correct answer intuitively.

The task stage of the TBL cycle will certainly help students in any oral test, and give them confidence to deploy what language they have, which will also help with fluency in writing. The planning and report stages will aid the production of accurate language and train students in editing and self-correction skills. The language focus phase will increase students' understanding of grammar. It also gives them a chance to select patterns and lexical phrases useful for their own areas of interest which can be incorporated into their writing. As the exams get nearer, planning and report stages can be done increasingly against the clock, to simulate exam conditions. Dictionary support can be withheld and students can begin to produce written work individually rather than co-operatively.

Exam technique is certainly important and students improve with training. Tackling the various types of questions can be done as a 'crash course' in the term leading up to the exam, although some students may feel more secure if it is brought in earlier. Traditional styles of exam practice can be adapted to groupwork, with students making up more testing items along the same lines as those in the exam.[2]

9.3.2 External exams with tasks

For EFL, there are many different types of external public exams available. As you will see in Appendix F, many of these now contain task–based components.

Pair and group tasks are commonly used to test a student's ability to communicate and co-operate in spoken interaction. Many set a variety of reading and listening tasks based on authentic materials. Some use the same reading materials for all levels, but grade the level of difficulty of the tasks. Since such exams reflect the practices commonly used in the TBL classroom, students will require much less in the way of exam technique training.[3]

If you feel that the exam you are required to teach for is not suitable for your students, talk to other teachers about the possibility of changing it. Write to examining boards for specimen copies of papers that you think might be more relevant to your learners. Circulate these among colleagues to show them what is available (addresses of examining boards are also given in Appendix F).

9.3.3 Progress testing with TBL

Suggestions for ways of helping students to monitor their progress were made in section 9.2.2 above. Informal tests are often useful.

'Review' day tests (see page 141) encourage students to review recent coverage by re-reading texts, and going through their language notebooks. 'Repeat task' days (see page 141) are another way of encouraging students to review their work and assess progress.

Pairs can either be asked to perform in front of the class, one after another, or two or three pairs can work concurrently at opposite ends of the classroom while the rest of the class (and the teacher) observe and make notes. Feedback may consist of three good things and one piece of advice for each learner. If you want to record the test tasks, ask for two volunteers to operate the cassette recorders. This leaves you free to organise the change-overs.

If you have a class of twenty-four, and you have done six main tasks since the last test, divide the class into four blocks, A, B, C and D. Number the students in each block 1–6. Ask the four number 1 people to make up two pairs to do task 1; the number 2 people to form pairs and do task 2, and so on. Each block observes their own learner and makes a note on their performance. If you do each task concurrently, at either end of the classroom, with quick change-overs, this could take as little as 15–20 minutes. Even if you do them one at a time, at two minutes a task, this will take around 30–40 minutes with quick change-overs. Keep public feedback till the end. To prepare for this kind of testing session, all learners will need to revise all the tasks.

Alternatively, you could record some pairs doing repeat tasks one week, and different pairs the next week. Play back the recordings, comment on the good parts, and give a few suggestions for improvement (see suggestions for handling feedback in 4.4.1).

9.4 Textbooks and TBL

While there are a number of task-based resource books on the market, there are as yet few genuinely task-based coursebooks. However, several coursebooks have tasks in, and teacher's books often suggest additional tasks. Text and resource books save teachers a lot of hard work, and serve as useful reference points for students. This section suggests how they can be appraised, adapted to and supplemented by TBL.

9.4.1 Appraising coursebooks for TBL content

It is important to analyse the contents with your students' needs in mind.

First of all, read the Introduction – this is usually in the Teacher's Book – to discover how the book is meant to be used, and what principles lie behind it. Many introductions state that a coursebook is 'communicative', but unfortunately this may just mean that there are pair activities where students practise using pre-specified forms but very few opportunities for true communication. Some resource books containing tasks which do stimulate real communication lack language-focused work, and fail to supply recordings which will help students improve their spontaneous spoken language.

Then look at the range and type of exposure to the target language in the Student's Book and on the cassettes. Ask questions such as those posed in Chapters 5 and 6, for example:

- Is there a balance of spoken and written, spontaneous and planned text?
- Is there a sufficient range of types of text?

Find how many activities in a typical unit give learners a chance to use the target language. Analyse these into two categories, asking:

- How many activities are intended to stimulate practice of specified forms – either on their own or alongside other language?
- How many activities are communication tasks – ones which require learners to use language freely to attain a goal or achieve an outcome?

Analyse the approach the material takes to language-focused work, asking:

- Is the grammar taught on its own? How is it contextualised?
- What about lexical phrases, collocations, and vocabulary building?
- Are there analytic consciousness-raising language exercises?
- Is spoken language studied as well as written?

You might need to adapt the balance of exposure (written and spoken) and activities promoting language use. Adaptation can involve omitting things as well as supplementing them. It can also involve finding a different way to exploit what is already there.

9.4.2 Adapting textbook materials to TBL

Opportunities for task-based learning can be provided by making minor changes in the way the original textbook materials are used.

- You could change the class management. For example, if you are planning to use a sequence of questions (either from the book or asked by you):
  - Instead of asking the whole class a question and inviting one student to respond, you might ask learners in pairs to consider the answer for thirty seconds or one minute, and then volunteer a reply. This in fact makes a series of mini task-planning-report cycles. You won't have time to ask so many questions, but you'll get far higher-quality responses, and a greater proportion of learner composing and talking time.

- You may simply need to change the order of two activities. Two examples follow.
  - If there is a reading text or a listening comprehension followed by a series of questions, introduce the topic then ask students to cover the text and predict answers to the comprehension questions before they read or listen (task). Students then tell each other their predictions (report), and read or listen to find out who guessed most accurately. Withhold the answer for as long as possible to promote student discussion and to encourage them to re-read the text or recording transcript to resolve any problems.
  - If your book follows a PPP cycle, you might begin with the free production activity – and use it as the basis for a task-planning-report cycle, introduced by a pre-task activity, doing some language focus work afterwards. You can select from the language presented in the book and show how it could have been used in the task. You may be able to supplement listening material by making a task recording beforehand (see Chapter 6). Learners can then study the language of the transcript, too. Set some controlled practice activities for homework instead of taking up valuable class time.

- You could change the balance of study in a given section.
  - For example, spend less time on practising and perfecting learners' production of the target pattern. Spend more on exploiting language from the texts or recording transcripts, or highlighting useful language that students have used in their own writing or in their task reports.

- You might try some activities with books closed. This introduces an element of fun and turns the original activity into a memory challenge task.
  - For example, list three things you can remember about one person/place/event in the story/text/picture.

9.4.3
Supplementing
textbook materials
with TBL

TBL features can also supplement existing textbook materials.

- Look out for good starting points for tasks (see Appendix A). For example:
  - With any picture or diagram play games like Memory challenge, 'True or not true?', 'Guess what is in this picture' (see 8.2.4).
  - Take the unit or reading text topic and think of a task based on personal experience related to it.

- Exploit reading and listening skills lessons for text-based task cycles. There are lots of ideas in Section 4 of Chapter 5. For example:
  - Ask learners to write their own prediction questions before they read or listen, as suggested for Text A in Focus 5. They then read each other's questions. After reading or listening to the text, the class discuss whose questions were answered.
  - After reading or listening, teams of four learners set other teams comprehension questions or quizzes. Encourage responding teams to give their evidence by quoting from the text.

Exploiting the texts and listening activities in this way maximises student spoken interaction, and increases motivation to read and listen several times, each time for a different purpose. It often leads on to a relevant writing activity, too.

- Exploit useful language from the texts for language focus work. Chapter 7 gives examples and detailed guidelines for this.

- Ensure writing activities have a purpose and an audience. Many writing sections in textbooks set out to give students practice in writing for its own sake, rather than in communicating through writing. Exam practice often entails writing for display, i.e. to show how much language a learner knows. In Chapter 4, section 5 we looked at the place of writing in the task cycle, and at ideas for ways of writing for a wider audience. Chapter 5, Section 4 offers many suggestions for using writing as a follow up to text-based tasks. Make writing activities purposeful.
  - Turn the preparation phase for a piece of writing into a group task – brainstorming, then ranking and sequencing the best ideas. Groups then plan how to do the writing, share it out and read and edit each other's work. Finally the writing is passed to other groups who have written on a similar topic to read and compare content.
  - Turn the writing activity into an opportunity to produce a reading puzzle for other students. Ask learners to include in their piece of writing a sentence that is either totally irrelevant or quite untrue. Other groups then read it to 'spot the stranger'.

- Ensure speaking activities give learners a purpose for communicating. Sometimes a 'discussion' activity can be developed into a task. For example a role-play or simulation such as: *Pretend your class is going to have a party. Say what you would like to eat and drink* can be turned into a more challenging and engaging problem, such as: *If you were given a budget of £20 to organise a party for your class, how would you spend it? Work in groups. Compare menus and reasons for your choices. Vote on the most original menu.*

Speaking activities, such as those in resource books, will often benefit from being followed by a planning and report stage, and from a recording of fluent speakers doing the same activity. This recording can then be exploited for language focus work.

Business language resource books often contain case studies and simulation materials to replicate business situations and stimulate the types of communication that are typical of business encounters. These often contain a spoken or written report stage. You could add to the learning opportunities here by recording learners' oral reports, and playing them back for appraisal.

9.4.4 Planning TBL input	Whether you are adapting or supplementing parts of your textbook to provide opportunities for task-based learning, it is important to look ahead over a week's or month's work, so that you achieve a good overall balance of exposure and language use.

You may decide that the texts themselves offer rich language opportunities but activities that stimulate talk are lacking. By inserting mini task cycles based on the texts and recordings, you can postpone or even omit some of the PPP language cycles. If the language on the syllabus doesn't occur, and you feel it is vital, cover it rapidly at the end of a cycle, and ask students to look out for further examples. You may have noticed some examples of the target structures in texts they have read previously, or in future texts; collect these for later and then set an analysis activity on them.

You may discover that your textbook offers a rather limited range of texts, or very little in the way of natural language. In that case you will need to introduce a greater variety of styles, text types and language by bringing in extra texts and recordings (see Chapters 5, 6 and 7 for guidelines).

Decisions about selecting texts and specifying language to supplement the textbook take us into the realm of syllabus design, a far wider issue, and one which is, sadly, beyond the scope of this book.

Summary

In conclusion, here is a list of the main advantages of adopting TBL.

- A task-based framework for language learning aims at stimulating language use and providing a range of learning opportunities for students of all levels and abilities.
- The role of tasks is to encourage learners to activate and use whatever language they already have, both for comprehension and for speaking and writing.
- The role of the task-planning-report cycle is to stimulate a natural desire in the learner to improve upon that language.
- Tasks based on texts and recordings of spoken language provide learners with a rich exposure to spoken and written language in use. This provides an environment which aids natural acquisition.
- The language focus component enables learners to examine that exposure, and systematise their knowledge of language structure.
- The texts and recordings used in task cycles form a pedagogic corpus of data for use in class. This provides a clear and familiar context for the teaching of grammar and other language features.

Adopting TBL is not a question of acquiring new teaching techniques – most of those necessary are already practised on teacher training courses. Neither is it a question of tacking TBL onto what is done already ('I already do tasks in my classes').

TBL is more a matter of perceptive and sensitive management of the learning environment. It involves examining existing beliefs and trying to look at learning and teaching in a realistic light. It entails coming to terms with the principles that underpin the components in a TBL framework and using them to create the right conditions for language learning. This in turn entails seeing the lesson outline as a framework which accommodates sustained learner activity.

In fact, for the teacher who has just introduced and set up a task-based cycle for the first time, the biggest challenge of all is possessing the strength of mind to stand back with confidence, and to let learners get on with their own learning.

Further reading

See *Challenge and Change in Language Teaching* by J and D Willis (eds), 1996, Heinemann ELT, especially the following papers:
T Woodward *Paradigm shift and the language teaching profession*
K Jennings and T Doyle *Curriculum innovation, teamwork and the management of learning*
D Ozdeniz *Introducing innovation into your teaching*
S Wharton *Testing innovations*

Notes

1 M Bygate in J and D Willis (eds), 1996.
2 L Prodromou, 1995.
3 S Wharton in J and D Willis (eds), 1996.

Appendix A:
Six types of task

This classification, which does not claim to be exhaustive, will help you generate a variety of tasks on whatever topic you have selected. For each type of task, it gives the outcome, broadly analyses the processes involved, then suggests some specific starting points and examples that you can adapt and build on.

Simple tasks may consist of one type only, such as listing; more complex tasks may incorporate two or more types, such as listing then comparing lists or listing then ranking. Problem solving may include listing, comparing and ranking.

After the starting points and examples, this classification also suggests follow-up tasks. All tasks involve speaking and listening. Many also entail reading and note-taking. All tasks can lead into a more formal oral or written presentation.

The task types classified here are introduced in Chapter 2. A more detailed breakdown of task types for use with texts can be found in Chapter 5, Section 4. Tasks specifically for beginners and young learners can be found in Chapter 8, Sections 2 and 5. Meta-communicative tasks, i.e. tasks that focus on language itself, are termed 'language analysis activities' in this book and are illustrated in Chapter 7.

1 Listing

Outcome Completed list or draft mind map (see Focus 5).

Processes Brainstorming, fact-finding

Starting points Words, things, qualities, people, places, actions, job-related skills:

- international English words, e.g. in sport, in pop songs
- things found in particular places, e.g. in the kitchen, on the beach
- everyday things, e.g. that you carry with you or that you often forget or lose
- qualities looked for in a product, e.g. a good pen, a stereo system
- qualities needed for particular jobs, e.g. teaching, being prime minister
- personal characteristics, e.g. of a TV celebrity, an astronaut
- features of a place, e.g. a holiday resort, a language school, a sports complex
- things you do to, e.g. prevent crime, plan a party, move house
- ways of doing things, e.g. remembering new words, cooking rice, saving money
- common questions, e.g. that guests ask hotel reception staff, that tourists ask tourist guides

Follow-up tasks
- **Memory challenge games** (lists and sources can be hidden and students asked to recall as many items as possible in a specified time).

- **Ordering and sorting tasks** (type 2) and **comparing** tasks (type 3) can be based on lists that students have made.

2 Ordering and sorting

Outcome Set of information or data that has been ordered and sorted according to specified criteria

Processes	Sequencing	Ranking	Categorising	Classifying
Starting points	Jumbled lists/sets of instructions/texts/news reports	Personal experience of methods/things/features that can be sorted according to specific criteria/personal values	Headings/half-completed tables/charts followed by sets of statements, data from various sources	Everyday things or events, lists of items, words
Sample tasks	• Put the days of the week into the correct order. • Order the instructions for making an international phone call/the steps for doing a magic trick. • Rewrite this news report putting the events into chronological order.	• Agree on the best ways to learn a new language/travel between two places/pass a driving test. • Rank these items in order of, importance/interest/usefulness/value for money.	• Group the statements under these headings: agree, disagree, undecided. • Complete this chart/table with information from the text.	• How many ways can you find to classify the food you eat daily/the things you do at home/the things you read regularly/the countries in this list? • Think of five ways to classify the clothes you wear/the animals in the picture.
Follow-up tasks	• 'Spot the missing item' – Students remove one item from a sequence, and read the list out for other pairs to spot it.	• Groups present their rankings for the class to reach a consensus through discussion and debate.	• Students justify their decisions to the class, or give an oral presentation of their completed table or a section of it.	• 'Odd one out' – Students make up sets of four or five similar items and add one that doesn't match. They exchange sets and see if other pairs can spot it.

3 Comparing

Outcomes

Vary according to the individual task goals, but could be the items appropriately matched or assembled, or the identification of similarities and / or differences.

Processes

	Matching	Finding similarities	Finding differences
Starting points	Information from two different types of source (e.g. visuals and text) that can be matched in order to identify someone or something	Two or more sets of information on a common theme (from personal experience / visuals / texts) that can be compared to find similarities	Two or more sets of information on a common theme (from personal experience / visuals / texts) that can be contrasted to find differences
Sample tasks	• **Descriptions** Listen to / read these descriptions of different people / places and identify which person / place is which. • **Narrative accounts** Read / listen to these accounts, e.g. of a car accident, and say which of the four diagrams most accurately portrays what happened. • **Following instructions** Match this text to the map or diagrams, e.g. to trace a route on a map, to complete a floor plan of a house, to assemble a model.	• Compare, e.g. two characters in a TV series, reports of the same event from different newspapers. • Compare your own version with the official or original version, e.g. compare your story ending with the original story, your solution with the one in the text. • Compare ways of doing things in different towns or countries, e.g. funding the arts, making coffee, cooking rice.	• 'Spot the differences', e.g. between two pictures, two story endings, two accounts of the same incident. • Jigsaw viewing, e.g. contrast a film / video sequence with a written account containing factual errors. Half the class see the video, half read the text, then they come together to identify the factual errors. • Contrast systems, e.g. of education in different countries, of lending libraries.

Follow-up tasks

Students design parallel tasks based on their own data, or make their own changes to the original data

	Matching	Finding similarities	Finding differences
	• e.g. after matching text to diagrams, students make floor plans of their own homes and describe these for their partner to draw.	• e.g. after finding similarities in news reports, students bring in other current newspapers with parallel news items.	• e.g. after finding differences between pictures, students change three things in their picture, rewrite the text including different factual errors or three additions and play 'Spot the differences'.

4 Problem solving

Outcome   Solution(s) to the problem, which can then be evaluated

Processes   Analysing real or hypothetical situations, reasoning and decision making

Starting points	Short puzzles, logic problems	Real-life problems, personal experience, hypothetical issues	Incomplete stories / poems / reports; visuals / snippets of audio or video recordings; concealed pictures, clue words for prediction and guessing games	Case studies with full background data, business and computer simulations

Sample tasks	• Cutting the cake
	What is the minimum number of straight cuts you must make to divide a round cake into eight equal pieces?
	• Crossing the river
	An old lady wants to cross the river with a wolf, a goat, and a cabbage. She only has a small boat and can only take two things at a time with her. How does she do it?
		• What advice would you give in response to this letter from an advice column?
		• Decide on the best two places – cheap but safe – for a young person travelling alone to stay in your capital city.
		• Plan a dinner menu for overseas guests within a given fixed budget. (Other constraints, such as diet, can be added later to increase the challenge.)
			• Make up your own version of the missing section / ending of the story / report.
			• Work out a possible story-line from these clue words / phrases / pictures / audio / video snippets.
			• Fill the gaps in this text with appropriate phrases.
			• Guess what's in this (covered up) picture / (closed) bag.
				• Social study of young offenders
				  Decide on the best action to take to stop them reoffending. Previous solutions and statistics for reoffending are given. (Offenders' family backgrounds to be initially withheld.)
				• Aid for development
				  Decide on three appropriate ways for your company / country to give aid to this developing country.
				• Product testing
				  Play and report back on computer simulation games.

Follow-up tasks   Students do a comparing task, presenting, justifying and discussing their solutions for the class to vote on the best one(s).

5 Sharing personal experiences

Outcome

Largely social and far less tangible than with other tasks. Sharing personal experiences is something we do very often in daily life: we may simply be passing the time of day, being sociable or entertaining or hoping to get to know others better. This kind of casual social talk can happen naturally during other task types and, because it is so common outside the classroom, should be encouraged.

Processes

Narrating, describing, exploring and explaining attitudes, opinions, reactions

Starting points

Anecdotes:

- on given themes, e.g. terrible journeys, silly accidents.
- about people, e.g. eccentric friends or relations, funny things done by children you know.
- about things you own(ed), e.g. a favourite toy, old shoes, memorable presents.

Personal reminiscences:

- about past routines and experiences, e.g. early schooldays, traditional festivals and celebrations, friends you used to spend time with.
- about single events you remember most clearly, e.g. moving house, visiting elderly relations, times of political / financial crisis.
- about past regrets, e.g. three things you most regret doing / not doing.

Attitudes, opinions, preferences:

- Find out what others think about films or TV programmes, personalities, current concerns and / or professional issues.
- Talk about your preferences and find people with similar ones, e.g. in leisure activities, places to shop, clothes.

Personal reactions:

- to situations, e.g. heights, frightening things, extremes of climate.
- What generally makes you, e.g. most annoyed, very happy, highly stressed, most relaxed.
- Quizzes, e.g. personality ones from quiz books.

Follow-up tasks

- Students select the funniest / most vivid / most memorable experience they have heard, tell the class and give reasons for their choice.
- Students tell another anecdote or personal story but it need not be true. Can the class guess whether it is true?
- Learners identify and summarise the reminiscences / opinions / reactions they found they shared with others.

Photocopiable

6 Creative tasks

Outcome

End product which can be appreciated by a wider audience. Creative tasks tend to have more stages than the usual classroom tasks. They can involve out-of-class research and are often referred to as 'projects'.

Processes

Brainstorming, fact-finding, ordering and sorting, comparing, problem solving and many others

Starting points	Creative writing and similar activities	Social/historical investigations and links	Media projects for the school or local community	Real-life rehearsals
Sample tasks	• Write a poem, short story, song or play, based on a literary text students have read or arising out of a programme they have seen. • Write diaries, e.g. for personal use, and/or to be read by the teacher but not by other students.	• Plan visits to local places, e.g. airport to interview passengers, company premises to report on products/processes, tourist office to investigate local tourism opportunities. • Talk/write to older inhabitants about changes to their lives, e.g. past customs, games they used to play, changes in eating/leisure habits over three generations. • Internet and email links, e.g. with twin towns overseas, overseas schools, research areas of interest on World Wide Web.	• Produce a class magazine or newspaper (one-off or regular issue). • Set up a display, e.g. on a local or topical issue or exhibition, e.g. of students' photographs. • Design and write a leaflet, e.g. for visitors to the school or town, or an advert, e.g. for a local product/entertainment. • Design, produce and record a short programme on audio or video, e.g. a local news documentary or a short drama.	• Students predict, script and perform an interaction that might occur in specific real-life situations, e.g. making a hotel booking, asking for directions or instructions for being interviewed for a job. These are then compared with spontaneous recordings of parallel situations or real-life circumstances.

Children's activities: done in small groups who then describe the process, e.g.

• make a model, paint a picture, prepare snacks.
• do a science experiment, test and report on makes of colouring pens.
• take part in a dressing-up competition, put on a show for other groups.

Follow-up tasks

• Other groups write a review of the end product.
• Learners keep a diary describing their progress on the project, and what they learned, with an evaluation of their work.
• Groups make a poster advertising their end product.

NB: Many other types of task can be adapted for young learners.

Appendix B: Overview of the TBL framework

Pre-task (including topic and task)

The teacher

- introduces and defines the topic
- uses activities to help students recall/learn useful words and phrases
- ensures students understand task instructions
- may play a recording of others doing the same or a similar task

The students

- note down useful words and phrases from the pre-task activities and/or the recording
- may spend a few minutes preparing for the task individually

Task cycle

Task

The students

- do the task in pairs/small groups. It may be based on a reading/listening text

The teacher

- acts as monitor and encourages students

Planning

The students

- prepare to report to the class how they did the task and what they discovered/decided
- rehearse what they will say or draft a written version for the class to read

The teacher

- ensures the purpose of the report is clear
- acts as language adviser
- helps students rehearse oral reports or organise written ones

Report

The students

- present their spoken reports to the class, or circulate/display their written reports

The teacher

- acts as chairperson, selecting who will speak next, or ensuring all students read most of the written reports
- may give brief feedback on content and form
- may play a recording of others doing the same or a similar task

Language focus

Analysis

The students

- do consciousness-raising activities to identify and process specific language features from the task text and/or transcript
- may ask about other features they have noticed

The teacher

- reviews each analysis activity with the class
- brings other useful words, phrases and patterns to students' attention
- may pick up on language items from the report stage

Practice

The teacher

- conducts practice activities after analysis activities where necessary, to build confidence

The students

- practise words, phrases and patterns from the analysis activities
- practise other features occurring in the task text or report stage
- enter useful language items in their language notebooks

NB: Some time after this final phase, students may like to repeat the same or a similar task with a different partner.

Appendix C: Five sample task-based lesson outlines

The aim of these sample lesson outlines is to exemplify the flexibility of the TBL framework in practice. They cover a variety of task and text types, and are suitable for learners at different levels and stages in a course.

The first two outlines focus predominantly on the use of spoken language, the next two predominantly on written. The last one offers a balance of both. Other lesson outlines showing the adaptability of the TBL framework are to be found in Chapters 5 and 6.

Although the language analysis activities focus on English, teachers of other foreign languages have found it possible to use the same outlines, with parallel texts / recordings, and to adapt the analysis activities to suit the features of other target languages.

The timings given are, of course, approximate. The outlines can obviously be adapted in various ways to suit learners in different circumstances.

**Outline 1
Picture puzzle:
find seven
differences**

> *The aim of this lesson outline is to illustrate a typical revision lesson covering familiar topics. The pre-task phase is, therefore, shorter than usual. This lesson also shows how a recording can be used at the end of the task cycle (see Chapters 2 and 3).*

Class and course background

Elementary, Spanish-speaking learners of mixed ability. Used to rule-based teaching but would like to learn to speak. They have completed the first four units of a topic-based coursebook (addresses etc, family, homes, uses of numbers) and have done simple tasks and puzzles. Lessons are 50 minutes long.

Starting lesson

Explain this lesson is mainly revision, and aims to revise words and phrases from Units 1–4, give ss different kinds of speaking practice and finally focus on question forms.

Pre-task (3–4 min)

1 Get ss to stand up, find a different partner from usual and sit down in their new pairs. Check they have at least one book between two. Keep them closed for now. They also need one sheet of paper between two, a pen or pencil and their language notebooks.
2 Introduce task – 'Find the differences' puzzle, like one they have done before (remind them) only with different pictures (see page 29). Each student will see both pictures. Together they have to find seven differences and write them down in note form. (Put an example (*cat on right / on left of sign*) on the board.) They will only have one minute. They should talk in English, but quietly.

Task cycle

Task (1 min)

Get them ready to start: *Find the pictures on page … and you have one minute from … NOW.*

Stop the task as soon as a few pairs have noted down seven differences (or when one minute is up). Ask how many differences others have found already.

Planning (8–10 min)

Tell all pairs to choose four differences they think the others may not have seen. They write them down in detail, and practise explaining them, so they can tell the whole class. Show them by expanding *cat* example on board.

Go round and help, noting useful phrases and writing some on left of board, e.g. *In picture A … the sign says … .*

Nominate the shy ones as reporters, and give them another two minutes to practise. Draw attention to phrases on board.

Report and listening (15 min)

Explain that they must listen carefully to other pairs. If they have the same difference, they tick it off. Once they have heard a difference, they must not report it themselves.

Each pair gives one difference (write these on board as they tell the class) till there are seven. Some pairs may still have more. Stop them from shouting them out (so they still have some to listen for later).

Announce recording of David and Bridget doing the same task.

Play recording. Ss tick off the differences they hear. (May need to pause after each one, and play it again.)

David:	*Okay? Another difference is the number of the house.*
Bridget:	*Yes.*
David:	*In Picture A it's thirty; in Picture B it's thirteen…*
Bridget:	*– is thirty. Oh!*
David:	*Oh, okay.*
Bridget:	*Oh. Do you think–?*
David:	*Doesn't matter. Thirty in Picture A and thirteen…*
Bridget:	*Thirteen in picture B. And this number's different.*
David:	*What number?*
Bridget:	*The phone number of Paul Smith and Sons.*
David:	*Oh yeah. So, the phone number of Paul Smith and Sons is – what? – in Picture A – is six three one nine oh. Six three one nine oh in Picture A…*
Bridget:	*Mmm.*
David:	*And six three three nine oh in Picture B.*
Bridget:	*Okay.*
David:	*Okay. How many have we got? That's three.*
Bridget:	*Three. How many do we have to have? Seven. Mm.*
David:	*How about the television – is that on? Yes. Oh no, the television is on, is it? – in the first picture–*
Bridget:	*Yes, it is!*
David:	*… and it's not on in the – in Picture B… that's – what have we got?*
Bridget:	*The television is on in Picture A but off in Picture B.*
David:	*Okay. Right. Anything else? Oh yes, the man's carrying an umbrella.*

Bridget: *Okay.*
David: *So what shall we put? The man...*

Collins Cobuild English Course Level 1, Unit 5, p. 120T.

Now ask class if any pairs have more differences? Ask them to give one each. Tell them the record total so far is 13 – can they beat it?

Language focus (15–20 min)	*Analysis and practice* From board: **1** Ss choose a useful phrase from each sentence and practise saying it. Delete the phrase immediately it is said. Delete other words gradually. This is called 'progressive deletion' (see page 111) and should be fun! **2** Ss read out all sentences in full, including the missing parts. Clean board. From transcript: **3** Ss hear recording again and follow it in the transcript. Pause tape sometimes to let them predict how next phrase will be said (intonation with stress on key words). **4** Ss read whole transcript and find twelve questions to classify in whatever ways they like (e.g. questions with *shall* or *get*; short questions/long questions; questions with/without verb, etc.). **5** Ss find two examples of the word *so*. Where does it come in the conversation? **6** If time, ss write down any new phrases they noticed. Bring class together and review analysis of questions. Practise short questions (point out many are without verbs) and then list questions with *shall, got, have* and practise them. Discuss use of *so*, and ask what word(s) are used in Spanish for this. Ss read out their phrases. NB: 4–6 can be done for homework and reviewed in class.

Outline 2
A sea journey

> The aim of this lesson outline is to illustrate the first lesson in a series
> based on a new topic. The pre-task phase will therefore be longer than
> usual, introducing topic lexis by various means including teacher anecdote
> and the use of a recording (see Chapters 2 and 3).

Class and course background

Intermediate/upper intermediate multi-lingual learners, mixed level, mixed
ability, ages from 16 upwards. Part-time class, two two-hour lessons a week.
They are beginning a textbook unit on sea journeys, which contains around
five tasks, leading into a short story.

Starting lesson

Announce new topic. Relate this to textbook unit.
Give overview of work for next two weeks, e.g. *By the end of this you'll have
talked and written about different aspects of journeys by boat, and read a short story
about a sea journey.* Ask them to bring to class anything they like that is linked
to the theme. Remind them main language features will be summarised at the
end of each week.

This lesson they'll be hearing a recording about a sea journey, then doing a
similar task – sharing their experiences of sea travel or boats. Language focus:
studying useful phrases and features of spontaneous English and comparing
these with planned English.

Pre-task
(15–20 min)

Aim: To introduce topic of sea journeys, and give class exposure to topic-
related talk, to activate and highlight useful words and phrases.
Starting points: three pictures of ships – big and small on rough and calm seas;
teacher's personal experience.

1 Talk about pictures one by one while putting them up on wall. Ask
   questions to assess class experience of topic, e.g. *Have any of you travelled by
   boat?/seen any TV programmes, films about sea travel?* Let class indicate their
   experience very briefly. (I'd tell them about my first experience in a small
   boat when the sea got really rough.)
2 Brainstorm with class on words and phrases. Organise on board as a mind
   map words about sea, boats, people, feelings, attitudes to sea
   journeys/being in boats.
   Bring theme round to *Are you a good traveller?* (and what this means, i.e.
   Do you get travel-sick on buses, in cars? or sea-sick?). Add other vital topic
   words that will come in the recording (see transcript below).
3 Announce recording of Rachel telling Chris about a sea journey. (Ss know
   her already from earlier recordings.) Write up alternatives to help them
   listen: *alone or with family? big or small boat? calm or rough sea? pleasant or
   unpleasant experience?*
   Play recording two or three times – 1) for gist (select words from board),
   2) for words and phrases they notice (add to board if useful), 3) if they want
   to hear it again.

Chris: *Are you a good sailor? Have you ever been seasick?*
Rachel: *Yeah I have been seasick, once. But I haven't sailed very much. Except in a–*

159

Chris: *Was that on a long journey?*

Rachel: *Yeah. In fact I'm quite a good traveller normally. But this was erm – er – not on a long journey, no. It was about twenty miles. And erm, coming – on the way back, it was a very small boat, and it was very hot, and me and the rest of my family were on this very – in the inside of the boat. And it was just like being in a – on a cork, carried by the water. And my brother started first, and then it just sort of spread like the plague.*

Chris: *Oh terrible.*

Rachel: *It was ghastly.*

Collins Cobuild English Course Level 3, Unit 20, p. 138T

4 Let them read task instructions from textbook. Give them two minutes' thinking time.

Task cycle

Task (3–4 min)

Ss do task in twos, then combine with another pair to re-tell their stories and compare their experiences. What did their stories have in common? Were any like Rachel's? Any groups that finish quickly can write down points they had in common.

Planning (5–10 min)

Each group of four selects two stories to present to the class.

Divide into pairs to rehearse them. Go round, helping if needed, and nominate spokespersons. Note down language points for highlighting later, such as any useful phrases that ss use.

Report (5–8 min)

Pick four or five pairs to tell their stories.

Class listen – their purpose is to note down details (warn them they must try to remember these for next lesson) and find what the stories have in common.

Give feedback on content. Review similarities and differences in their stories.

Set homework: plan a first written draft of the story, changing one detail, to be polished and presented to class in next lesson.

Language focus (15–20 min)

Analysis and practice

1 Dictate/write on board five good phrases from stories ss told in task cycle. Write up five corrected phrases/sentences with a word that caused problems missing for ss to discuss their meaning and complete them.

2 Based on transcript of Rachel's story. Ss read and circle useful words and phrases. Discuss which of these are typical of spoken language, and which of planned, or written language (see page 32 for typical spoken phrases).

3 Hand out version of planned story. Ask ss to discuss how this differs from the spoken transcript. Then they can underline all past tense verb forms.

Rachel: *I'm quite a good sailor normally. But this time, I was with my family and we were on a very small boat and it was like being on a cork on the water. We were all sitting inside the cabin and it was really hot. My brother started being seasick first and then it just spread like the plague. It was ghastly*

4 Ss write down other language features from lesson that they want to remember.

NB: 2 and 3 can be done for homework.

**Outline 3
Spiders: a
success story**

> *This is an example of a lesson based on a reading text. It contains a wide range of specific language-focused activities illustrating the starting points for language analysis activities as described in Chapter 7.*

Class and course background

Intermediate learners, monolingual, mixed-level class. They have already talked about phobias, and done a listing task on all the things they have heard people can be frightened of. They have also completed a more open task, where they told each other about what they had been frightened of as children. A few people have mentioned insects and spiders briefly, and students have found out who in the class is afraid of spiders. So there is no need for a lengthy pre-task phase.

Starting lesson

Explain there will be two task cycles in this lesson. These will lead into reading a newspaper report about a woman with a serious phobia about spiders. She lived with her husband near a large town, but could never be left alone in case she saw a spider (possibly write main topic words on board: *woman – phobia about spiders*, etc.).

Pre-task (2–3 min)

Explain the first task: in pairs ss to brainstorm and list three consecutive steps they might take to help cure this woman of her phobia about spiders.

**Task cycle 1
(Speaking)**

Task 1 (2–3 min)

Pairs list possible ways to help her get over her phobia.

Planning 1 (2–3 min)

Pairs rehearse how to explain the steps they recommend, and justify the order they are in.

Report and reading 1 (10 min)

Pairs tell the class their proposals and justify them. The class listen and count how many different ideas they come up with.

   Let the class discuss and vote on which four steps might be similar to those in the newspaper report. Write these on the board.

   Give out the texts with the missing line in Focus 5. Ask students to read to see whether their four steps were in the report. Finally ask which pair had the most steps that were similar.

**Task cycle 2
(Reading)**

Task 2 (4–5 min)

Ss read the text again and discuss in twos where the 'lost line' must have come from.

Planning and report 2 (2–3 min)

They tell each other where they think the line fits and why. Do not tell them if they are right or wrong. (If they all agree, no need to prolong the report!)

   Give out the text with the line in place, so they can see if they were right. (They will need the complete text for the next phase.)

Language focus
(20–35 min)

Analysis and practice

Each of the activities below can be followed by a review, hearing what ss thought, and bringing out some of the ideas in the notes below. In some cases, ss may benefit from a brief practice activity. (I would aim to do activities 1, 2 and two others in class and set 4.3 (on *to*) for homework.)

1 Main theme: Spiders

Circle all the phrases which refer to spiders, including those with pronouns, e.g. *saw one*, *removed it*. Join up the circles with straight lines, to get a lexical chain (see example below). Ss can then compare chains to see if they have found the same set of references.

NB: In order to do this, learners will have to focus on aspects of textual cohesion. They may notice the use of plural forms (and the word *one*) to express spiders in general. They can distinguish phrases that contrast with the idea of a real spider, e.g. *doodles resembling spiders*. These points can be highlighted at the review stage.

SPIDERS

*a success story
from the new organisation
Triumph Over Phobia (TOP).*

ONE woman was so afraid of spiders she could not be left in a house alone.

If she saw one she would climb on the table and not be able to get down until somebody came into the room and removed it.

During her first TOP meeting, she noticed doodles on a page which resembled spiders and she suddenly recoiled in horror. She was eventually persuaded to look at photographs of spiders in books, then leave the pages open in a room so she saw them each time she walked in. Her husband began to move the position of the book and change the page so she saw a different one each time.

After three weeks she was given a plastic spider at a TOP meeting and took it home. One of the group took a real spider in a jar to the next meeting, where it was gradually moved nearer to the sufferer. She later agreed to take the real spider home and gave it the name Bernard.

Two and a half months after first going to the group her phobia had gone.

The Daily Telegraph 24 January 1994

2 Time and sequence

Ask ss to find between eight and eleven phrases or single words that express the notion of time. Which ones denote the passing of time and thus help to signal the stages in the cure of the phobia? (There are seven or eight of these.)

NB: This highlights a very common function of time phrases – signalling the structure of a sequential narrative. It also shows that not all stages are explicitly signalled, and learners may need to look for less obvious linguistic clues, as in *began to ...* above.

A further focus on adverbs of time could be achieved by asking where the words *suddenly*, *eventually*, *gradually*, *later*, and *first* occur in the time phrases. Ask ss in pairs to read the phrases with these words out loud and notice where there might be similar stress patterns.

3 Place and position

Ask ss to look for around twelve phrases expressing the general notion of place and position. Subdivide these into three or four categories: those referring to
- her house, e.g. *left in a house alone*
- the spiders themselves, e.g. *in a jar*
- position or movement, e.g. *moved nearer to the sufferer*
- the meeting, e.g. *to the next meeting, going to the group*.

4 Common words highlighting grammar points: the passive voice and uses of *to*.

4.1 Ask ss to find four phrases with the word *was*. Which three have a similar structure? (*She was eventually persuaded to look at photographs/she was given a plastic spider / it was gradually moved nearer.*)
Ask ss if they know exactly who persuaded her to look at the pictures, who gave her a plastic spider, and who moved the spider nearer to her? Does it matter that they don't know?
Ask where else in those sentences they could put the words *gradually* and *eventually*.

Either

4.2 Ask ss to find six phrases with the word *to* and notice which verbs it goes with. Ask them if they can divide these phrases into two categories.
There is one phrase where you can omit the *to* and still have a grammatical sentence. Ask them to find it.

or

4.3 Tell ss these common uses of the word *to*:
   a) as a preposition indicating movement towards something or someone, e.g. *They have just moved to Kendal.*
   b) before an indirect object e.g. *I wrote three letters to the headmaster.*
   c) following a verb like *want* before an infinitive, e.g. *I tried to kick the door open.*
   d) denoting purpose or intention *in order to ...*, e.g. *I came in today just to see you*.

Now they try to decide which category each example below belongs to.

> table and not be able **to** get down until somebody came
> Her husband began **to** move the position of the book
> took a real spider in a jar **to** the next meeting, where it was
> gradually moved nearer **to** the sufferer. She later agreed
> She later agreed **to** take the real spider home and gave
> months after first going **to** the group her phobia had gone.
> ran on the spot for ten hours **to** stay alive. Peter Emerson, aged
> reported him missing **to** the police. Peter, who lives in
> I tried to kick the door open and **to** pick the lock but
> We've each got **to** say a little bit about our favourite

4.4 Underline the other verb phrases in the examples below which have the same patterns as this example: *She was eventually persuaded to look at photographs.* (These can include any part of the verb *be*, i.e. *was, will be / is*, etc.)

I was asked to help out at the butcher's shop.
You will normally be required to work one weekend day.
He was just told to go home and fetch it.
She is being encouraged to rest more.
You are advised to travel light, carrying no more than one...
They were more or less forced to accept an alternative.
You are constantly being reminded not to leave your luggage unattended.

NB: Some of these sentences may be unfamiliar to learners. Ask them to think of contexts in which they might hear or see them used.

Review analysis and get ss to write useful language in their books. If time, ask them to do a 'gapped example' quiz round the class, using examples from their notebooks.

**Outline 4
Romania:
an economic
report**

> *The aim of this outline is to illustrate a range of language-focused activities suitable for ESP texts in general (see Chapter 7). This lesson is based on the start of a text brought by one of a group of ESP (Business English) students.*

Class and course background

Small group of business people with interests in Eastern Europe. They have rusty lower-intermediate-level English and wish to broaden their business vocabulary and improve their reading of economic texts. They bring with them magazines like *Time* and *Newsweek* which can be exploited for more examples.

Pre-task (5–10 min)

1 I would ask the class to tell me (as non-expert teacher) what they already know about the current economic scene in Romania. I'd ask about the chief economic adviser and whether they think Romania is meeting IMF (International Monetary Fund) and World Bank requirements. Their main points can be written briefly on one side of the board.

2 Explain they will be reading the text of part of an interview held in 1994 with the chief economic adviser. It has lots of useful vocabulary and specialist phrases.

3 Ask which five of these six phrases are likely to appear in the text of the interview. Can they explain to me what they mean (after discussing this in pairs first)?

transition to a market economy   *industrial production*   *balance of trade*
general surge in profits   *trade deficit*   *money supply*

Task cycle (10 min)

Task

Ss read both columns in order to:
• find out who is being interviewed and what his overall purpose seems to be;
• discuss how far the speaker answered the interviewer's question.

Romania: Adviser outlines economic scene

Misu Negritoiu has played a prominent part in Romania's transition to a market economy... At present he is chief economic adviser to the president, one of the key figures in Romania's process of economic development. In an interview he discussed aspects of Romania's economy.

Q. Is Romania currently meeting IMF and World Bank requirements?
A. We are doing better than expected. The balance of trade was excellent in the first months of the year and up 40 per cent on the same period of 1993. The trade deficit now stands at about $200 million. The money supply is high. Industrial production has increased 20 per cent in the first half.

Planning and report

Each pair plans their responses then gives them to the class. The purpose of the report stage is to see if ss all agree, and if they don't, to discuss further.

Language focus
(15–20 min)

Analysis

Focus on useful forms by asking ss in pairs to do the following:

1 Phrases implying importance and authority

Find three phrases in the left-hand column which emphasise that Misu Negritoiu is an authority on the subject. Which words express the notion of importance?

2 Phrases implying success and increase

Find five or six phrases in Misu Negritoiu's answer (right-hand column) which express the notions of success and increase.

Ask students whether the trade deficit of $200 million is actually good or bad news, and why. (It's not clear to me as a non-expert.)

NB: The lexical phrases identified through both the above analytical activities illustrate various types of common collocations (see 2.3.1). *Better than expected* is a fixed phrase; *played a ... part in...* and *up 40 per cent on the same period* are semi-fixed phrases; *key figure* is a very common collocation.
The balance of trade was excellent and *the money supply is high* illustrate two very typical types of noun phrase: one with *of,* and one with noun plus noun, and the lexical items themselves (e.g. *balance of trade*) are typical of economic text. *Trade* would be a useful word for ss to do a dictionary exercise on.

3 Specialist/topic lexis: structure of noun phrases

3.1 Find five noun phrases with the word *economy* or *economic.* What other phrases with these words do learners know? Get them to experiment with creating phrases by putting *economy/economic* together with words like *crisis* and *system.*

3.2 Find two phrases with the word *trade.* What other kinds of words are often found with the word *trade?* Can they find some more examples in a newspaper, journal or dictionary? Are they all the same grammatically?

3.3 Say what all these phrases have in common structurally: *market economy, key figure, World Bank requirements, trade deficit, money supply.* (They are all made up of two or more nouns together.)

3.4 Say which phrase is the odd one out structurally and why: *market economy, key figure, trade deficit, money supply, industrial production.*

Practice

Expressions with numbers: Memory challenge game.
Tell ss to turn the text over. Write these numbers on the board: $\frac{1}{2}$ 20 40 200 1993. Can they remember the whole phrases they were in? Give them one minute to read the text again, without writing.

Then, again without looking back at the text, they write the phrases down from memory. They check to see if their partner has the same as them. Then read them out to the class to discuss before reading for a final check.

For homework, ss can either prepare a first draft of a two-minute presentation in answer to the same interview question on a different East European country or prepare a list of questions they would like to ask the economic adviser. (They will ask each other these in the next lesson.)

**Outline 5
Survey on
favourite
school subjects**

Like Lesson Outline 2 this outline gives an example of a TBL lesson on a new topic. Thus it has a long pre-task phase, with a task recording to help students understand what to do. It also exemplifies a range of language-focused activities highlighting phrases which express specific notions and functions (see Chapter 7).

Class and course background

Large monolingual class of mainly young adults from a range of backgrounds. Late elementary level, but very mixed. This is my second lesson with them. As back-up, I have copies of the six best pieces of last year's ss' written work on the same topic, to be used either this or next lesson.

Pre-task
(10–15 min)

1 Introduce topic and purpose of survey by asking ss what subjects they studied at school (see Focus 2, Task 7). Don't ask if they liked them or not.
2 Make a list on the board. Ask them to classify subjects – writing them in groups (e.g. languages, sciences, etc.) for later use.
3 I would tell class about subjects I liked and hated and, briefly, why (two or three minutes). Class then read task instructions: *Tell your group what were the school subjects you liked best and least. Explain your reasons.*
4 Organise groups of four with a chairperson. Give ss three minutes' individual thinking time to plan what subjects they will talk about, and what they will say.

Listening
(8–10 min)

Play recording to give groups some idea of how to do task. This is just the first few minutes of the task and they will hear about two out of four people's preferences (Caroline's and Stephen's). Play it a second time. Put a tick or a cross with an initial C or S by the relevant subjects on the board. Let ss ask about and write up a few useful phrases. (Remind them they will be able to study the transcript later, so no need to go into great detail now – approximate comprehension is sufficient.)

Catherine: *We've each got to say a little bit about our favourite subject at school, and which were the ones, erm, that we liked the least and for what reasons. Why don't you start?*

Caroline: *Right, well. My favourite subject was always English, I think because I liked writing stories. The least favourite was always Maths. I was awful at it. I think I, erm, didn't concentrate on some vital bits and missed out and then it just got worse and worse. I used to sit at the back and giggle quite a lot. And, er, so it was pretty disastrous, really.*

Stephen: *I liked science subjects, but I think that was because the teachers were very much better in that than in subjects like French which I really didn't like at all. I didn't mind things like Maths and English, because I could do them, but it – the languages, French, Latin, Greek, got a bit, you know – I got a bit behind, and the teachers weren't that helpful, so I didn't like those as much…*

John: *What did you dislike?*

Stephen: *Well, French…*

Collins Cobuild English Course Level 2, Section 58a

Task cycle 1 (Speaking)	*Task (4 min)* Chairperson should allow each student to speak for not more than one minute. The group can take notes if they wish. Chairperson should speak last. *Planning (5–8 min)* Each student should report about someone else. (This increases their motivation to interact further, check facts, etc.) Chairperson hears them rehearse. Students should aim for about half a minute's talk. Group can ask for help if unsure of any points. Write any useful words/phrases they ask for on board (for later practice). *Report (5 min)* Purposes: to find out which subjects were the most and least popular, and the most common reasons why. Also to discover if men/women like/dislike the same subjects. Students listen and take notes. Explain they will need these in order to write the conclusion to their survey next lesson.

Task cycle 1
(Speaking)

Task (4 min)

Chairperson should allow each student to speak for not more than one minute. The group can take notes if they wish. Chairperson should speak last.

Planning (5–8 min)

Each student should report about someone else. (This increases their motivation to interact further, check facts, etc.)

Chairperson hears them rehearse. Students should aim for about half a minute's talk.

Group can ask for help if unsure of any points. Write any useful words/phrases they ask for on board (for later practice).

Report (5 min)

Purposes: to find out which subjects were the most and least popular, and the most common reasons why. Also to discover if men/women like/dislike the same subjects.
Students listen and take notes. Explain they will need these in order to write the conclusion to their survey next lesson.

Language focus
(15–20 min)

Analysis and practice

Play the tape while students read the transcript to find the following:
1 Phrases expressing likes and dislikes of school subjects. Each student writes speakers' positive and negative reactions in two lists.
   Review these and then ask if there are any school subjects ss felt the same about. Ask which expressions might be useful to them.
2 Phrases denoting or implying levels of achievement in these subjects. Ss decide whether the speakers were good or bad at them, then discuss in what ways these phrases could be classified.
3 Phrases giving reasons for speakers' attitudes to these subjects.

NB: In identifying these, learners will need to make inferences and read between the lines; not all reasons are preceded by explicit verbal signals such as *because*. Some reasons have no signals, others are signalled afterwards by a word like *so*.

4 Three examples of the word *that*. Each use of *that* has a different meaning. Ask which one could mean which and which one means something like *very*. (This use of *not that* + adjective is quite common in spoken English.) What does the other one refer to?
5 Features that are typical of spoken English. Ask if there are also some useful phrases students might need in a written survey.

Task cycle 2
(Reading)

If time (now or next lesson), ss can read what last year's groups wrote about their teachers, and prepare a report in which they summarise the main points and compare their findings with their own results.

For homework, ss write a first draft of what their group found out. This will be worked on in class next lesson, and then a final version of the small-group report will be read by other groups. This can lead to writing a whole-class survey report.

Appendix D: Groupwork appraisal sheets

These sheets are reproduced from *The Shropshire Talk Project* (see Acknowledgements). By changing 'assignment' to 'task' you could adapt them to TBL classes.

Groupwork self-assessment sheet   **Z1**

Assignment: ....   Name: ....

Date: ....

Did you   – listen to other people?   ....

        – respond to other people's ideas?   ....

        – help to organise the talk?   ....

        – help others in the group?   ....

        – explain your ideas clearly?   ....

        – understand the ideas?   ....

        – enjoy the discussion?   ....

Did everyone in the group   – join in?   ....

                   – listen to each other?   ....

                   – help each other?   ....

Has the talk helped you to understand the subject?

Has the groupwork made you think?

What parts of the assignment did you do best?

What parts of the assignment did the group do best?

How would you improve this assignment if you had to do it again?

How could you improve your own groupwork?

How could your group improve its work?

Please use the back of the paper to add further comments if you wish.

Group roles: Making a transcript / Analysing talk   **Z2**

Making a transcript

Record 4–5 minutes of your group talking.
Listen to the recording, and choose 1–2 minutes to copy in writing.
Make a written copy of the chosen part of your tape.

You will need to decide – how to show who is speaking
                          – how to show a pause
                          – how to show coughs and grunts and laughs
                          – how to show when two people are speaking at once

Remember that people will not always speak in full sentences!

Analysing talk

Either listen to the tape, or read the transcript carefully.

– Are all members of the group involved?
– Does any one member of the group talk too much?

Who – starts things off?
     – provides the ideas?
     – organises the discussion?
     – helps and encourages others?
     – asks questions?
     – provides information?

Does anybody – stop others from speaking?
              – not listen to what has been said by others?
              – not allow others to speak?
              – make fun of other people?
              – stop the group from exploring more deeply?

Prepare a brief report on the discussion commenting on   – the discussion as a whole
                                                          – each group member

Appendix E: The most frequent words of English

These two frequency lists have been compiled from the British National Corpus (BNC). The BNC spoken corpus is made up of around 50 per cent natural spontaneous conversations recorded as people went about their daily lives ('demographic' material), and around 50 per cent sources of spoken language that students might be exposed to, such as broadcasts, public/government talks, current affairs and news commentaries ('context-governed' material). The BNC written corpus is made up of a wide range of written texts from a variety of sources.

Most of the top 50 words form essential elements in common patterns. Most of the top 500 words have at least three different uses and meanings, and frequently occur in lexical phrases of various kinds. Close study of these words, their meanings and their patterns as they occur in their natural contexts will give us new insights into grammar and collocation. Language focus activities based on common words and typical patternings are illustrated in Chapter 7.

The top 200 words of spoken English

the	there (pronoun)	an	'cos (conjunction)	let	her (determiner)
I	just	so (conjunction)	something	course	probably
and	or	will (modal verb)	bit (noun)	week	may (modal verb)
be	would (modal verb)	take	should (modal verb)	ask	little
you	can (modal verb)	some	could (modal verb)	over	school
it	no (adverb)	could (modal verb)	his	talk	must (modal verb)
a	then	make	into	than	different
of	she	one (number)	no (determiner)	still (adverb)	old
to (+ infinitive)	this	on (adverb)	him	number	child
in (preposition)	there (adverb)	how (adverb)	more	many	feel
have	all (determiner)	like (preposition)	us	another	leave
that (determiner)	them	in (adverb)	back (adverb)	thank	question
we	see	by (preposition)	like (verb)	call	away
that (conjunction)	now	three	use (verb)	new	job
they	come	who	tell	man	remember
get	as (conjunction)	look	quite	problem	out (preposition)
to (preposition)	your	put	okay	also	pay (verb)
do	up	year	all (adverb)	of course	house
what	mean (verb)	as (adverb prep)	right (adjective)	never	sure
for	when	really	day	work (noun)	last
not	about	any	first	money	end (noun)
but	which	here	work (verb)	keep	part (noun)
go	very	good	why	used (modal verb)	whether
he	from	where	only	anything	move
on (preposition)	because	other	need	more	else
know	thing	give	pound	her (pronoun)	own (det/pron)
say	right (adverb)	down	about	happen	today
well (adverb)	people	way	much	area	hear
think	me	their	point (noun)	big	before
if	out (adverb)	our	again	fact	every
at	my	actually	off	even	nice
with	time (noun)	sort (noun)	might	too (adverb)	place
so (adverb)	want	lot	find	through	
yes		one (pronoun)	try	always	

The top 200 words of written English

the	would (*modal*	also	how	feel	well (*adverb*)
of	*verb*)	about	our	company	never
and	this	so (*adverb*)	day	over	off
a	if	come	because	high	course
be	her	give	down	number	provide
in (*preposition*)	there	me	through	thing	school
to (+ *infinitive*)	can (*verb*)	new	so (*conjunction*)	area	about
have	all (*determiner*)	now	both	leave	country
to (*preposition*)	do	any	must (*modal verb*)	against	large
it	make	may (*modal verb*)	want	most	member
for	who	first	government	there	away
that (*conjunction*)	what	your	own (*det / pron*)	under	all (*adverb*)
with	go	such	child	might (*modal verb*)	try
on (*preposition*)	its (*determiner*)	only	tell	need	house
he	that (*determiner*)	than	become	here	hold
I	see	people	still (*adverb*)	ask	out (*preposition*)
not	take	good	too (*adverb*)	much	without
by	time (*noun*)	think	back	mean (*verb*)	different
at	into	should (*modal*	more	show (*verb*)	within
you	up	*verb*)	work (*noun*)	us	during
from	some	her (*pronoun*)	life	party	keep
his	him	way	system	another	call (*verb*)
but	could (*modal verb*)	use (*verb*)	however	work (*verb*)	point (*noun*)
as (*conjunction*)	year	man	on (*adverb*)	service	although
which	when	find	woman	problem	local
or	them	between	after	put	begin
they	more	like (*preposition*)	each	after	end
she	other	in (*adverb*)	case	again	most
an	my	look (*verb*)	seem	over	few
say	out	where	great	hand	follow
we	get	just	group	small	always
as (*adverb*)	no (*determiner*)	very	old	place	turn (*verb*)
their	then	even	part	while	
will (*modal verb*)	know	many	world	no (*adverb*)	

NB: Both lists are made up of 'headwords', i.e. the word *be* includes *am, is, are, was, were, been* and *being* and their abbreviated forms. Likewise *get* includes *gets, got,* etc. and *thing* includes *things*.

The part of speech is only given where it is useful to distinguish between different grammatical uses of the same word form, e.g. to show that *like*, the preposition, is more common than *like*, the verb. It must also be remembered that most common words, like the verb *see* and the noun *case*, have more than one meaning.

How useful are these words?

The table below shows what proportion of spoken and written text is made up of the most frequent word forms.* It demonstrates quite clearly how important the common words of English are.

The most common	25	word forms account for	29%	of spoken text and	29%	of written text
"	50	"	36%	"	36%	"
"	100	"	46%	"	42%	"
"	500	"	66%	"	56%	"

*Source: The Cobuild Bank of English: figures based on a written corpus of 196 million words and a corpus of unscripted speech of 15 million words.

NB: This table is based on word forms rather than 'headwords' as in the tables above. This means that *have, has, had, having* are counted as separate items. If the calculation had been based on 'headwords', then the percentages would be even higher.

Appendix F: Task-based examinations (English)

In recent years most of the major examinations have been revised or replaced, bringing them more into line with good classroom practice. Communication tasks have been included in many examinations, within the constraints required by examination conditions – constraints of security, time, limited assistance from teachers and collaboration between learners. This new outlook means that these examinations provide learning targets which are now more compatible with task-based language teaching.

The table below surveys the examinations which include communication tasks. It includes international examinations in general/social English and largely excludes ESP exams and those for young learners. It also indicates the coverage of each examination (reading, writing, listening, speaking) and the level. Levels are based on the 1 (beginner) to 9 (very advanced/bilingual) scale of *The ESU Framework*, Carroll and West 1989, Longman, updated as *English Language Examinations from Britain*, West and Walsh 1992, English Speaking Union.

For further details of these examinations and for sample papers, you should contact the examination boards:

NEAB   Northern Examinations & Assessment Board (formerly JMB) Manchester M15 6EX

Tel: 0161 953 1180   Fax: 0161 273 7572

Oxford/ARELS   The Oxford-ARELS (Association of Recognised English Language Schools) Examinations
Ewert House
Ewert Place
Summertown
Oxford OX2 7BZ

Tel: 01865 54291   Fax: 01865 510085

Pitman   Pitman Qualifications
1 Giltspur Street
London EC1A 9DD

Tel: 0171 294 2471   Fax: 0171 294 2403

UCLES   University of Cambridge Local Examinations Syndicate
EFL Division
Syndicate Buildings
1 Hills Road
Cambridge CB1 2EU

Tel: 01223 553311   Fax: 01223 460278

ULEAC   University of London Examinations & Assessment Council
Stewart House
32 Russell Square
London WC1B 5DN

Tel: 0171 331 4000   Fax: 0171 331 4044/45

Examination	Reading	Writing	Listening	Speaking	Level
					9
Oxford-ARELS Diploma			✓	✓	8
ULEAC Certificate of Attainment in English 6	✓	✓	✓		
UCLES Certificates in Communicative Skills in English (CCSE) 4	✓	✓	✓	✓	7
Pitman ESOL* & Spoken ESOL Advanced	✓	✓	✓	✓	
ULEAC Certificate of Attainment in English 5	✓	✓	✓		
UCLES Certificate in Advanced English (CAE)	✓	✓	✓	✓	6
UCLES Certificates in Communicative Skills in English (CCSE) 3	✓	✓	✓	✓	
Oxford-ARELS Higher Certificate	✓	✓	✓	✓	
Pitman ESOL & Spoken ESOL Higher Intermediate	✓	✓	✓	✓	
NEAB University Entrance Test in ESOL	✓	✓	✓	✓	
ULEAC Certificate of Attainment in English 4	✓	✓	✓		
UCLES First Certificate in English (FCE) (From 1996)	✓	✓	✓	✓	5
UCLES Certificates in Communicative Skills in English (CCSE) 2	✓	✓	✓	✓	
Pitman ESOL & Spoken ESOL Intermediate	✓	✓	✓	✓	
ULEAC Certificate of Attainment in English 3			✓	✓	
UCLES Preliminary English Test (PET)	✓	✓	✓	✓	4
UCLES Certificates in Communicative Skills in English (CCSE) 1	✓	✓	✓	✓	
Oxford-ARELS Preliminary Certificate	✓	✓	✓	✓	
ULEAC Certificate of Attainment in English 2		✓	✓		
UCLES Key English Test (KET)	✓	✓	✓	✓	3
Pitman ESOL & Spoken ESOL Elementary	✓	✓	✓	✓	
ULEAC Certificate of Attainment in English 1		✓	✓		
Pitman ESOL & Spoken ESOL Basic	✓	✓	✓	✓	2
					1

* English for Speakers of Other Languages

Bibliography and References

ABDULLAH, S 1993 *The role of video recording for role play to encourage oral communication for learners of EFL* Unpublished MSc dissertation, LSU Aston University, Birmingham

ALBAN, G 1992 *An analysis of group discussion: competition or co-operation between girls and boys* Unpublished MSc dissertation, LSU Aston University, Birmingham

ALDERSON, A and LYNCH, T 1988 *Listening* OUP

ALLAN, M 1985 *Teaching English with Video* Longman

BASSNETT, S, MCGUIRE, S and GRUNDY, P 1993 *Language Through Literature* Pilgrims Longman Resource Books

BRADFORD, B 1988 *Intonation in Context* CUP

BRAZIL, D, COULTHARD, M and JOHNS, C 1980 *Discourse Intonation and Language Teaching* Longman

BRAZIL, D 1994 *Pronunciation for Advanced Speakers of English* CUP

BROWN, H D 1994 *Principles of Language Learning and Teaching* Prentice Hall Regents

BYGATE, M 1987 *Speaking* OUP

BYGATE, M. TONKYN, A. and WILLIAMS, E. 1994 *Grammar and the Language Teacher* Prentice Hall

BYGATE, M 1996 'Effects of task repetition; appraising the developing language of learners' in WILLIS J and WILLIS D 1996

CARTER, R and MCCARTHY, M 1995 'Grammar and the Spoken Language' in *Applied Linguistics* 16/2 141–158

COOK, G 1989 *Discourse* OUP

COOK, V 1991 *Second Language Learning and Teaching* Arnold

COOPER, R 1993 'Video, Fear and Loathing: self-viewing' in *The Teacher Trainer* Vol. 7/3

CORDER, S PIT, 1986 *Talking Shop* reprinted in Rossner, R and Bolitho, R (eds) 1990

COULTHARD, M *An Introduction to Discourse Analysis* Longman 1985

COULTHARD, M (ed) 1992 *Advances in Spoken Discourse* Routledge

CRYSTAL, D 1992 *The Cambridge Encyclopedia of Language* CUP

DOUGHTY, C 1991 'Second language instruction does make a difference: Evidence from an empirical study of SL relativization' *Studies in Second Language Acquisition* 13/4: pp431–69

DUFF, A and MALEY, A 1990 *Literature* OUP

ELDRIDGE, J 1994 *Code-switching in a Turkish Secondary School* Unpublished MSc dissertation, Aston University, Birmingham and forthcoming in *ELT Journal* Vol 51 1997

ELLIS, G and SINCLAIR, B 1989 *Learning how to Learn* CUP

ELLIS, R 1986 *Understanding Second Language Acquisition* OUP

ELLIS, R 1993 'Talking Shop. Second Language Acquisition Research – how does it help teachers?' *ELT Journal* 47/1:3–11

FOSTER, P 1996 'Doing the task better – how planning time influences students' performance' in WILLIS J and WILLIS D (eds) 1996

GARVIE, E 1989 *Story as Vehicle* Multilingual Matters

GIVON, T 1979 'From discourse to syntax: grammar as a processing strategy' in T. GIVON (ed) *Syntax and Semantics* Vol 12: *Discourse and Semantics* New York Academic Press

GORE, J 1995 'Groups and tasks: let's take a closer look' in *British Council Teaching Centres Network News*, Issue 10

GRELLET, F 1981 *Developing Reading Skills* CUP

HADFIELD, J 1990 *Communication Games* Nelson

HADFIELD, C and J 1992 *Writing Games* Nelson

HOLME, R 1991 *Talking Texts* Longman

JENNINGS, K and DOYLE, T 1996 'Curriculum innovation, teamwork and the management of change' in WILLIS J and WILLIS D (eds) 1996

KÖKSAL, A 1993 *Task-based methodology: an investigation into oral accuracy improvement* Unpublished MSc dissertation, Aston University, UK

KROLL, B (ed) 1990 *Second Language Writing* Cambridge CUP

LAKOFF, G and JOHNSON, M 1980 *Metaphors we Live by* University of Chigago Press

LARSEN-FREEMAN, D and LONG, M H 1991 *An Introduction to Second Langue Acquisition Research.* New York. Longman

LEWIS, M 1993 *The Lexical Approach* Language Teaching Publications

LEGUTKE, M and THOMAS, H 1991 *Process and Experience in the Classroom* Longman

LIGHTBOWN, P M 1985 'Great expectations: second language acquisition research and classroom teaching' in *Applied Linguistics* 6/2

LIGHTBOWN, P and SPADA, N 1993 *How Languages are Learned* OUP

LINDSTROMBERG, S (ed) 1991 *The Recipe Book* Pilgrims Longman Resource Book

LITTLEJOHN, A 1983 'Increasing learner involvement in course management' *TESOL Quarterly,* 17.4

LONG, M and CROOKES, G 1992 'Three Approaches to task-based syllabus design' *TESOL Quarterly,* 26,1

MALEY, A and DUFF, A 1990 *Drama Techniques in Language Learning* CUP

MASCULL, B 1996 *Cobuild Students' Usage* Cobuild/HarperCollins

MATTHEWS, R FRANCIS, P and BAIN, R *Talking to Learn: The Shropshire Talk Project*, Shropshire County Council in association with MacMillan Education 1987

McCARTHY, M and CARTER, R. 1995 'Spoken Grammar: what is it and how can we teach it?' *ELT Journal* 49/3 1995

MOHAMED, S and ACKLAM R *Beginners' Choice*, Longman 1992

NATION, P 1990 *Teaching and Learning Vocabulary* New York Newbury House

NATTINGER, J and DECARRICO, J 1992 *Lexical Phrases and Language Teaching* OUP

NUTTALL, C 1996 *Teaching Reading Skills in a Foreign Language* London, Heinemann

OCHS, E 1979 'Planned and unplanned discourse' in Givon T (ed) *Syntax and Semantics* Vol 12: *Discourse and Semantics* New York Academic Press

OZDENIZ, D 1996 'Introducing innovations into your teaching' in Willis, J and Willis, D (eds)

PAWLEY, A and SYDER, F 1983 'Two puzzles for linguistic theory: nativelike selection and nativelike fluency' in Richards J C and Schmidt R (Eds) 1983 *Language and Communication*, Longman

PRABHU, N S 1987 *Second Language Pedagogy: a perspective* OUP

PRODROMOU, L 1995 'The backwash effect: from testing to teaching' *ELTJournal* Vol 49/1

RAMSEY, G 1989 *Plenty to say* Longman Speaking Skills series

RIBÉ, R and VIDAL, N 1993 *Project Work Step by step* Heinemann Handbooks for the English Classroom

RICHARDS, J 1990 *The Language Teaching Matrix* CUP

ROSSNER, R and BOLITHO, R (eds) 1990 *Currents of change in English Language Teaching* OUP

SCHMIDT, R W 1990 'The role of consciousness in second language learning' *Applied Linguistics*, Vol.11/2

SCHMITT, N and SCHMITT, D 1995 'Vocabulary Notebooks: theoretical underpinnings and practical suggestions' *ELT Journal Vol 49 /2*

SINCLAIR, J M 1991 *Corpus, Concordance and Collocation*, OUP

SINCLAIR, J M and COULTHARD, M 'Towards an Analysis of Discourse' in COULTHARD, M (ed) 1992 pp1–34

SKEHAN, P 1994: 'Second Language Acquisition Strategies, Interlanguage Development and Task-based Learning' in Bygate, M Tonkyn, A and Williams, E (eds) 1994

SKEHAN, P 1996 'Second Language Acquisition Research and Task-based Instruction' in WILLIS, J and WILLIS, D (eds) 1996

SKEHAN, P and FOSTER, P (in preparation) 'The influence of planning and post-task activities on accuracy and complexity in task-based learning' *Thames Valley University Working Papers in ELT* Vol. 3

SWAIN, M 1985 'Communicative competence: some roles of comprehensible input and comprehensible output in its development' in GASS, S and MADDEN, C (eds) *Input in Second Language Acquisition* Rowley, Mass: Newbury House pp.119–39

TOMLINSON, B (ed) forthcoming 1997 *Materials Development in Second Language Teaching* CUP

ULIJN, J M and STROTHER, J B 1990 'The effects of syntactic simplification on reading EST texts as L1 and L2' *The Journal of Research in Reading* 13: 38–54

VALE, D and FEUNTEUN, A 1995 *Teaching Children English* CUP

WALLACE, C 1992 *Reading* CUP

WHARTON, S 1996 'Testing Innovations' in WILLIS J and WILLIS D (eds) 1996

WHITE, R and ARNDT, V 1994 *Process Writing* Longman

WILLIS, D 1990, *The Lexical Syllabus* Collins Cobuild

WILLIS, J and D 1988, *The Collins Cobuild English Course Teachers' Book* Level 1

WILLIS, J and D 1989 *The Collins Cobuild English Course* Levels 2 and 3

WILLIS, J and WILLIS, D (eds) 1996 *Challenge and Change in Language Teaching* Heinemann ELT

WILLIS, J forthcoming 1997 'Concordances in the classroom without a computer' in Tomlinson, B (ed) 1997

WOODWARD, T 1996 'Paradigm shift and the language teaching profession' in WILLIS, J and WILLIS, D (eds) 1996

WRIGHT, A 1996 *Storytelling with Children* OUP

WRIGHT, A, BETTERIDGE, D and BUCKBY, M 1984 *Games for Language Learning* CUP

Index

Key

Page 36

1 Classifying tasks

Applying Prabhu's three categories, tasks 1–9 in Focus 2 could be classified thus:

Tasks 1 and 2: information-gap.

Task 3: both information-gap and, possibly, reasoning-gap, since the memory challenge aspects of the task (once the information has been exchanged) are not otherwise accounted for.

Task 4: reasoning-gap.

Task 5: information-gap.

Tasks 6 and 7 (done with a partner or a group): both information-gap and reasoning-gap, since learners are asked to find things in common and compare reasons. Some people feel that task 7 also has an element of opinion-gap.

Task 8: both opinion-gap and reasoning-gap; in justifying their opinions, learners are likely to be exchanging the reasons for their choices.

Task 9: both reasoning-gap (learners are solving a problem and each making their own reasoned contributions) and possibly also opinion-gap (they may well have attitudes and opinions they want to share, based on their own professional experience). It would be possible to turn task 9 initially into an information-gap task by giving different, possibly overlapping, sets of information about the company to each student in the group.

From this exercise it can be seen there is not necessarily a single clear-cut way of classifying each task. And there are elements in some tasks that cannot be fully accounted for in this three-way classification.

2 Closed and open tasks

a. Teachers generally feel that tasks 1 and 2 are the most specific since they have very concrete outcomes; tasks 5 and 8 also have very specific goals.

b. Within the broad themes that are given, tasks 6 and 3 offer learners the chance to talk about many different aspects of the people they choose; 7, 8 and 9 provide opportunities for them to elaborate on past experiences, to exchange anecdotes and (in the case of 9, and possibly 8,) to share relevant professional expertise.

c. This, of course, depends on the backgrounds of the learners. Most teachers feel that task 4 is a good task for near beginners because it provides a lot of vocabulary, followed by 1, then 2, or possibly 5.

Page 38

Discussion Points

a. During the pre-task phase, learners get exposure to the teacher talking, and possibly from a recording of the task being done by other people. They may also gain exposure from reading the task instructions and working out how to do the task. During the task cycle they will get exposure to each other talking or writing, as they do the task, as they plan how they will report on it, and then exposure from listening to each other as they report formally to the class. The language focus component gives repeat exposure to the language already used in the text or recording. They also hear the teacher and the class talking about it, and see it in a written format.

c. Correction is likely to be most effective at the planning stage, when students are preparing to talk in front of the whole class, and naturally want to be accurate and avoid making mistakes. If corrected during the task, when students are focusing on meaning, correction of form is unlikely to be noticed and retained. Also, shy students may be discouraged from contributing. To be corrected in public, during the report phase, could well be embarrassing for students; however, tactful feedback on language they used after the report (in a less public forum), or during the language focus phase, is usually welcomed.

d. With the language focus phase coming after the task cycle, the language to be studied will already have been processed for meaning and much of it will now be familiar to learners. In other words, the recent topic and task, together with the recording and/or text, provide a clear, holistic context for the study of specific language forms.

These three points will be further developed in chapters 3, 4 and 7.

Page 44
Odd one out

The odd one out is a *long dress* because the rest can all be men's clothes. Some students identify *black trousers* because it is in a plural form. But generally in 'odd one out' games, the focus is on the meanings rather than the forms, unless otherwise stated.

Page 51
Material Appraisal 1

a. You will need to activate relevant vocabulary and set the scene. Here are two suggestions: As the class watch, do a very rough drawing on the board of a scene similar to the ones in the Find the Difference pictures, but with the house, the people, etc. in different places, and with different details. As you draw each item, get the class to guess what it is you are drawing/going to draw next. Describe and speculate about the people as you draw them. *Okay. So here's a man carrying a large bag – where do you think he's going?*

Alternatively, do a *Picture Dictation* pre-task. You give the instructions, choosing items that are in the pictures to be used for the task, and each student draws their own picture, following your instructions. For example *Take a large piece of paper. Now, on one side – either on the left or on the right, draw a house with three or four windows and a front door. Draw another, smaller house next to it. There is sign near the house – it says "For Sale". Draw some people standing together outside,* etc. It is better if your instructions are not too precise, then all the students' pictures will have several differences. When they have completed their pictures, take two pictures, hold them up and point out their differences to the class. Do this with several pairs of pictures. Encourage the class to join in. Finally students in pairs could compare their own pictures.

b. You will need to get the class used to asking questions to find out what is in their partner's picture. So, choose (or draw, very roughly) a picture similar to the ones they will be using. Hold it up, back to the class, so that only you can see it, i.e. so the class cannot see it. Set a time limit. Tell the class to ask you questions about it, so they can find out what is in it, then write a list of what they have found out. Finally show them the picture so they can check their lists.

Planning 4

a. Task 4, Family members.

b. Two alternative suggestions:
Think of two teachers you remember – one for negative reasons, another for positive reasons. Tell the class about each one in turn. Include an anecdote or two, describe the kinds of

things they used to do, and perhaps say what your classmates thought about them. Then discuss with the class why you remembered each one so well, bringing out (or asking them to remember) the positive and negative aspects.

Or use two written descriptions of teachers remembered by previous students (one for positive and another for negative reasons). Ask students to read and compare them. Finally discuss the positive and negative aspects.

Page 66
Spiders

The lost sentence was originally after *and took it home* in the second to last paragraph. The full text can be read in Lesson Outline 3, page 162.

Discussion Points (b) and (c) are expanded on in section 5.5, pp 81–82.

Page 83
Material Appraisal 3 Grading tasks

To provide the easiest route, begin with (b), because it gives a lot of visual support and paraphrases some of the less common words used in the text. The least effective task would probably be (d) because it requires only mechanical recognition of the key words to complete it, and thus does not encourage interpretation of the text.

Most teachers rank the *Lost sentence* task as more difficult than any of these, because it requires a very detailed reading and under-standing of the stages in the cure. But the degree of difficulty would depend on what was done in the pre-task phase. Beginning with task (b) above, or a pre-task brainstorm on ways to cure spider phobias, task (a), would make it easier to follow the sense of the text and find where the sentence might fit.

Page 100 Focus 7
Analysis activities

a. Positive phrases that students normally identify include:
my favourite subject
I liked writing stories
I liked science subjects

I didn't mind things like... because I could do them (point out here the word *do* means *was successful in them/did them well.*)
Negative phrases:
my least favourite was always Maths
I was awful at it
missed out
it just got worse and worse
so it was pretty disastrous, really
subjects like French, which I didn't really like at all
I got a bit behind
The teachers weren't that helpful (note this use of *that* as a modifier)
I didn't like those as much
Point out uses of words / phrases like *pretty, a bit, that,* to modify adjectives / adverbs – these are all common in spoken English.

b. Phrases which refer to time can be classified thus:
  – referring to a specific point in time:
    yesterday morning
    just before closing time
  – referring to a length of time (duration):
    spent the night
    for ten hours
    for 14 hours
    for about ten of the 14 hours
  – referring to a point in time relative to another event:
    immediately
    at first

c. Phrases with *of*:
  one of the key figures
  Romania's process of economic development
  aspects of Romania's economy
  the balance of trade
  the first months of the year
  Many of these are common lexical phrases (e.g. *key figure, balance of trade*) and can be learnt by heart. Point out that nouns such as *process, aspects, balance* have very little meaning on their own, and so are nearly always followed by a more specific word which adds the full meaning.

d. The word *any* is used when we want to be non-specific, to mean *all/ every/it doesn't matter which.* If we use the word *some* we are being more specific. (Compare: *I like any classical music. I like some classical music.*) The rule that *any* must be used in questions and negatives is misguided. *Any* is used just as often in positive statements. *Some* is used in questions which are specific in their reference, e.g. *Would you like some salad?*, i.e. *the salad that is on the table.*

e. *...with the white hair* – category 2
...purple with cold – category 4
...with a bit of wire – category 3
...with his parents – category 1
...with you sitting there – category 4

Page 102
Concordance analysis

Most of the phrases with *in* here refer to place. Two only (14, 15) refer to time.

6 shows that *in* can be used with emotions. More examples are: *in fear/embarrassment/anger.*

7 could be considered a sub-set of 'place' expressing a written document; we say: *in magazines/journals/my letter of*, etc.

11 Similarly, *in* can be used with a speech event: *in a speech/broadcast/talk/lesson*, etc.

12 and 13 show that *in* can be used for processes; *play a (...) part in* is a useful set phrase.

16 and 17 show *in* used with names of subjects, professional fields, e.g. *experienced in child care*, etc.

What other uses of *in* might students know? (*In groups/pairs/threes; in* with languages: *in French* and so on.)

This analysis activity could lead on to a dictionary exercise, where students look up *in* in a learners' dictionary to find more examples like these and add useful phrases to their notebooks.

Pages 106–107

In all activities where students are asked to identify phrases, encourage them to identify and quote a larger chunk rather than just a minimal phrase. This helps them to see how the phrases relate to other units of meaning, and to notice prepositions and other common collocations.

a. Other phrases referring to the cold:
...with his teeth chattering
...his face purple with cold
Still freezing
It was bitterly cold
Expand students' vocabulary by building on

these phrases. Examples follow:
Freezing point/melting point/boiling point/breaking point/bursting point.
Purple with cold/blue with cold/white with fear/red with anger.
You can be *freezing cold* or *boiling hot; nice and cool* or *nice and warm!*

b. See key to page 100 b. above.

c. Most learners find around eight. Note the various ways of referring to the boy and adding more detail, e.g. *Peter Emerson, aged 15,* – these are typical of newspaper reporting style.

d. There are around eight. Note the four different ways in which the shop is referred to.

e. Of the three verb phrases with *had* (i.e. past perfect tense), two phrases – *parents, who had reported him missing* and *staff had gone home* – need to remain in the past perfect, to ensure we understand this had already happened earlier. One phrase – *I had gone into the cold store* – could equally well be in the simple past form – *I went* – since the time frame is made explicit by the phrase *just before closing time.*

g. The uses of verb plus *-ing*: (further examples you can give students are added in brackets).
 – describing someone or something:
   Staff arriving for work
   Still freezing
   someone playing a joke
   (*I saw him standing by the door*)
 – after parts of the verb *to be*:
   I was wearing
   (*we've been reading*)
 – following verbs like *start, stop*:
   and began shouting
   (*stopped smoking*)
 – following words like *after/before/on*:
   after being locked in
   (*On seeing his face*)
 – as an adjective with a noun:
   freezing point
   closing time
   (*opening hours*)
 The pattern *reported him missing* (with a reporting verb) is rare; however, we often use *-ing* after verbs of perception: *saw them coming/noticed her smiling* if we want to stress the process or continuity of the action.

Compare: *saw them come* where the moment of arrival is important, rather than the process of arriving.

So the particle *-ing* seems to have a descriptive function and/or implies an action that happens for a length of time (even a very short time).

h. Categories for verbs ending in *-ed*:
   – past participle/passive in meaning:
   spent the night trapped in
   after being locked in
   – simple past form:

Peter immediately telephoned his parents
the door locked behind me
I tried to
I realised
   – past perfect form:
   who had reported him missing
   – Other past simple forms:
   spent
   ran
   found
   began

i. See g. above.